Beyond Words

Beyond Words

*The Story of Sensitivity Training
and the Encounter Movement*

Kurt W. Back

RUSSELL SAGE FOUNDATION
New York

Publications of Russell Sage Foundation

Russell Sage Foundation was established in 1907 by Mrs. Russell Sage
for the improvement of social and living conditions in the United States.
In carrying out its purpose the Foundation conducts research
under the direction of members of the staff or in close collaboration
with other institutions, and supports programs designed to develop
and demonstrate productive working relations between social scientists
and other professional groups. As an integral part of its operations,
the Foundation from time to time publishes books or pamphlets
resulting from these activities. Publication under the imprint
of the Foundation does not necessarily imply agreement
by the Foundation, its Trustees, or its staff with the interpretations
or conclusions of the authors.

Standard Book Number: 87154–077–0
Library of Congress Catalog Card Number: 73–182935

Russell Sage Foundation
230 Park Avenue
New York, N.Y. 10017

Printed in the United States of America by Connecticut Printers, Inc.,
Hartford, Connecticut.

First printing: January 1972
Second printing: July 1972

To
M. L.
Love Beyond Words

"Whoever you are—
I have always depended on the kindness of strangers."

Blanche DuBois
in
Tennessee Williams's
A Streetcar Named Desire

Contents

Preface

In this book I have tried to capture a development in the science of man at the climax of its career as a social movement. I have included the social science background necessary to understand the techniques, and have made use of biography, sociological analysis and current history to examine the status and significance of the techniques in current society. In combining different methods I have attempted to do justice to this recent development which presents so many diverse facets.

In trying to complete a picture of the intensive group process, sensitivity training, T-groups, encounters and their off-shoots, I have used several methods including conceptual analysis of relevant writings, sociological analysis of societal trends, interviews with key individuals, and personal experience and observation. Although I did not conduct evaluation research for this study, I have analyzed and summarized existing studies of the experience. Renewed interest in formal evaluations and studies under way may soon relieve the gloomy picture of the state of the research shown here.

An exploration of this kind is always risky, especially in a field continually sprouting new developments and controversies. I am, therefore, greatly indebted to Russell Sage Foundation for its confidence and patience, and particularly to David C. Glass and to Orville G. Brim, Jr., president of the Foundation. Both men were helpful and supportive throughout.

Every project depends on the cooperation of many people and this study is no exception. First of all, I am grateful to many individuals, prominent as originators, developers, practitioners, critics or consumers of group techniques, who willingly gave their time for lengthy interviews, even though they did not always agree with the perspective of the questions. Some of them are quoted or otherwise included in the text, but the information all of them provided forms the background for the entire volume.

In obtaining information, the skill of the interviewer is crucial. I was helped immensely by Sheila R. Oelfke and Bryden M. Gordon. Only through their efforts, charm and poise in a variety of interview situations and through their persistence in obtaining relevant materials was it possible to gather all the information needed for this project. In developing the study from raw data to final manuscript I am especially indebted to two co-workers. The work Joanna D. Morris undertook included putting the transcript of the interviews into usable form, collecting and analyzing the research projects, checking out the final references, and other tasks too numerous to list. Judith B. Leavell helped in producing the manuscript, including typing and editing several versions, each subsequent one bearing the imprint of her incisive suggestions and revisions. I appreciate the assistance of all four in the successful completion of this project.

Part I

PROLOGUE

Chapter 1

The Pilgrim Underneath

"One can only speculate on the next state of symbolic and ritual crystallization and how soon it will appear. Yet on this one can be dogmatic. However different the rituals and interaction forms turn out to be from 'traditional religion,' the demands of the human condition will begin to reshape the cultural dimensions to provide effective emotional outlets for the fundamental crises of existence both for the individual and the group."[1]

Geoffrey Chaucer in the *Canterbury Tales* describes the tradition of twelfth-century pilgrims going every spring to holy places. Partly they were driven by religious convictions; but in part they were searching for a change of routine, a transformation of themselves, and relief from distress and illness. They were also looking for companionship, and as he describes it, they had a merry time in their groups. They probably were looking, too, for something more: strong emotions which could transport the pilgrim from his mundane existence and create a unique experience he might cherish for a while or even for the rest of his life. And thus, before and after Chaucer, men have longed to go on pilgrimages.

Today we still find them going. For many, the old shrines have lost their magic. The modern pilgrim has often lost his belief in a saint who can help him, but his need for the singular experience a pilgrimage can give is still present, although few would admit it in these times. A great portion of today's pilgrims are looking for strong

[1] E. Chapple. *Culture and Biological Man.* New York: Holt, 1970, 324.

3

group experiences. Thus, on weekends and during the summers they journey to places that call themselves by different names: T-group centers, encounter group centers, and human potential centers, among others.

These centers may appear novel, but they conform to an old tradition, the human need for a pilgrimage. Some of the essential historical constituents of pilgrimages may have been lost, but perhaps something equivalent has been gained. The basis for the pilgrimage has always been some ulterior motive: a sacred belief, a religion, or an ideology. The culturally acceptable goal for a pilgrim was preparation for afterlife and seeking intercession of the saints. The modern pilgrim may not seek rewards in the afterlife, in fact, he frequently rejects belief in it. He does not make a pilgrimage to seek the hereafter, but the here and now. He seeks frankly those experiences sought only indirectly by his ancestors. Today's pilgrim can say that all he is seeking is an encounter with others, help in solving his personal problems, and a strong experience, and that no otherworldly power is needed to give it to him. In justifying this argument, the modern pilgrim claims a scientific understanding of the forces he experiences.

The scientific point of view, especially dealing with interpersonal relations and the study of society and the human being, has been widely accepted only within the last century or so. Science has its own rules, justifications, and logic in explaining what happens in various social situations. For many people today, the mantle of science can be spread over many activities whose legitimacy might otherwise be questioned. Thus, with the rise of science, many actions whose basis for justification was formerly religion, the state, or other authorities, obtain a new sanction, and the scientific mantle covers areas of life and social activity that have little to do with science.

If we wanted to study the pilgrimages of Chaucer's time, we would have two ways open to us. First, we could look at the whole social setting of the Middle Ages in England or in Western Europe, in relation to the social values attached to the shrines, the religious orders, the feudal society, and the needs of the people. We could look at pilgrimages as social facts, as historical developments, or as a phenomenon that could be explained in these terms. Alternatively, however, we could view the pilgrimages as the pilgrims themselves would have viewed them. By accepting the rules of the church, the possibility of miracles, the intercession of saints, and the power of a priest to enjoin actions, we could derive a logic that would explain the pilgrimages in religious terms, probably the only description of the pilgrimages acceptable to the citizens of those times. This logic of explaining ancient pilgrimages would, however, be unacceptable to the present-day historian or sociologist.

In attempting to understand modern pilgrimages, we can likewise view them in two ways. We can describe the whole social context, and get their picture as a social phenomenon. Or we can view them from the inside out, accepting at face value the experiences of the participants, seeing how they are rationalized, and how they fit into the rules and the explanation of society and systems the pilgrims themselves accept. For a full understanding of today's pilgrimages, as well as of the older ones, a combination of the two approaches is desirable. The contrast between these two approaches is smaller today than it was for the social historian and the theologian in other times. The language of social science that the investigator uses in looking at the ancient and modern pilgrimages as a social phenomenon is the same language that the pilgrims themselves try to use.

Modern pilgrimages to the centers for group processes, encounter, and personality growth are, in their present form, a quite recent development. Only within the last half of the 1960's have they attracted attention among the general public and in the popular media. Magazine articles, books, movies, television shows, all have popularized sensitivity training and personal growth and have lent to the centers the aura of a popular movement. Most of the articles and books describing the pilgrimages have been written from the inside, by pilgrims and clerics, as it were. Participants have described their experiences in T-groups, their weekends in encounter centers, the various games and techniques to which they have been exposed. They tell of unexpected revelations, conflict, despair, and joy, spontaneous love-feasts, and sudden, if ephemeral, enthusiasms. Trainers and group leaders have described their guiding principles, the rationale of their practices, and the events as they saw them, given their presuppositions. These writers have performed a valuable service by giving travelogues of the new landscapes on the American scene.

The time has come to stand back from the immediate scenery and take a look at how sensitivity training fits into the whole picture, where it comes from, what its meaning is, and what it portends. There are difficulties connected with this undertaking. The initiate will maintain that a person who is not part of the movement cannot understand the experiences of insiders. Today, the economically sophisticated social scientist can easily point out the trading and commerce function of medieval pilgrimages and play down the genuine religious fervor among the participants. At the time, however, he would have faced angry denials. The devout pilgrim might have rightly claimed that only his experience and his point of view could be validly considered.

Taken to its logical extreme, this conflict leads to an insoluble dilemma. The observer who is looking at the movement from the outside is somewhat handicapped by the fact that he cannot explore the depth of feelings which may constitute the only true meaning for the initiate. Does it then become impossible to study a movement unless one is completely convinced of its validity? A similar argument has been made about the so-called drug culture. People who are not addicts cannot completely understand the drug experience, and people who are addicts are, from many points of view, not very trustworthy witnesses. We must accept a less than ideal compromise of methods. We shall proceed through the whole series of available evidence, some of it derived from my own experiences, some by participating in groups, some by participating in discussions and interviews with people connected with the movement, and some from all other kinds of available evidence. Thus, in contrast to many of the other documents, this will not be a personal testimonial of a pilgrimage. It will be a critical, analytical discussion of a social movement, what it means for today's society, its promises, and its threats. I will, of course, be partially influenced by my own experiences in connection with this movement.

The search for intensive group experiences is the central focus of the movement we are trying to describe. Because this search has pervaded society to such an extent, it is futile at this point in the argument to construct a rigorous definition of sensitivity training.[2] As a substitute, we shall describe the incident to which its birth in its present form can be traced, and sketch the growth and diversity it has attained in the quarter-century since.[3]

No unusual cosmic event is recorded for early August, 1946,

[2] The terminology of the intensive group experience is not standardized. We shall use *sensitivity training* as the general term for the group methods described here, *T-group* if we refer specifically to the technique developed at Bethel and by the National Training Laboratory, and *encounter* for the technique associated with Esalen and the Western Behavioral Science Institute. The exact provenance of these terms is discussed at appropriate places in the text.

[3] The basic source for the Connecticut workshop is R. Lippitt, *Training in Community Relations.* New York: Harper, 1949. This has been supplemented by personal interviews with participants.

around a small teachers college in Connecticut. Nevertheless, historically the time was crucial. The first anniversary of the explosion of the atomic bomb was approaching. Many people thought of this time as the dawn of a new age, the atomic age. By the same token, the old era of endemic war and depression was ending. For almost two decades society had lived in a constant state of crisis, brought about mainly by the failure of social and interpersonal relations. The Great Depression had marked the failure of economic arrangements in society and of relations between different groups within it. The rise of the strong aggressive ideologies of fascism, communism, and nazism had marked the breakdown of the relation between man and man. The final culmination of this breakdown, the Second World War, had shown even greater failures in human understanding. The same period, however, had seen a great rise in scientific exploration, which in physical science had culminated in the explosion of the atomic bomb. Social sciences had progressed less spectacularly. Social research had been stimulated by the problems of the New Deal and the war years and by support from government. Social scientists set themselves to understanding the failures of the previous decade, and at the same time to substituting scientific understanding in areas that previously had been within the provinces of religion, ideology, and personal philosophies.

The historical setting, if not the physical one, was propitious for a new dawn. At New Britain Teachers College, a group of adult educators, public officials, and social scientists held a summer workshop designed to explore the use of small groups as a vehicle for personal and social change leading to the solution of burning social problems. The aim of the program was the training of officials in intergroup relations agencies; however, an equally important aim was to develop techniques in face-to-face groups and to learn more about how they function.

We shall meet many of the staff members of the workshop again as prominent leaders in the sensitivity training movement. The educators' team, particularly the group leaders, Kenneth Benne, Leland Bradford, and Ronald Lippitt, had been involved in different studies of the ways in which groups could be used to solve the problems created by depression and war. Benne's work had been in connection with educational philosophy, Bradford's in the training of indigenous teachers in literary and adult education programs, and Lippitt's in investigating the environmental study of groups. The research team came from the newly organized Research Center for Group Dynamics at Massachusetts Institute of Technology, where

Kurt Lewin attempted to fuse theory and research on groups into a unified field. The public officials and representatives of intergroup organizations, especially the American Jewish Congress, were conscious of the importance of group anchorage for the preservation and effective change of attitude. The three types of participants were, moreover, not totally distinct. Some of these individuals had their feet in more than one camp. Many of them had collaborated previously, and Lewin's influence had affected the theoretical orientation of many members.

It is not surprising, therefore, that the group as such was the focus of interest. The participants were divided into three groups, each with its own trainers and observers, and the development of each group was to be the touchstone of the success of the workshop. It was hoped that there would be an emerging unity in each group, a recognizable character that would make the group the unit of change. Thus, the training staff as well as the research staff watched carefully the progress of the groups and reviewed the events within the groups in great detail.

For this purpose the staff gathered in the evenings to discuss the daily events in the training groups. One evening, to the surprise of the staff, and probably somewhat to its dismay, three "delegates" from the trainees appeared at this session and wanted to listen to the discussion. Lippitt describes the scene and its aftermath:

> And on this particular night, three of the trainees, three school teachers who hadn't gone home that evening, stuck their heads in the door and asked if they could come in, sit and observe and listen, and Kurt [Lewin] was rather embarrassed, and we all were expecting him to say no, but he didn't, he said, "Yes, sure, come in and sit down." And we went right ahead as though they weren't there, and pretty soon one of them was mentioned and her behavior was described and discussed, and the trainer and the researcher had somewhat different observations, perceptions of what had happened, and she became very agitated and said that wasn't the way it happened at all, and she gave her perception. And Lewin got quite excited about this additional data and put it on the board to theorize it, and later on in the evening the same thing happened in relation to one of the other two. She had a different perception on what was being described as an event in that group she was in. So Lewin was quite excited about the additional data, and the three at the end of the evening asked if they could come back again the next night, and Lewin was quite positive that they could; *we* had more doubts about it. And the next night the whole fifty were there and were every night, and so it became the most significant training event of the

day as this feedback and review of process of events that had gone on during the work sessions of the day. And as Ken Benne, Lee Bradford, and I discussed this, actually it was at a hamburger joint after one of these evenings, we felt the evidence was so clear that the level of our observations of the phenomena about these sessions were a major basis for reorganizations of perceptions and attitude change and of linking up to some degree attitudes and values with intentions and behavior.[4]

If any starting point for the movement can be identified, it was this incident. From it grew the multitude of workshops, laboratories, training programs, books, and tapes which, in the intervening decades, have promoted the work on feedback, group-confrontation, encounter, and process-analysis. In this incident, ideology, pragmatism, opportunism, transcendence, and scientific method form a curious combination which has given its stamp to the movement.

At this junction it might be instructive to note the backgrounds of the principle actors involved. The undisputed intellectual leader of the group was Kurt Lewin.[5] He had developed an exciting theory in psychology—field theory—that attempted to look at the individual in relation to his relevant environment, his "life space." Even more important, he had introduced new methods of observation to psychology that made it possible within the psychological laboratories to study volition and emotion instead of the traditional fields of sensation-perception and learning. During the previous decade he had turned his interest to social problems. Taking the group as the unit of concern, he applied the concepts of direction, change, influence, and power to the whole group, talking about members as integrated parts of the group in the same way he had described parts of the personality as regions within the person. At the Research Center for Group Dynamics at MIT, recently founded under his direction, he had started a program of systematized experimentation with small groups, as well as what he called "action research," a combination of social research, action, and research evaluating action that allowed bold ventures in research. In this context he had shown his capacity for translating ultimately abstract concepts into exact research. To

---

[4] Personal interview.

[5] An exposition of Lewin's life and work is given in A. Marrow, *The Practical Theorist*. New York: Basic, 1969. The bulk of Lewin's writing is published in four volumes: *Dynamic Theory of Personality*. New York: McGraw-Hill, 1935. *Principles of Topological Psychology*. New York: McGraw-Hill, 1936. *Resolving Social Conflicts*. New York: Harper, 1948. *Field Theory in Social Science*. New York: Harper, 1951.

this interest as a scientist he added a human involvement in the primary problems of the day.

The three trainers all agreed with these main trends, although their respective emphases, corresponding to their backgrounds, were on different aspects. Ronald Lippitt had been a student of Lewin, and together they had conducted the first experimentation with whole groups. He combined his early interest in group work with his later training in psychological research, employing group leadership and cooperation with volunteer organizations, while at the same time feeling a responsibility for research in the context of the group work.

The other two group leaders, Leland Bradford and Kenneth Benne, had been involved in adult education for a long time. Bradford had been led to his present interests through his work in New Deal agencies. One of the main problems he had dealt with had been the development of teachers for adult education and literacy programs. Few teachers were available; they had to be able to be trained quickly, and further, they were preferably drawn from the same group as the people to be taught. These circumstances led Bradford, after consultation with many leaders in teacher-training programs, to consider group methods in teacher training where the group members essentially trained each other. Bradford had, therefore, a chance to observe group methods of teaching and the effect of group interaction on the individual at first hand, on quite a large scale, and in a novel situation. He remained committed to the transformation of educational methods for use with adults outside educational institutions.

One of the educational experts whom Bradford had consulted was Kenneth Benne. Benne had been impressed by the problems of adult training and by the need for new methods. He had been interested originally in philosophy of education; his philosophy was strongly influenced by John Dewey's emphasis on the importance of methods, tolerance, and in a general democratic ideology. Most recently, at the Teachers College of Columbia University, Benne had had the opportunity to enlarge upon his theoretical analyses and also to put them into practice. The unity of the autonomous group at Teachers College had also led him to interests in group methods and especially to a consideration of the leader's role.

These, then, were the leaders of the workshop. The peculiar combination of talents and interests certainly had a great influence on subsequent developments. The common interests of the leaders in teaching outside the classroom and in teaching persons not commonly thought of as students, the search for correctives for certain trends in the society in an educational context, and the application of relevant principles of social psychology were the common ground from which they could proceed. Lippitt's commitment to research in group dynamics, Benne's intensive study of pragmatism, and Bradford's involvement with practical problems of adult education led each of them to give his personal contribution to this mix. Lewin, with his ample ability to create new theoretical revolutions, inspire novel research techniques, and see relevant psychological principles embedded in social problems, could direct the issues coming out of this workshop into a new system.

With this nucleus, the incidents during the evening discussion period of the workshop assumed a peculiar significance. From experience and theory the leaders believed that the workshop could produce groups as units within which the trainees could find their way to new achievements. In spite of their extensive backgrounds, they had few concrete ideas how this group formation would come about. The research staff, consisting mainly of hardheaded, empirically oriented graduate students from Harvard and MIT, kept questioning the events, and especially the evidences of group development. It may be significant that the three students on the staff, Morton Deutsch, Murray Horwitz, and Melvin Seeman, did little to promote the movement, while becoming prominent social psychologists in their own right. Lewin's reply to their questions was essentially to consider the group as something fragile, young, just developing, which could not be hurried along but should be watched with tender care. The techniques used at the workshop consisted mainly of discussing common problems within their communities, role-playing some possible actions and responsibility, and giving attention to actions of the group members.

The presence of uninvited guests at the staff meetings revealed the fascination this last aspect had for the trainees. As teachers they had themselves observed and discussed their classes. They were attracted to discussions of their own actions, although it might have been a strain for them. More important, these sessions put the groups at the center of the discussion. It was not the individual who was analyzed and discussed, but his place in the working of the whole group.

At this juncture the important decisions were made which mark this event as the birth of a whole movement. The discussion of events, which the participants renamed "feedback," assumed the central position in future workshops. This discussion, so attractive to the members, could serve as an experience that would give the group an emergent unit, making the group itself a basis of change. It is unclear what happened as the outcome of these discussions; Lippitt's own evaluation of the results of the workshop showed generally weak effects though some enthusiasm. He did not discuss any evaluation by the participants of the evening discussions; however, all the leaders were certainly impressed by the reaction.

These ambiguous results led to a decision to repeat the workshop, but without a central topic such as intergroup relations. Instead, the focus was to be on group relations as such, on member relations, group procedures, and the influence of the group; in general, those features that could produce a change in the participants, an undefined change that would make them better group members and leaders. This workshop was to be held the next year, 1947, at the Gould Academy in Bethel, Maine.

The decision to continue the workshops and to focus on group development started a trend affecting many fields of applied social research and social science, and many professions. Less than twenty-five years later, the types of workshops have proliferated; schools, industries, and government agencies use them in several guises. Thousands of participants go each month to some center to experience group methods. The many centers themselves have become a multimillion-dollar business, and almost every month mass media describe some of the more sensational aspects.

This rapid success from modest beginnings is a noteworthy social phenomenon. It represents the rise of a new profession, of a new way of spending one's leisure time, of new approaches to management, education, sociability, psychotherapy, and other fields. The manifestations of intensive group methods are varied; but through all of them runs a thread leading back to those first evening sessions at New Britain. The discovery of the value of self-confrontation and evaluation and the strong personal experiences connected with them has shown itself to be of unexpected value.

Chapter 2

Social Science and Social Movement

"The borrowed authority of science becomes a powerful prestige symbol for unscientific doctrines."[1]

THE APPROACHES

How can we account for the surge in popularity of sensitivity training? Let us first locate the field of sensitivity training as we can see it at this point. Originally, sensitivity training was designed as a technique for teaching people how to work in groups and how to work more effectively with other people. Central to this technique was the discovery of the effectiveness of immediate feedback, of the here-and-now orientation, and of concentration on the group process itself. These features were not original inventions; however, the crucial discovery was that these procedures could bring about intense emotional experiences among most participants in sensitivity training groups. These three features, the concentration on the immediate group process, the emphasis on personal relations and personal remarks, and the resultant subjective experiences, can be used tentatively as a definition of sensitivity training.

This combined emphasis on technique and experience has become the basis of an ambiguity in sensitivity training. As a new technique it should be evaluated by its consequences, merits, and drawbacks, and thus its spread should be dependent on its demon-

[1] R. Merton, "Science and the Social Order," in *Social Theory and Social Structure*. Glencoe, Ill.: Free Press, 1957.

strable results. It would seem doubtful, however, that this has been so. In this vein, it may be instructive, therefore, to compare sensitivity training with another new discovery that came to the fore at about the same time. Some enthusiasts of sensitivity training have compared its impact with that of the discovery of atomic energy, asserting that atomic energy gave us a great amount of physical power to control the physical universe, and sensitivity training gave us the power to control the personal universe. This may be an interesting analogy, but we can also see glaring differences. Development and increased use and understanding of atomic energy have proceeded along the established lines of research by proving certain hypotheses and by development on the basis of established results. True, if we take the whole context into account and study the history of atomic energy, we can find some social reasons, even interpersonal reasons, why this particular development was favored, why certain lines of research were undertaken and others were not. Clearly the wartime conditions, the relationship of several theorists to each other, the relationship between scientists and policy makers, all had their influence in controlling the course that the development of atomic energy took. However, the theoretical and practical implications of atomic energy and its actual use are objectively determined and can be explicated in textbooks, showing the logical line of thought. In this way, atomic physics has become an accepted scientific development. On the other hand, there has been little identification of people who say they believe in atomic energy or use it in contrast to those who do not. And we can find few secondary benefits to belief in atomic energy, such as making believers happy or segregating them as a distinct group in the population because they do believe so or do not believe so. A development such as atomic energy follows the model of rational scientific endeavor. A human enterprise, it can be studied as a historical fact or a sociological development, or shown in interpersonal relationships. Its main impetus, however, comes from the acceptance of this evidence according to the rules of scientific method.

Sensitivity training, on the other hand, has spread in a different way. One of the indicators of this difference is the paucity of research results pointing to positive effects. Here we note the apparent paradox that an effort which has enlisted the aid of many social scientists, which has been sponsored by several academic and research organizations, has produced so little research about the procedures and outcomes of the technique. Even more surprising is the apparent lack of concern about this state of affairs. Early concern

about evaluation studies has given way to explanations of why traditional evaluation of effects would be inappropriate.

In fact, an investigator's concern with assessment techniques
is frequently taken as an expression of hostility. When inquiring
about evaluation techniques, I was admonished, "Do not try to prove
things; give yourself a chance to live the experience." I was also
given many reasons why evaluation techniques would not work. For
instance, one former participant of a sensitivity training laboratory
who had become a staff member explained to me that the main effect
he could trace in himself had been a career decision made three
years after his laboratory participation. Could such an event be captured by statistical techniques? Alfred Marrow, an enthusiastic pro-
ponent of the laboratory method in industry, especially for management, remarked that executives in his organization did not show so
much change in behavior as a greater willingness to listen to others
and a general openness in social interaction. Changes of this kind
rely more on personal testimony than on measurement. Marrow, like
many others, used the indisputable increase in use of the method,
especially by hardheaded businessmen, as evidence that sensitivity
training is successful.[2] On the other hand, hardly anybody actively
worries about the lack of research results (see Chapter 13). The feeling that something important is accomplished, and that joy and involvement are generated, is sufficient for devotees of the technique.

Perhaps a better analogy to the spread and influence of sensitivity training may be the spread of drugs in the same period. In the
early 1940's several new psychoactive drugs were discovered, notably
LSD, and the physiological reactions could be studied in great detail.
Interest in research application of these drugs spread rapidly
through scientific laboratories, and their use correspondingly increased, so that in ten years the use of tranquilizers and other drugs
in psychotherapy became an accepted procedure in the psychiatric
community. Here again we might trace the development of drug use
through some of its social and interpersonal features. In some regard the spread of drug use followed the model of accepted scientific
development. But usage among the general public and the establishment of a "drug culture" had little to do with the proved effects of
drugs. People declared themselves for or against drugs, and being in
favor of them implied a certain societal identification: belief in the
drug culture and the gradual relationship of drug use to a way of
life. Some of the drugs used, such as marijuana or heroin, had been

[2] Personal communication.

15

available and used for a long time. In order to understand the spread of drug usage, we would have to look at its presence in society, at the needs within society it fills, and at the peculiar constellation of social, personal, and cultural factors that led to its rapid rise in favor.

We do not want to say that sensitivity training is the same kind of activity as drug use, any more than it is a scientific achievement comparable to the use of atomic energy. Both are examples illustrating that innovations can take different paths. If man were an ideal rational being, the spread of a new method would proceed along the lines of evidence, assessment of results, verification, and adoption. If man were carried away completely by impulse, then spread would occur through gratification of immediate needs and emotional contagion, like a fad or a hysterical epidemic. In actuality, man is neither. Scientific development does not proceed along purely rational lines of disinterested thinking, but is dependent on social and institutional factors. On the other hand, the course of a social movement is frequently dependent on verifiable facts which form the basis of some serious scientific study. The mix of the two forms a continuum between a scientific innovation and a social movement. Therefore, it may be well to consider the adoption of a certain innovation by looking at it both ways. One can look at its core of scientifically verifiable facts, study what the scientific theories are, and how they have been verified. We can call this the "internal approach." One can also look at the social and emotional conditions and needs which give rise to a social movement of that kind. In this case, we do not have to concern ourselves with the confirmation of scientific fact by some method of proof and verification, but with the relationship of the beliefs and the corresponding action to the needs of the total society. This we could call an "external approach." These two approaches correspond to definitions of science and of social movements. The contrast between the two is not as complete, of course, as an exposition of this kind makes it seem; but this exposition delineates the conceptual differences.

Sensitivity training seems to have an intermediate position on our continuum of scientific innovations and social movements. In its more recent development, it has come closer and closer to the kind of social movement that spawns its own culture, its own devotees, and its own problems, while spurning scientific verification. On the other hand, it was originally much closer to scientific fact. It was couched in the framework of theories of social psychology and group therapy, having at its core social psychological theory and scientific method. Confusion sometimes arises if the language of scientific method is still used in the movement when it is not appropriate at all.

A great part of this book will be devoted to showing the relation of social psychological facts and the general method of social science to this development of a social movement. In order to do so, we have to concentrate first on the external approach, the conditions that facilitated group dynamics to become a social movement to the current extent. The range of possible mixtures between rational decision and emotional spread is most pronounced in innovations dealing with personal conduct. In this field there has been a long-standing confusion between two approaches: determining what man shall be and developing a theory of what man is. In general, the former has been connected with religion, the latter with science and its application in technology.

The religious approach is older, and until quite recent times was the only approach. According to this view, people were to be changed to agree with a scheme conforming to some higher authority. The whole change process could not be justified without this appeal. The perfect state to be attained was sufficient justification for any attempts at personal change, whether initiated by the person himself or by society. It is significant in this context that one of the change agencies of this kind, the Jesuit organization, was accused of having as its guiding principle, "The end justifies the means."[3]

As long as personal change is viewed as part of the responsibility of religion, it is tied in with other aspects of religion, such as a consistent picture of the world and a feeling of the sacred. The cognitive and emotive sides of religion blend easily with its educational practices, so much so that it is difficult for many to separate these different aspects of religious world view.

The influence of religious ideals has dwindled in recent times. We may even say that it is completely ineffective today for a large sector of the population. Even secular ideologies have lost their influence as motives for molding people according to some ideal. In spite of this rejection of ultimate principles, a sense of dissatisfaction with oneself and with others remains acute in society. In this context, the new techniques of change come to the fore.

The second approach to personal change is based on science. The rise of scientific thought to a place of great importance is rela-

[3] Cf. R. Fülöp-Miller. *The Jesuits.* New York: Capricorn Books, 1963, 150–156.

tively recent and has brought about a major change in the society. Levi-Strauss has contrasted most effectively "savage" and "modern" thought.[4] Modern thought is experimental, pragmatic; it looks at what works in a particular situation without trying to fit each piece immediately into a consistent world view as the primitive, mythic religious view had done.

Bereft of justification through ulterior aims, the modern intellectual turns to science as the guide for solutions to his dissatisfaction. This trust in science leads to several new developments. Process is emphasized instead of the goal, and change itself becomes the principal focus of attention. In conformity with scientific procedures, some evidence is organized with regard to the mechanism and outcomes of the procedure used. Although the value of the change is not necessarily a subject of concern and is normally left to the assessment of the client, the professional practitioner of change techniques is committed to a searching inquiry into the change process itself.

Thus the scientist, and particularly the social scientist, has succeeded the priest as the guide to personal change and, it might be said, to spiritual search. His point of view dominates the field in which man is seeking escape from feelings of inadequacy and guilt. Change in language has accompanied the changed perspective. Terms such as guilt, depravity, and salvation are avoided; instead we have illness, neurosis, and therapy, and even terms such as alienation, mechanization, and spontaneity.

This concern of science with human interaction has brought scientists into close contact with other leaders of society who have been traditionally concerned with the same problems. The authority to set standards for self-development or conduct with others had previously been based on supernatural sanction. These beliefs have constituted the whole ethos of a society, a reaction to the total situation of the society and the ability of the culture to deal with internal and external strains while still keeping a consistent systematic unity. The scientist's procedure is different. He treats each problem according to its own parameters, proposing a solution that explains a situation in its own terms, without the necessary implication of a whole world view. This procedure has worked in the physical and biological sciences, although sometimes the scientific approach has had such obviously great implications that attempts at innovation have had severe repercussions. The controversies surrounding Galileo and Dar-

[4] C. Levi-Strauss. *The Savage Mind.* Chicago: University of Chicago Press, 1966.

win began to resemble social upheavals. Study of, and attempted changes in, human behavior are even more likely to affect society's basic assumptions and thus interact strongly with other interests within the society, especially religious ones.

It is not surprising, therefore, that sensitivity training has had religious undertones since its beginning. In its drifting away from strictly scientific procedures it has assumed the religious function of providing a consistent world view and some of the emotional aspects and controls of religious ritual. It has tended to become a religiously oriented social movement. Thus, when using the external approach we shall have to trace the many connections between sensitivity training and religious behavior.

EXTERNAL APPROACH: THE SOCIAL MOVEMENT

In the external approach, we treat sensitivity training as a social phenomenon and inquire into its place in society, its function and its relations to other social events. In this context, it is best to treat it within the framework of the theory of social movements.

In general, a social movement can be viewed as a response to a need society does not fill for a number of its members. The specific direction it takes as well as its spread depend on a variety of circumstances, such as the nature of the existing social order, what the movement can and cannot provide for its members, the appeal of the main leaders and the other protagonists, the viability of the new idea, and processes of control exerted by the society.

Theorists have listed essential factors for the success of a social movement. For instance, Smelser distinguishes five factors influencing the development of social movements: *structural conduciveness*, the openness of channels for action within the existing structure; *strain*, conditions that show the lack of capability of the existing stimuli to satisfy certain factors; *generalized beliefs*, which indicate some diagnosis for the failure and proposals for eventual solution; *precipitating events*, which dramatize both the strain and possible avenues of adjustment; and finally, *social control*, the measure in which the existing system can contain and channel the emerging movement.[5]

Another sequence has been defined by Blumer: *unrest*, where people are becoming susceptible to new appeals; *popular excitement*, an agreement on the causes of the difficulty and sharpening of the

[5] N. Smelser. *Theory of Collective Behavior*. New York: Free Press, 1963.

objectives; *indoctrination,* the emergence of a definite set of beliefs and of mechanisms, such as leadership, to disseminate them, and finally *institutionalization,* when the purposes of the movement are carried out.[6]

In both of these schemes, which are representative of sociological theory in this field, we notice the importance of a belief system validated mainly by its relevance to social problems, not by any systematic proof.

The central point of interest is the collective inclusion of indoctrination steps. This belief in indoctrination techniques represents an innovation in the way in which ideas are disseminated by the movement. In contrast to a model of rational adoption, the nature of the information spread is not important in itself; it is only important within the context of the needs within the society and the events that dramatize them. Verification of these beliefs is not necessary. Instead, beliefs are validated if they actually meet the needs they are supposed to fulfill. Thus, in contrast to the model of rational dissemination, the social movements model accounts for acceptance of new rules by the context, not by the information itself.

It is not surprising that evaluation of the effects of sensitivity training has not progressed in the more than two decades of the development. We may even understand now why this deficiency has not been a matter of great concern among the scientific and nonscientific members of the movement. Nevertheless, the positive feelings that advocates experience are indicative of current needs within society as well as evidence of the nature of the movement. We are not dealing here simply with a new technique which can be characterized and whose effects will be accepted if beneficial and discarded if detrimental. What we are dealing with is a new movement, a new faith, whose basic tenet is that some of the ills of society can be overcome.

This reasoning shows us the way for the external analysis to proceed. The central concern is to describe the nature of the new faith, its manifestations in different contexts, and their effect on the society. To understand the development of the movement we must also identify the conditions which led to the rise of the generalized belief (in Smelser's terms) namely, the structural conduciveness and strength in the society, or the basis of the unrest. Further we must consider the mechanism by which the generalized belief has stabi-

---

[6] H. Blumer. "Collective Behavior," in A. M. Lee (ed.), *Principles of Sociology.* New York: Barnes and Noble, 1951, 165–222.

lized into a social movement, the precipitating events and the social control mechanisms. We have seen already the specific event that triggered the ideas basic to sensitivity training. The further history of the movement shows the implication of the event and their incorporation into organized action.

INTERNAL APPROACH: LANGUAGE OF SCIENCE

The field of sociology that can guide us in the internal approach to the study of the sensitivity training movement is the sociology of science. The scientific community is primarily self-sustaining; validation of facts and beliefs is accomplished within a community of peers. Thus, the establishment of scientific fact proceeds within a small community of professionals who accept their own rules of scientific method and who frequently are the only ones who can understand the whole course of argument. Sociology of science must therefore investigate the mechanism and channels by which consensus is given and which encourage progress of scientific pursuit in new directions.[7]

The reliance of the scientist on his own community does not result in the separation of his knowledge from exterior reality. On the contrary, the rules of scientific evidence are designed to ensure that accepted scientific pronouncements are in accord with observed fact as well as with the ongoing theoretical framework. The main characteristic of the scientific enterprise is that this kind of checking, verification, and encouragement can only come from the scientific community itself, not from a desire for popular approval and success. The sociologist of science must therefore investigate the process of communication among scientists, the personal contacts, formal relations, and written communications. The conditions for the spread of a new scientific idea have not been codified and catalogued. By following the argument presented above, we can propose a sequence, however.

The development of a new scientific idea will be motivated by a felt *difficulty* or *lack* in the present system of knowledge; this can be considered analogous to the first steps in the development of social movements which Smelser called "structural conduciveness" and "strain." It is felt here almost exclusively in the scientific community. In specific cases this difficulty may be very small, prompting a creative scientist to convince his relevant audience that such a need ex-

[7] N. Storer. *The Social System of Science.* New York: Holt, 1966.

ists. The second step is the *formulation* of the new idea, justified according to the accepted standards of the particular science and, therefore, comprehensible and acceptable to the relevant group of colleagues. Next is the *dissemination* of the idea through established channels, publication, speeches, and participation in formal and informal meetings. In this way, the new idea enters the mainstream of scientific thought. The final step is the establishment of a social network to maintain interest in the topic and to promote necessary criticism and additional work in the field. This stage may be called *institutionalization* and consists in part of assembling a framework within a university or research organization, collecting students, and creating personal channels of dissemination such as journals and professional associations.

Sensitivity training has aspired to legitimation by this method as well as by becoming a social movement that responds to needs of the larger society. Its origin within the scientific community, the language used in some of the reports, and the rise in the prestige of science make it necessary to study sensitivity training as a scientific movement.

Let us turn to the relationships that the exterior and interior approaches have to the peculiar progress of sensitivity training as a social movement. Sensitivity training does not fit into the conventional model of social movements. Many persons involved in developing and strengthening the movement would deny that they developed a technique capable of dealing with specific problems or designed to regenerate society or bring man secular salvation. Articles on sensitivity training in its earlier phases have emphasized the importance of specific techniques against any wider implications which would follow. In fact there is some strain within the fold between those who try to fit the scientific mold and those who want to spread the message to the world.

JUNCTION OF EXTERNAL AND INTERNAL APPROACHES

Only since the second half of the 1960's has the social-movement wing become prominent; at that time, sensitivity training was discovered fully grown by the popular media. Magazine pieces were followed by television and radio shows, films, and general public excitement. The twenty years prior to this time were spent in a more ambiguous stage. Sensitivity training was discussed in professional publications, some of which were created expressly for this purpose, but also in publicity written to attract participants to different workshops and other events.

This overlap between popular and professional interest makes the distinction between the internal and external paths to understanding important. In the early phases, the trainers stressed the purely rational, technical aspects of sensitivity training. It was sold as a tested and testable procedure that would improve the workings of groups and develop successful trainees into better group members and leaders. Discussions of sensitivity training focused on the procedures first, and then on their effects on the participants and the groups involved. This is the internal approach: examining the procedure in its own terms and discussing only the features consciously introduced by the planners.

The combination of internal and external approaches is not unique. On the contrary, it seems to be a common feature of movements that attempt to change people. There is always an internal theory, which explains the procedures in terms the participants can accept; and an external point of view, which looks at the whole procedure as a general process in the society. Not only the distinction between, but the connection of the internal and external approaches becomes crucial as well. One theory showing the connection between them has been proposed by Jerome Frank in *Persuasion and Healing*.[8]

Frank proposes a set of necessary conditions for the kind of intense experience we find in encounter groups. They include (1) a recognition of a condition that makes a person different from (usually inferior to) the rest of society; (2) the existence in society of a group of qualified persons who, through special guild training, have achieved a recognized competence in dealing with this condition; (3) a socially reinforced belief by the sufferer in these practitioners and in the efficiency of their techniques; (4) a separation of the sufferer from his usual environment and status preparatory to treatment; and (5) the encounter between sufferer and practitioner resulting in a strong experience by which the sufferer can recognize that a reintegration into effective living has become possible. The kind of role the practitioner assumes, the definition of the complaint of the sufferer, and the particulars of the cure will depend on the prevailing culture and beliefs. They may be interpreted in a religious, medical, or political way. The cure may be expulsion of bad spirits,

[8] J. D. Frank. *Persuasion and Healing*. Baltimore, Md.: Johns Hopkins, 1961.

release from sin, psychotherapy, thought control, or expansion of potentialities. The sufferer's experience in all these cases is similar, but it is interpreted differently according to the viewpoint employed.

Frank's theory applies to religious as well as scientific-based methods. The difference between the two lies in the attitude of the practitioner, his training, the differential emphasis on total vs. piecemeal effect, and the kind of evidence accepted. Religious justification is of one piece; it is transmitted by authority as well as training and it is not subject to revision according to empirical results. The scientific approach rejects reliance on authority or charisma, emphasizes substantive training, and relies on a definite empirical method. The social controls on, and responsibility of, each practitioner are correspondingly different. The religious practitioner is right according to his own inspiration as long as the client holds the same belief. The scientific practitioner is right according to the accumulated body of knowledge which is subject to verification by himself or another qualified person.

Frank's work is directed mainly toward therapy and especially the importance of the proof of the claims of different schools of psychotherapy. Parenthetically, he draws attention to a new form of social movement which takes as its center an accepted scientific advance. This is the topic that concerns us here and that constitutes sensitivity training as a social movement.

The kinds of internal theories Frank discusses fall into several categories: magical, religious, political, and scientific. Thus he uses the same system to explain the workings of shamanism, Catholic shrines, Communist thought control, and psychoanalysis. The techniques used must be consistent with the base of the theory. What is sufficient for our purpose is that science can function in the same way as the more traditional theories of magic, religion, and ideology. It has been traditional to contrast science with those bases as being a rational method encroaching on older systems and trying to replace them. The difference might have been exaggerated, however. As science began to usurp the older bases of belief, so it gradually was influenced in turn by the mechanisms by which these belief systems have influenced human action, independent of rational proof. A closer look at this phenomenon will enable us to understand better the role of the scientific base of sensitivity training in its becoming a social movement.

The treatment of methods of personal change in *Persuasion and Healing* will be considered as simple "debunking" by the followers of each procedure. Thus, Communists may be offended by the treatment of thought control and the Russian penal system, Catholics by the discussion of Lourdes, and psychoanalysts by the description of their therapy, although they may agree on Frank's interpretation of the other two and all of them can understand the interpretation of shamanism among the Northwestern American Indians. Using some theory external to the one preferred by the practitioner does not imply a negative view, however. The use of such a device does not denigrate the theory discussed.

The ambiguity between external and internal approaches and the concomitant stresses have been hallmarks of the history of sensitivity training. It is reasonable to believe that the planners promoted their theories of the functioning of group training in good faith and that they tried to develop a technique according to these principles. Some of these theories and practices might well have validity outside the movement and would repay serious investigation. Nevertheless, almost from the start the social-movement features interjected themselves among the pedestrian mechanisms of the workshop. These features included the selection of members and the indoctrination of believers. Their presence is shown in the movement's implicit acceptance of a deep, nontestable belief, the placing of value on the intuitive feeling of being right or changed or saved, and the development of mechanisms to channel this energy into consistent efforts. These features were just as much a part of the training as the reliance on social science that led to empirical and largely unsuccessful research.

The central beliefs of social movements and techniques of personal change have had traditionally a magical, religious, or at least ideological base, a core of sentiments functioning through emotion or direct experience. Many current social movements are still nonscientific in their beliefs. Many people in present-day society no longer recognize religion as a motivating force, however, and experiences of the last decades have left them disillusioned with political ideologies from left to right. Thus, the core or central belief of a movement must find a different justification. Frequently, the same persons who reject the trapping of formal religion can accept the authority of science. Science thus has become the core of a series of social movements, from Christian Science to scientology.

We have here a new development in the rise of social movements. If science becomes the central belief, the function of this belief comes into direct opposition to the main characteristics of science, which are replicability and testability, that is, the nature of evidence. Evidence in the scientific sense may be retained, but it

25

becomes essentially irrelevant in the acceptance of new ideas spread by the movement.

Society today has a number of these movements, a kind of science put into the framework of a social need. Social science has tried to fill the gap left by the secularization of society. Best-seller lists abound with new theories which give solutions to personal, spiritual, or social problems in scientifically tested ways. The spectrum of these movements ranges from those with a strong scientific base, such as psychotherapy or management, to those with a scientific coating of essentially religious or ideological ideas. It is not that simple to distinguish the scientific and ideological elements. We shall find that the sensitivity training movement in particular draws from both sources. The basis for understanding these movements lies in their use of scientific method combined with an emotional appeal to unmet needs in the society.

In this light, we can examine the origin and development of sensitivity training. The staff of the Connecticut workshop was committed to finding a process of changing people through group action. When the trainees attended the sessions that discussed the events in the day's groups, a new dimension of experience opened. Although no effect on the groups was established, the reactions of the participants, their continued attendance at the meetings, and the enthusiasm they evoked showed the appeal of this procedure. In the formal evaluation of the workshop no attention was paid to the possible effect. The essence seems to have been the experience for itself.

In addition, the action orientation of the trainers would make them sensitive to any method that found acceptance by the trainees and gave hope that expansion of this procedure might prove even more exciting in the future. They were clearly impressed by the positive reaction from a group of representatives of the people they were trying to reach.

It is unlikely that there was at first a real intention to start a social movement, however. The leaders had some deep ideological commitments to democracy, increased participation, accelerated social change, and improved intergroup relations, as well as an affinity for such terms as group decision, group growth, and change agents. But they were also in varying degrees committed to the scientific method. Essentially the social psychologists in the group wanted to establish principles of group functioning and attitude change. In addition, a team of research scientists and graduate students from Harvard and MIT, who were seemingly instrumental in the start of the movement, looked with some amusement at the efforts to create groups as if they were hothouse flowers. They, too, reinforced the importance of the scientific method.

The atmosphere in the workshop led to a combination of faith and knowledge. The immediate subsequent history reflects this tension. Almost immediately, despite skepticism about the success of the current workshop, it was decided to conduct another workshop the following year and to center it on group techniques, especially group feedback and similar self-confrontation. Thus, the discovery of a new solution for social problems was accepted and the group committed itself to its pursuit. Concurrently, the research effort was also to be experimental, and thus a balance with scientific validation was to be established. Out of this program came the first training laboratories at Bethel, Maine, which have continued to be the center of the movement.

Part II

THE SOCIAL SETTING

Chapter 3

The Pursuit of Happiness

"America is, in my experience, the only country in the world which is, for better and for worse, squarely, uncompromisingly, in the twentieth century."[1]

Sensitivity training is a procedure that uses group action as an end in itself. The principle of feedback is of primary concern in sensitivity group meetings. Second, taboos of ordinary society are reversed: frankness substitutes for tact, self expression for manners, nonverbal techniques for language, and immediacy for responsibility. Norms that have evolved to ensure the smooth and continual operation of society are rejected. The newly adopted standards of behavior are conducive to a strong emotional impact. A third feature which may seem contradictory is the strong commitment of the sensitivity training movement to the justification of its procedure through scientific method alone and not through religious or ideological commitments. Emerging from these three characteristics of sensitivity groups is a fourth, general one, the overarching stress on the value of change, a change whose direction is not necessarily determined.

This constellation makes sensitivity training different from the social movements usually treated in the sociological literature. It did not develop in response to physical deprivation or social discrimination; neither does it emphasize a strong ideological or doctrinal split in society. It takes as its point of departure the need for new forms

[1] A. Alvarez. *Under Pressure*. Baltimore, Md.: Penguin, 1965.

31

of self-expression and interpersonal relations; and it tries to use the language of science in justifying these needs and pointing to their fulfillment. This different type of social movement presupposes within the society a new constellation of conditions which led to its development. Thus, we could look for conditions that promote dissatisfaction in a generally affluent society, insecurity about life style and goals, as well as unsatisfying interpersonal relations. And we could see where previously successful channels for remedying this situation are now closed.

This description of society fits certain aspects of the contemporary scene, especially in the United States. As the trend to an affluent, mobile, restless, and secular society has progressed furthest in this country, it seems likely that new ideas developed by social psychologists and educators will be most easily taken up and transformed into a social movement in the United States. In other societies this trend has not been so strong: sensitivity training may grow but rarely transcends the institution in which it developed.

MOBILITY

Geographic mobility has always been a basic fact in American life. Migration is traditional in a country established in the last three centuries through population movement, first as immigration and then as migration to the West. Mobility has had its impact on society and its effects have been dealt with through the establishment of institutions such as civic clubs, social groups, and voluntary organizations, where newcomers could find contacts in the community. Throughout American history, there has been an emphasis on institutions and behavior patterns that aid the rapid assimilation of newcomers into a new community group and also ease the difficulty of separation from the old. Observers of the American scene have commented on mechanisms that promote rapid assimilation: the easy, but superficial access to sociability, the mechanisms of integration into the social network, and the means of maintaining contacts among mobile groups.

New patterns have emerged from this traditional mobility. The last few decades have seen new population movements from the rural areas to the cities, from the cities to the suburbs, and a renewed push toward the West, Southwest, and the South Atlantic and Gulf areas. Except for the migration of Negroes from the South into the cities, this movement has been primarily an affair of the well-

32

educated, technically and professionally skilled group. The move to the suburbs, which constitutes the bulk of intrastate movement, has been primarily a middle-class phenomenon, especially for those who are also mobile in a social sense. Interstate mobility has involved, by and large, a small section of the population. This sector is primarily comprised of the higher-educated groups and persons in certain professional and technical occupations, but not necessarily the peak income occupations.[2]

The main recipient areas, such as the new suburbs and the West, especially California, have also been the primary centers of sensitivity training and encounter groups, pointing up the direct connection between mobility and sensitivity training. Encounter groups have become a respectable "lonely hearts club" for newcomers or those without roots in a community. The new norms of immediacy and letting oneself go to a strong emotional experience are conducive to rapid integration into a new setting as well as departure without emotional damage.

Sensitivity training also provides instruction for a mobile society or a mobile subculture. W. Henry summarized the problems of successful change.

> The *scene* of social mobility, in this classic case, though not necessarily for all cases, is an interactive scene. The characteristics of this interactive scene are:
> 1. Goals and values are learned by the mobile person in interaction, and they are *practiced* in such a setting.
> 2. Lifestyle changes imply a significant amount of actual social *participation* with individuals who already hold the position toward which the mobile individual is moving, and altered or reduced participation with those abandoned.
> 3. Social space changes can involve less marked, or less broadly based, interaction, especially in the case of the male where occupational advancement is a crucial condition for mobility. For the

[2] D. Bogue. *The Population of the United States*. Glencoe, Ill.: Free Press, 1959. H. Eldridge and D. Thomas. *Demographic Analysis and Interrelations,* Vol. III of *Population Re-Distribution and Economic Growth in the United States*. Philadelphia: American Philosophical Society, 1965. P. Fellin and E. Litwak. "Neighborhood Cohesion under Conditions of Mobility," *American Sociological Review*, 28, 1963, 364–376. J. Ladinsky. "Occupational Determinants of Geographic Mobility among Professional Workers," *American Sociological Review*, 32, April, 1967, 258–264. U.S. Department of Commerce, Bureau of the Census. *Population Characteristics*. Series P–20, No. 188.

woman whose mobility is not based principally upon occupation, social participation remains the crucial condition.[3]

Thus, in social as well as physical mobility many individuals have lost the cues they both gave and received to establish an identity within their society. This privation may be felt deeply in loss of identity and a search for identifying symbols. Sensitivity training promises to teach one how to read the cues given him as well as how to send out the most favorable cues. Feedback techniques try to make a person aware of how he impresses others as well as give him a chance to check his own impressions of himself. The training group enables him to improve his adjustment to the group and to gain a trust in his ability to adapt to many new situations. The ethos of the groups also promotes belief in a new or real identity where the restricting and varying norms of society are less important, and the authentic self, that is, what a person would like to believe himself to be, is the only important fact to consider.

Toffler has discussed the concept of modular man who plugs in only part of his personality in any relationship and hardly ever involves his whole self.[4] Clearly the modular person has little trouble in adjusting to new situations and breaking them off, which would run counter to the idea that people have a strong need for at least some total relationships. Whether or not these relationships are basically necessary, tradition has been on the side of total involvement, and the term "alienated" comes readily to mind to describe the modular man. Sensitivity training offers the experience of total involvement in a relationship of very short duration, accepting the basic situation of transiency without forcing one to resort to the modular relationship.

The relationship of the mobile society to sensitivity training has been recognized by its adherents. Bennis and Slater have exalted the *Temporary Society*,[5] see in it a transition to true democracy, and describe sensitivity training as a mechanism to create adaptive organizations for a new society. However, Slater in a later book, *The Pursuit of Loneliness*, is more pessimistic about contemporary American society.[6] He points out as its main features the rejection of in-

[3] W. E. Henry. "Social Mobility as Social Learning: Some Elements of Change in Motive and Social Context," in M. B. Kantor, *Mobility and Mental Health*. Springfield, Ill.: Thomas, 1965, 31.

[4] A. Toffler. *Future Shock*. New York: Random House, 1970.

[5] W. C. Bennis and P. E. Slater. *The Temporary Society*. New York: Harper, 1968.

[6] P. E. Slater. *The Pursuit of Loneliness*. Boston: Beacon Press, 1970.

terpersonal relations—from do-it-yourself projects to decline of public transportation—and an inability to solve social problems on the spot, preferring to ignore them. In this context he feels migration has been the main mechanism in American history for man to escape the solution of local problems. He sees in sensitivity training a procedure that can overcome these deficiencies of society, giving people practice in interpersonal relations where they were not previously accustomed to them. Sensitivity training is thus an excellent synthetic community experience for a population that has lost the meaning of "community" but not its sentimental appeal.

Carl Rogers, who has taken more and more the role of a major prophet of the sensitivity training movement, sums up his beliefs on the relationship of mobility to laboratory training as follows: "I believe there will be possibilities for the *rapid* development of closeness between and among persons, a closeness which is not artificial, but is real and deep, and which will be well suited to our increasing mobility of living. Temporary relationships will be able to achieve the richness and meaning which heretofore have been associated only with lifelong attachments."[7]

AFFLUENCE

One of the striking facts about the period in which sensitivity training has spread is the increased affluence of a great part of the population. Simply stated, this means that a majority can avoid worrying about their subsistence. The reputation of the United States as an affluent country has had a long history; but the period immediately following the Second World War saw abrupt changes in the direction of affluence. Statistics show the extent of wealth in the aggregate. Family income more than doubled in the decade from 1939 to 1949, resulting from several factors: an increase in the percentage of the population in higher-paying occupations, in the average income within each occupation, in the number of income receivers for each family. We do not have to dwell on income statistics to make this point; the spectacular increase in expenditures for products that had only recently been luxury items—televisions, cars and second cars, boats, travel, and the arts—bears witness to the effect of increased affluence.

These statements do not imply that poverty has not persisted in

---

[7] C. R. Rogers. "Interpersonal Relationships U.S.A. 2000," *Journal of Applied Behavioral Science, 4,* 1968, 268–269.

a considerable segment of the population. However, during the period from 1945 to 1960, many people became prosperous, possessed most items of necessity as a matter of course, and more and more came to expect items of luxury.[8] The dominant political and social ideas during this period also stressed the prosperity of the majority and tended to overlook the distress of the minority. Popular books by respected economists and social philosophers, such as Galbraith's *Affluent Society* and Potter's *People of Plenty,* emphasized the self-image of a society that had solved its basic economic problems.[9] Preoccupation with poverty reappeared only in the early 1960's.

Thus we find a considerable segment of society feeling wealthy and economically secure and enjoying a high standard of consumption, especially in comparison with the preceding decades of depression and war. These conditions had important consequences for the development of sensitivity training.

The first and most obvious consequence of affluence is the availability of funds and time. This affluence was a motivation for the movement to develop in the direction it did. Many laboratories and encounter sessions are financed by fees charged to the participants. Because a large percentage of personal and corporate income is available for luxuries, it is possible to collect high tuitions from individuals or for participants to be financed by sponsoring organizations. Sensitivity training thus becomes part of the expense-account economy. The recreational aspect of sensitivity training laboratories has been very prominent from their beginning. The newly found leisure of the prosperous is still too unusual to be used exclusively for recreation or other seemingly unproductive activities. An attractive compromise solution has been the combination of recreation with presumably elevating situations, a traditional American solution, at least since Chautauqua and revival days.

The other effects of affluence may be more subtle, but they may point to motives for the inception of sensitivity training. The direction of the whole economy has been away from an economy of scarcity. Improved technology and greater exploitation of raw materials and energy sources have made it possible to produce goods and products in great quantities. Production itself has decreased in impor-

---

[8] H. Miller. *Income of the American People.* New York: Wiley, 1965. A. Toffler. *The Culture Consumers.* New York: St. Martin's Press, 1964. S. De Grazia. *Of Time, Work, and Leisure.* New York: Twentieth Century Fund, 1962.

[9] J. K. Galbraith. *The Affluent Society.* Boston: Houghton Mifflin, 1958. D. M. Potter. *People of Plenty.* Chicago: University of Chicago Press, 1954.

tance in the economy; many people assume that technically it is possible to provide all the goods necessary. It must be remembered that the formative years of sensitivity training occurred during the period before fear of the population explosion and ecological imbalance became widespread. Thus, society could turn away from focusing on production and survival problems and concentrate on efforts to make economic life more rewarding and pleasant as well as efficient. As economic necessities decline in importance, concern about the manner and social conditions of production increases. As in the whole society the proportion of people involved in primary agricultural extraction and manufacturing production declines, so in each organization, management becomes bigger and more important than direct production. This in turn leads to a self-conscious examination of interpersonal relations.

Similar mechanisms are at work in the individual. The necessity for survival and fulfillment of such basic needs as food, shelter, and clothing have throughout history engaged the full efforts of man, and the ambition not to have to worry about their adequate fulfillment has been realized by only a few. Correspondingly, people have expected that achievement of these needs could bring happiness or at least lasting satisfaction.

Many who were able to achieve such a fortunate state found that it did not bring happiness or even satisfaction, however. The newly affluent discovered quickly that other needs were not satisfied; these needs were less easy to define but frustration was manifested in boredom, feelings of worthlessness, lack of excitement, and other indicators stereotyped as the symptoms of affluent suburbia. Psychologists began to attack this problem. They learned to distinguish several kinds of drives. Earlier biological biases considered drives not basic to survival as less important. Later theorists, especially those writing in the period under discussion, acknowledged that other drives share an equal importance with survival drives. A. Maslow, one of the most influential of these theorists, has also been one of the leading thinkers of the sensitivity training movement.[10] He distinguishes between D (depletion) and E (enhancement) drives, recognizing that the survival forces must be satisfied before the enhancement drives can reach their full strength. The importance of

[10] A. Maslow. *Motivation and Personality*. New York: Harper, 1954; and *Eupsychian Management*. Homewood, Ill.: Dorsey Press, 1965. Other theories can be found in works by philosophers and psychologists from B. Russell, *In Praise of Idleness*. New York: Norton, 1935; to D. Katz, "The Functional Approach to the Study of Attitudes," *Public Opinion Quarterly*, 24, 1960, 163–204.

enhancement drives is becoming more and more widely recognized. Effective social motivation for middle-class adults in today's society may be stimulated more by enhancement drives of self-realization, excitement, and creativity than by stability-producing drives of security or satisfaction of basic biological needs.

SECULARIZATION

Mobility and affluence have given many people, especially educated white-collar workers, a need to find a new center of interest, a new way of seeking meaning in life and of arousing strong emotional experiences. Guidance for the solution of these problems has been traditionally the function of religion. As we have indicated before, this route has become unacceptable to many people, especially the affluent mobile group.

Glock and Stark have provided an effective framework for analyzing the position of religion in the life of a person and its function in society.[11] They distinguish five dimensions: the *ideological*, which consists of beliefs which adherents are supposed to hold; the *intellectual*, which includes information on the basic tenets of faith and the practices appropriate to adherents; the *experiential*, which encompasses religious emotions or experiences of ultimate value associated with religion; the *ritualistic*, which refers to specific practices; and the *consequential*, which constitutes the secular effects of religious membership. This last dimension is considered separate from the others as it concerns itself with the relation of religion to the rest of society, while the other four are concerned with religious affiliation only.

The first four dimensions can be looked at as two groups of two. The ideological and intellectual dimensions describe what the adherent of a religion is supposed to know; they represent religion as a way to understand the value of the universe and man's place in it. The experiential and ritualistic dimensions refer to special feelings associated with the religious realm and socially determined practices in handling emotions. Psychologically, the first group represents the cognitive aspects and the second group the emotive one.

Throughout human history these two aspects have been intimately connected. Man has turned to religion to understand facts about himself and about nature, and has expressed strong ineffable

[11] C. Y. Glock and R. Stark. *Religion and Society in Tension.* Chicago: Rand McNally, 1965.

feelings about them. It has been difficult to distinguish these two in real situations. Search for ultimate reality has typically been connected with religious experiences and ritual. Sociologists of religion since Durkheim have shown how the cognitive and emotional sides are aspects of an ideal of society and an important basis of social integration.[12]

The last two centuries in the Western world have witnessed a natural experiment separating the different functions of religion. The tenets of religion have become of declining importance. The rise of a society that relies on secular knowledge rather than religion for the final truth has been unique in history. The advancement of science has systematically undermined the influence of religion. By explaining the physical universe, the nature of life, the position of man in the biological realm, the nature of the psyche and of society, science has proposed knowledge that has substituted for the revelations of religion. For many, therefore, religion is not needed anymore as a basis for understanding the world. As the cognitive value of religion has been discarded, the influence of religion as a whole has subsided.[13]

The close connection between the cognitive aspects of religion and the ethical and emotional aspects was recognized during the rise of science. The obstacles such scientists as Galileo, Darwin, and Freud had to overcome are too well known to need elaboration. Opponents of these scientists were correct in implying that the whole fabric of religion was one, and that undermining the cognitive side of belief might have consequences for other areas of religion that would not be logically necessary. This has happened; the need for a religious explanation of the universe has reached a low level. We have now a situation in which we can observe the independent functioning of the other components of the religious experience.

As long as a recognized religion has a strong hold on a society it provides sufficient justification for expression of emotions. In the seventeenth and eighteenth centuries, religious justification began to fade, partly as a consequence of the rise of science, and also as a reaction to intense struggles to which religious conflicts had led, especially those occurring in the seventeenth century. The period of the enlightenment was the first to champion science against traditional religion. Sufficient scientific knowledge had been gained to

[12] E. Durkheim. *The Elementary Forms of Religious Life*. London: Allen and Unwin, 1915.
[13] B. Wilson. *Religion in a Secular Society*. Baltimore, Md.: Penguin, 1966 gives extensive documentation of this trend.

make this step possible. The denominational struggles in Europe had also produced a need for relative peace, and the wars of the eighteenth century were quiet dynastic struggles, as opposed to the religious wars of the preceding century. Ultimate aims reappeared, however, this time as secular aims and ideologies, and the succeeding one hundred fifty years saw wars and violence of unprecedented ferocity based on conflicts of secular ideology. The period immediately preceding the birth of sensitivity training had seen the extremes to which ideological aims dominated society, for example, in Germany and Russia. In the United States, however, a distrust of any ultimate aims in favor of concentrating on means and processes became an accepted philosophy. This approach had been expressed before in the pragmatism of James and Dewey. It is significant that the original philosopher and theorist of the sensitivity training movement, Kenneth Benne, was a student of Dewey. But beyond this direct intellectual descent, belief in process as opposed to goals was very much within the spirit of the times and the country.

Evidence seems to show that the emotional needs that religion has served still persist. What had been easily justified by religious aims is being rediscovered as having value in its own right. The decline of the cognitive aspect of religion and the distrust of ultimate aims leave ritual and emotion on their own. We do not really know much about the need for these experiences, how strong they are normally, and how much they are influenced by differential experience. This is a novel situation in human history which leads to a strong emphasis on the intense experience, behavior, and ritual found in group experience. We find an intensive search for new forms in which old religious rituals can be accepted by a modern, science-believing generation. This development has been reinforced in the rise of a phenomenon which has been called "civil religion,"[14] the investing of institutions, documents, and officials with those emotional values that divine religion has had in other places. Among possible alternatives, sensitivity training clearly fulfills many of the specifications: it talks a scientific language, it promises both personal growth and instrumental ability, it promises a definite, set-apart, change experience, and includes special ritualistic behavior. It gives an air of scientific respectability to the feelings people have previously sought in a religious experience.

[14] R. Bellah. "Civil Religion in America," *Daedalus*, 26, Winter, 1967, 1–21.

THE CHANGING SOCIETY

The implications of these three trends in contemporary society —mobility, affluence, and secularism—include the need for new tools to deal with these unprecedented problems. The years have brought a plethora of books dealing with the problems afflicting society. Recurrent themes throughout these books are the high value placed on change, on individual regeneration, and on adaptation to flux for its own sake.

In each historical period and in each cultural setting, institutions have developed and practitioners have arisen to make men more perfect, to reduce the gap between their abilities, their needs, and the social demands put on them, and to give them the most harmonious life possible, appropriate to the condition of the society. Experts in human improvement have treated men singly, in groups, and as whole societies. These experts have a heavy responsibility. They claim the right to manage and reconstruct the basic life style of other individuals, be it for the individual or the common good. In exercising this power they accept certain responsibilities toward the society and toward the individuals they deal with. These persons may be regarded as the model of professionals; in examining their performance, we deal with the privileges and responsibilities of professionals.

The practice of human improvement has advanced along two main lines: developing man to what he *should be* and beginning from a theory of what he *is*. As long as religion united the cognitive and emotive aspects of life, the whole field of change was a religious question. While science has become more and more important, developing man to what he should be has still been viewed as a function of religion, the sacred part of society, but finding a theory of what man is has become a function of science, the material or cognitive part of society.

The influence of religious ideals is completely ineffective today for a large sector of the population. Even secular ideologies have lost their influence as motives for molding people according to some ideal. General social aims are discounted; regeneration is based on individual improvement, detached from social institutions. This philosophy of personal change became formalized in the 1960's,[15] but its origin can be traced to the concern with psychotherapy and other change techniques without ultimate aims that became crucial in

---

[15] C. Reich. *The Greening of America.* New York: Random House, 1970.

previous decades.[16] In this context, new techniques of change came to the fore, namely, the approach to personal change based on science.

Let us take the description of a T-group given by a former T-group trainer.

> I think where it started was that part of T-group operations where people looked at each other's roles and told each other how they perceived each other. This is a very attractive thing for some people to do, so this then became sort of pulled out and made kind of the central theme and central purpose. I have quite serious objections to doing that; that is I like it fine in a context of a group trying to get a job done. I think then I can look at behavior and accept criticism. But I don't like it when it's in a vacuum, and when the discussion centers around what do I think of you, what kind of person are you? I think under these conditions nobody knows what to do with the information, . . . the comments made are more likely to talk about the guy who is doing the perceiving than the guy he is perceiving. And by and large it is a mischievous enterprise and an anxiety-producing enterprise. Of course that explains something of what happens. The group goes through these tremendous anxiety phases at the beginning and then begin to develop solidarity, and then begin to develop a kind of uneasy complacence in trusting each other, and then they feel tremendous relief, and so they go out saying, "God what a wonderful experience; we went into the depths and came out of it." And it's a conversion experience.[17]

The last comment is significant. If it is a conversion experience, then we face the question, what have they been converted to? Clearly the whole technique is more geared to ideology as a motivating factor in social change than to force, but here participants undergo the experience for the sake of change itself, not for an ultimate aim. Techniques similar to the ones used in T-groups have been used before, but with an ultimate aim in mind rather than just a simple change experience.

We can see here the value put on change, on the regeneration experience, pure and simple. The impression that sensitivity training is worthwhile, that a usually rigid group of modular men can form a unit, and that "real" scientists conduct the meetings, makes the change experience acceptable. The vocabulary of change, "change agents," "gut-learning," "spontaneity," "authenticity," is all directed toward some change from everyday life, no matter what. In the same

[16] P. Rieff. *The Triumph of the Therapeutic*. New York: Harper, 1966.
[17] Herbert Thelen. Personal interview.

vein, Kenneth Burke has put forth the concept of the "God-term," the term which represents the principal value in a society. Change might be such a term now. Weaver has said that change is an ultimate word in our society.[18]

NATIONAL DIFFERENCES

It might not have been coincidence that the birth, growth, and greatest spread of the sensitivity training movement occurred in the United States. The same ideas of group dynamics, interpersonal workshops, and organizational change had arisen independently in England. There, however, these exercises stayed almost exclusively within professional confines, mainly the organizations that started them, and were conducted for clients with specific problems. Sensitivity training did not arouse the indiscriminate attention of a major population group. Thus, while intellectually the scene was ready for the intensive group method, the social situation was not ripe for its spread to the society at large.

The Tavistock Institute of Human Relations in London is an interesting case in point.[19] Tavistock had been a clinic, psychoanalytic in orientation but hospitable to interdisciplinary work, since 1920. Interest in group psychotherapy and in work with social problems created procedures and ideas similar to those later developed in sensitivity training. In fact, during the early 1940's some of the staff suggested facetiously that a sign should be erected over the entrance reading, "Here and Now Starts Here." The Second World War brought new situations for group work; leaderless group techniques were designed for crew selection and training. Immediately after the war, two projects were set up which used principles related to group dynamics: A. T. M. Wilson and Trist designed special communities for returning prisoners of war, and a group worked on the problems of the ailing and nationalized coal industry.

Although the ideas of the Tavistock group had developed independently, and were primarily integrated into the psychoanalytic

[18] K. Burke. *A Grammar of Motives.* New York: Prentice-Hall, 1952, Chap. II. R. Weaver. "Ultimate Terms in Contemporary Rhetoric," *Perspectives USA, 11,* 1955, 122–141.

[19] For the history of the Tavistock Clinic see H. V. Dicks. *50 Years of the Tavistock Clinic.* London: Routledge and Kegan Paul, 1970. For the contacts between Lewin and Tavistock, see A. Marrow, *The Practical Theorist.* New York: Basic Books, 1969; I. Yalom, *The Theory and Practice of Group Psychotherapy.* New York: Basic Books, 1970, especially 150–151.

thought of Melanie Klein, the staff had direct contact with the American sources of the sensitivity training movement. Lewin's work especially was known and appreciated by the Tavistock staff even in the 1930's, and personal contact was made between Trist and Lewin in 1945–46. In fact, Lewin was invited to spend 1947–48 (the years of the first workshop) at Tavistock, but his sudden death prevented this plan. The relationship between the American and English groups has continued to be close. The Research Center for Group Dynamics and Tavistock jointly publish their research journal, *Human Relations;* representatives from Tavistock visited the early National Training Laboratory and visits have been exchanged since. The Tavistock theory and practice is recognized as one of the pillars of intensive group work.

In spite of all this parallelism and interaction, there has been one fundamental distinction between the Tavistock approach and all American approaches. The English approach is conducted for special clients—organizations or individuals—with distinct problems. In Britain itself, Tavistock training is practically concentrated within the Institute, with rare exceptions. Some former staff members are now conducting the training at different places, such as Bristol or Leeds. The whole program has stayed a tightly knit operation, without appeal to laymen, and probably little known to the general public outside of those with direct professional concern.

The Tavistock approach is usually considered one of the main branches of sensitivity training, but it has never become a social movement. Instead, it concentrated on specific problems which the members of the Institute tried to solve. It did not send out any proselytes, any missionaries supportive of the group, and in fact, most of the Tavistock work (except for a recent offshoot in the United States) is done at Tavistock Institute itself. We have here a control condition we can use to see the conditions that prevented this same kind of group development as that in the United States from becoming the center of a social movement, and caused it to stay completely within its own professional boundaries. From the point of view of our study, it is fortunate that here we have found a control group with the same caliber of staff, similar theory, and even some connection with the center of sensitivity training, but did not take the role of a social movement.

Tavistock staff members in conversation are quite appalled about some of the developments in the direction of social movements in the United States. They are committed to a consistent theoretical approach to solutions of specific problems and are repelled by what they might consider emotionalism and sensationalism, for instance, the casual direction of a laboratory session or encounter group. Eric Miller tried to express his feelings in this metaphor: "When I go to Washington (that is, the National Training Laboratory) I would wear my waistcoat; if I were going to Bethel I would button it up closely; but if I were going to California, I would wear two."[20] Only during the late 1960's has sensitivity training in open groups appeared in England. In 1970, a tabloid-like paper, *News of the World*, featured an interview about the training given the actors in *Oh! Calcutta!* as follows: " 'Our sexual effects were eliminated, one by one, and replaced by what he [the director] called sensitivity.' There wasn't much sensitivity on the stage when I watched sketches about lustful wife-swapping and assorted fornication but I let that pass."[21]

In other countries where no indigenous movement has existed, American influence has sometimes generated a demand for training centers. Where this development has been successful, it has confined itself to an academic and professional setting. As we shall see, even the purely professional contacts have sometimes been strongly resisted: NTL's first "mission" to Sweden, for instance, ended in failure because Swedes simply could not accept the outward forms of informality, for example, first-name calling and interruptions, which the Americans considered to be the signs of spontaneity.

The reason for this difference in spread of the movement seems to be that the trends we have identified as the social base of the sensitivity training movement are weaker in other countries. The sheer size of the country and its migratory traditions make geographic mobility more common in the United States than in Europe, where the lack of a well-integrated business empire makes the businessman as well as the academician less mobile. Similarly, there is less affluence, and the urgency of postwar rebuilding has made the need for necessities still paramount for the greater part of the population. Religious influence may not be any stronger in many European countries than in the United States. Nevertheless, the shift from organized religion historically has been toward secular ideologies with a definite orientation toward a future goal, such as Marxism or fascism. There is little basis in tradition for a cult of experience.

This last point, the subjective tradition, may be the most important one. Statistically, differences in mobility, affluence, and secularism between countries certainly can be found. But the im-

[20] Personal interview.
[21] *News of the World,* Aug. 21, 1970, 3.

portant point is that the whole national ethos favors these trends in the United States and is an opposing force elsewhere. The belief that change is good, including both social change and personality change, that wealth is a characteristic of the country, and that social progress is part of the religious heritage is an integral part of American history. The same trends can be found in other countries but in opposition to older beliefs in future goals. In a sense, the American beliefs may be said to be characteristic of the twentieth century and adapted to technological and organizational changes.[22] The beginning of a sensitivity training movement in other countries may be a sign of a similar trend. The difference was summed up neatly by Dorothy Stock Whitaker, an American expert and sensitivity training leader now living in Britain: "A British housewife would not go to a session of this kind without a definite aim. After all, the British have not been told that the pursuit of happiness is an inalienable right."[23]

This comparative analysis has reinforced the inference that sensitivity training as a social movement is a reaction to strains in modern life, especially in the United States. It satisfies needs generated by novel conditions that the traditional institutions, especially religion, cannot fill. Sensitivity training may be more a symptom of what ails society than a cure for its ills.

[22] For an examination of cultist movements in the United States based on these conditions, see O. E. Klapp, *The Collective Search for Identity*. New York: Holt, 1969.

[23] Personal interview.

Chapter 4

Chronicles of the Movement

"And the Word became Flesh . . ."

We can now understand the meaning of the Connecticut workshop within its social context. The workshop was designed precisely for that part of the population most susceptible to this new movement. The trainees included people engaged in interracial work, professionals, people involved in education and community work—all were people who were dissatisfied with themselves, their effectiveness in dealing with an important problem, and their relation to the dominant issues of society. In other times, people in a similar predicament might have sought spiritual comfort, ideological inspiration, or confirmation of their weaknesses; but here they were looking for help in the form of improving their techniques of dealing with other people and through the growth of group consciousness.

At this point the backgrounds and particular contributions of each of the leaders should be given more attention, adding to their introduction in Chapter 1. The dominant leader in the workshop was Kurt Lewin. Lewin had been a versatile innovator in many fields of social psychology. In his early work in Germany he had devised a theoretical system able to include emotion, need, and will, and still be subject to rigorous experimentation. In his later work in the United States, he expanded this system to include social psychology, especially a developing theory of group structure and action. Here, too, he developed both theory and experimentation jointly and inaugurated some of the pioneering studies in experimental social

47

psychology. At the same time, he had an abiding interest in social problems and the way in which social science could be used to handle some of the crucial problems of the time. In addition, rare for an academic social psychologist, he kept up interest in, and connections with, professionals in fields allied to social science such as social work, adult education, health education, and nutrition. Because of his many involvements, he was primed for a situation such as the one that developed in Connecticut. He was attuned to the needs of the times, and at the same time was able to use a unique situation for training and to integrate it into a theoretical scheme. His developing interest in groups had led him to use the workshop to study how groups develop and whether groups really could evolve unique growth patterns and personalities.

The other members of the staff of the laboratory fitted in with various aspects of Lewin's work. Ronald Lippitt, who had been his student and had conducted some of the early experiments with groups, had been interested in group leadership but was working as a leader mainly in order to better understand group processes.

Leland Bradford, on the other hand, was primarily interested in adult education. His later importance in the movement was so great that we shall describe his involvement in his own words. Bradford mentions many of the people who were instrumental in starting the interpersonal workshops. They had worked together on similar problems and were ready to accept a new revelation. We can let him introduce the other leaders of the early phase.

> I think it was partly a combination of people, because if I hadn't met Ron Lippitt, I'm sure it wouldn't have moved that way. If I hadn't met Ken Benne I don't think he would have been involved, so in a sense it was people. But I think there were other factors that made it relevant, and for me there were a number of them. Early in the adult education movement, there was a lot of work on group discussion; it wasn't on group process, it was just on group discussion . . . which in a sense, I suppose, implied kind of working things out together in groups rather than unilateral decisions. The second thing that seemed to be an impact, for me anyway, was the New Deal days, where we were facing social problems not too dissimilar from the times here: extreme poverty, people on relief, need to have made work, the need to develop educational systems. So in WPA in Illinois we set up adult education programs, nursery school programs, workers' education programs, housekeeping programs, all kinds of things. The problem then came, how do you pick people who haven't done that sort of work, and who were in a sense psychologically demolished by being on relief and so on, and almost revive

them and give them skills they didn't have in a very short period of time? How do you do things which aren't done in the normal tradition of training people in skills? The example I always think of was we had a week to train a teacher. Well, a college of education had four years. And what could you do in a week? Most of them, except for Ken and Max Goodson, said it couldn't be done. Tradition said it took four years. And secondly we ran into the fact that we had supervisors who didn't know an awful lot more than the people they were supervising. And so there was a problem of how do you manage a group of people who are struggling in a new field? And I think the war was another factor in this thing. The war threw everything out of balance. It also called for the use of all the new knowledge that could be found. It made the request for behavioral science knowledge to be used, what there was of it, and Murray's work in OSS, and Lewin's work and everybody else's . . . you know, were trying to do things. And I think this brought an urgency. My war experience was different from Ken's and Ron's, because I was Training Director for two federal agencies. First the Immigration and Naturalization Service, then the Federal Security, and the problems we faced, how do you suddenly train an awful lot of people to be supervisors or foremen? They used a pattern they call it now the . . . JRI, Job Training, and Job Relations, and Job Methods. These programs were in a sense experience-based. We started one by saying, OK, you tell me how to tie a knot, and obviously you can't do it. Show me how to tie a knot; well, that doesn't work either because the mirror reversed. So you really have to train the guy by giving the experience. It was the guts of experience-based learning. I went through that course, and I hated it, so I tried to modify it, and make it more complex. The need was present and the jobs that I got myself into, I looked desperately for help, and I turned to Ken for his ideas, to others, and I met Ron and got extremely intrigued with his interest and knowledge. He brought me into touch with all the network he knew of Kurt, and Al Zander, and Jack French, and so on, and then toward the end of the war, Ron said he would like to work with me, so I got him as my assistant in the Federal Security Agency. And we experimented in one hospital and so on. Both the accidental meeting of people and the need of the times, both the New Deal days and the war days, brought a new stimulation.[1]

These people then easily reached a decision to have another training laboratory, this time focused more on the meaning of groups than on any particular problem. Support was obtained not only from the Commission for Community Interrelations, but from the Office of Naval Research and the Carnegie and Field Foundations as well.

[1] Personal interview.

The proposed workshop was designed on a larger scale and attempted to include all possible methods which could be used in working with groups, including sessions which were directed toward general group problems, basic skill training groups, and interest groups related to the special ideas and problems of the delegates. It also included efforts to make the whole workshop an almost autonomous community. For this purpose, the workshop was located in a somewhat inaccessible region in northern Maine.

> Bethel is a very interesting place, because although it is a very small town, it has a preparatory academy there which is also a public high school; they're combined. And . . . one of the residents of the town had lived there for years, and had gone there as a patient of a so-called psychiatrist, and stayed on, and outlived the psychiatrist and had his home there, and was a very wealthy man from Cleveland, and gave a lot of money to the academy which permitted them to build some fine buildings. But these buildings were not being used in the summertime so that seemed to be a very good place for NTL to be.[2]

The association with Bethel has persisted over the years to the point that Bethel has become synonymous with at least one branch of sensitivity training. Thus, an attempt was made to create a cultural island that would provide a feeling of community living as well as promote group development.

This self-conscious approach to developing a culture was balanced by an increased research staff, which included anthropologists, clinical psychologists, and social psychologists, to investigate different aspects of the training process and the group atmosphere.

Preparations for the new workshop were intensive. During the year of preparation, Lewin died, and the organizers of the first laboratory, now a large expanded group, were without a center or charismatic leader.[3]

Thus what came to be called the First National Training Laboratory for Group Development brought together a group with varying aims. The primary purpose of the laboratory was to teach the

[2] Hugh Coffey. Personal interview.

[3] Material on the early years of the National Training Laboratory for Group Development comes in great part from personal observation and interviews with most of the persons mentioned in the text. Other sources are Marrow's *The Practical Theorist;* L. Bradford, J. R. Gibb, and K. Benne, *T-Group Theory and Laboratory Method.* New York: Wiley, 1964; and the "Landmarks" issue of the *Journal of Applied Behavioral Science* (3, No. 2, 1967).

delegates to be more efficient in their work within groups. Delegates were selected to represent government, industry, and civic organizations. In spite of attempts to find power people, the typical delegate was more likely to be the president of the PTA, a middle-management official in industry or government, or a public health worker. Whatever the ultimate aims of the laboratory or the staff members were, a major effort had to be made to give training in group techniques to these delegates. Thus a central part of the staff were the three trainers from the Connecticut workshop—Leland Bradford, Kenneth Benne, and Ronald Lippitt—with several additions: Paul Sheats, Alvin Zander, and Robert Polson. Again these additional staff members represented some varying interests. Zander's background was similar to Lippitt's, that of a university-oriented social psychologist with interest in group work. Polson was a sociologist interested in rural extension work. Prior to coming to Bethel, Sheats was almost wholly committed to adult education and mass media at Town Hall in New York. The training staff was inclined toward applications, but included a strong academic social-psychological orientation.

In addition, there was also an expanded research staff under the leadership of John French. He had been active mainly in personnel management and research, but he was intending to return to a university position. The functions of the staff included possible aspects thought to be important in the workings of the group. The largest part of the staff worked on observation of the groups themselves. These observations were made on the morning groups, the basic skill training groups. There were five of them, one for each trainer with a constant group membership. Observations of the groups were made using different methods, including a type of interaction process being developed by R. Freed Bales who later perfected the method and made it a standard instrument. Also used were a somewhat more global group-process observation and the time-honored total-observation method to catch anything the first two types of more formal observation might have missed. Another part of the research staff was engaged in clinical assessment, over-all studies of personality changes that might take place among the delegates and the leaders, and intensive studies of a selected subsample of leaders and delegates. In addition, there was a special staff for immediate analysis of data and anthropological observation of the whole group as a cultural phenomenon. The staff further included administrative personnel, some students who doubled as delegates and staff members, and some of the staff members' families who helped in various ways.[4]

The different orientations of the leaders gave the group some creative excitement but also caused tensions which foreshadowed the later development of the movement. In all three of the main personnel groups—delegates, training staff, and research staff— these different orientations could be found. Among the delegates this consisted of a difference in outlook regarding what they wanted from the lab. Some came for purely professional reasons. They knew exactly what they wanted to learn (new techniques for handling their job), listened when something came up that might interest them, and if they were successful, picked up one or two techniques they could use.[5] Those people had a rational approach and were somewhat skeptical about the lab, but probably were fastest in applying the substance they learned in actual practice. Another group came to understand more about group process. Those delegates, mainly students, were sometimes later recruited into the movement as future team leaders. But probably the largest group came without any definite purpose in mind, merely to obtain some new experience or try out some idea, perhaps in a vague search for social betterment. Within the workshop they were extremely cooperative, participating in different aspects of the training and acting as subjects. For instance, a group of five volunteers was recruited for a special discussion group where they and the leaders would undergo intense personality assessment as well as more intense observation during those group meetings. Near the end of the lab they had one session in the laboratory tradition of feeding back to them their behavior and reactions. The volunteers were prominent members in their workshop, people who were very active, and assumed leadership in many areas besides this special research participation. More than ten years later, I met two of the members of this group separately and under such different circumstances that at first I did not make any connection with the Bethel experience. Both of them brought up the Bethel experience spontaneously as something that worried them very much,

[4] Some indications of the fruits of this research effort and an incidental description of the first National Training Laboratory is found in L. P. Bradford and J. R. P. French, Jr. (eds.), "The Dynamics of the Discussion Group," *Journal of Social Issues*, 4, No. 2, Spring, 1948.

[5] The principal example of this effect is documented in the article by L. Coch and J. R. P. French, "Overcoming Resistance to Change," *Human Relations*, 1, 1948, 512–532, which describes a successful experiment in making workers accept a work simplification procedure.

and both mentioned that they had learned from the experience never to leave themselves open to other people's criticism. Most of the participants did not undergo such strong traumatic experiences, however, and stayed with the movement as faithful alumni.

Similar differences in orientation could be seen among the staff members. By the nature of their job requirements, the training staff was more interested in learning and change, while the research staff possessed more scientific and detached attitudes. In fact, the roles sometimes overlapped. Some of the trainers with more academic backgrounds viewed their groups as an example of face-to-face encounter, and also succeeded in getting their trainees extremely interested in research. Other trainers were more interested in developing a group atmosphere and in promoting the group mystique. At the last session of the workshop, all the trainers made a conscious decision to create a sacred experience, and to have the trainees leave with an almost religious feeling. The final evaluation session was held by the research staff after the last exalted training meeting. Some of the informal observers, who had almost become participants in their groups, remarked that it was hard for them to leave a churchlike experience and then be presented with facts and figures in an evaluation session. Testimonials of "I have been changed" lasted until the departure of the delegates. The research staff tried a more detached orientation, but there was an interesting division between the people who were making the more formal observations and were rotated to ensure reliability, and the informal observers who stayed with the groups and eventually acted more like participants than observers. This could be seen, for instance, in evaluations of the different experiences. The formal observers made judgments comparing the groups and were quite amused at some of the failures, whereas the informal observers always defended the groups, saying one had to understand what the people were doing.

Looking at the workshop dispassionately from the training and research points of view, it is hard to see whether it was a success or a failure. Hindsight can tell us that theory of group performance was insufficiently clear at the time to warrant such an elaborate study; neither was the methodology developed which could measure and analyze the wealth of possible data; this included such purely technical deficiencies as the difficulty in handling measures of interaction and sociometric data without a computer and such enduring problems as the integration of quantitative and qualitative osbervations. Likewise, the training experience seems to have been an important aspect for many who went through the workshop. Nevertheless, it was, and still is, hard to say what the trainees learned, with the exception of those who went in order to pick up some specific purposes and techniques. From the point of view of the whole laboratory, though, it was certainly a success. From what was ambitiously called the First National Training Laboratory in Group Development has come the National Training Laboratory every year since, and different laboratories and satellite groups have sprung up in other locations.

The effects of the first laboratory were evident on its parent organization, the Research Center for Group Dynamics. Some of the staff members who had been very impressed by the workshop intended to conduct training groups as part of their regular academic schedule. However, the more academically oriented staff members of the Center were opposed to this idea. A discussion developed, but it was decided not to make the general staff seminars into group feedback sessions. This decision showed that T-groups, or basic skill training groups as they were called at that time, could never become equivalent to group dynamics but became a special branch. This was one of the early signs that the National Training Laboratory was a movement in its own right and not just another method for applying behavioral science techniques.

The sensitivity training movement developed during the following years in three periods: 1946 to about 1954, when new methods were being tried, and an experimental atmosphere prevailed; the middle 1950's to the early 1960's, when methods were consolidated and became somewhat fixed (the T-group especially was developed during those years); and finally, the period of the 1960's, when waves from new sources moved in on the movement, and the whole movement underwent change and expansion. It appears that in 1971 we are at the beginning of a new period in which the different branches of the movement are trying to assess the effects of this sudden expansion and change.

THE HEROIC PERIOD

The first years of the National Training Laboratory were years of experimentation. The excitement generated in the first workshop promised expansion into many directions. Bethel could become a place where students and experimenters would find a field situation in which to investigate the relationships between individual and group dynamics. It could become a training ground for professionals working with groups and a site for supplementary training for personnel in group work, community work, adult education, and other new and developing professions. Or it could be a haven for those concentrating on the problem of group action itself. This was the course eventually taken.

Of course, no immediate decision was made to proceed in this way. Several possibilities were tried. New staff was recruited from different fields: people who had experience in different kinds of behavioral science, and who had the motivation for, or interest in, novel methods of group work and therapy.

Staff alterations and variations in composition of the delegates (trainees) reflected the varying changes in emphasis. One year the emphasis was mainly on personality factors, and additional clinicians and psychiatrists were added to the staff. This step toward interpreting the laboratory method as therapy for normals was soon retracted, especially because the traditional psychodynamic theory did not mesh easily with the more social orientation of the lab. At the other extreme, in a later year general semanticists were invited to study the language and communication processes of the laboratory. We can see these as attempts to link the laboratory process to existing social science. Parallel with these efforts was research which was less concerned with the development of the groups themselves but used groups as good examples to study the relation between individual and group characteristics.

In the same way, the composition of the trainees changed. For instance, in one year the Episcopal church sent a great number of priests to the training session. From this session derived the influence that sensitivity training has in many churches, especially the Episcopal. Lippitt mentions that the nature of the group composition was one of the main problems of this experiment. The original assumption was that

> people who came from different backgrounds in professions and occupations would be confronted with having to get past their own occupational language, their own occupational imagery and assumptions by having to find common ground with folks in other occupations. And also that people who were strangers to each other would be freer to initiate a new culture than those who knew each other. Another development was that of occupational labs, in which instead of having people who were strangers and occupationally heterogeneous, occupational labs began to develop of people in the *same* occupational roles, with religion labs co-sponsored with the National Council of Churches, and there began to be the Middle Management labs of Arden House for industrial people and corpo-

55

ration presidents' labs and we began to get homogeneous occupational role groups. Out of that developed what was called the "Family Lab," and the family meant people who worked together back home, in the same department or company. So in addition to the occupational labs, we had labs for back home, and out of this began to develop the whole concept of team development, so that the faculty of the school would be a lab client. This began to hook up the whole training activities of NTL with another area of work which was "OD" [organizational development].[6]

Group composition was one area in which the original orientation of the laboratory was changed. The initial idea of using strangers as a means to bring the trainee out of his shell was found deficient, because the exact structure of the group was important. Change in a specific direction could be effected more easily in homogeneous groupings; permanency of specific changes, such as in actual work settings, would be guaranteed by adjusting the work structure of the training group to the structure of the real situation. However, in this case a general training plan would have to be sacrificed to the particular circumstances of application. Transfer and generality of training are thus in direct conflict.

Lippitt mentions three basic assumptions in addition to that of group composition which were found to be faulty during this period of experimentation: one was the cultural island, the disconnection of the trainees from their usual settings; another, a main idea of the cultural island theory, "to give the individual a chance to examine with feedback and a chance to experiment, a chance to develop some patterns of behavior in which they would be having as the main purpose of this experimentation and this opening up or looking at themselves the transfer to their occupational roles." And the third was that the major learning experience was connected with leadership and functioning in groups. These were the early assumptions of Bethel designed to use the peculiar group process as a means of occupational improvement; rejecting these assumptions was a cause as well as a consequence of the lessened importance of transfer of training. The training group was not intended to be the only, or even principal, teaching device in the laboratory. For instance, "theory input," or classical lecture method, was added as well as exercises of all kinds. The widespread experimentation during this time also included psychiatric and sociological orientations, general semantics, and psychodrama.

[6] R. Lippitt. Personal interview.

What of the group technique itself? Kenneth Benne describes its evolution.[7] The main problem was that the training group was loaded down with too many responsibilities. In the First National Training Laboratory the basic morning group was called the BST (basic skill training) group. Here the members discussed relevant and widely applicable problems of their occupations, practical leadership and membership skills, and lived through the emotional experiences of the group as well. Benne describes the function of the BST group under the heading, "The Separation of Extraneous Training Functions from the T-Group." He shows the conflicts that occurred because of the ambiguity of the group: the trainer experienced role conflict between being a teacher of practical problems and a trainer; he could not be a lecturer and a helper at the same time. The trainees used the occupational context of the group sessions as a means of resisting the pressure occurring in the early stages of group development. Finally, the inclusion of outside topics also conflicted with group training in a purely procedural manner. If group problem solving is taught within a group, the solutions must be applicable within the group session itself, which is not possible with "back-home" problems. On all these counts, the original basic skill training groups led to conflict.

Benne shows in detail how the T-group developed out of the BST group. This first happened by adding new, clinically oriented staff. Within two years, in 1949, the name T-group (training) appeared, and the original core group, Bradford, Benne, and Lippitt, were deposed from active leadership of the T-group while remaining in power positions as far as the whole laboratory was concerned. The more clinical orientation of the actual leaders pushed the groups further toward therapy groups, much to the dismay of the original core leaders. The "old-timers" had two reservations: the "normal" trainees had come to the laboratory for education, not therapy, and crossing the borderline toward therapy was a violation of the implicit contract between the laboratory and the trainees. Further, the format was considered too limited to bring about any real deep-seated therapeutic changes. In spite of these misgivings, the T-group proved a popular and enduring innovation. Additional types of groups were designed to take over the functions discarded by the T-groups, such as A-groups (activity), which were homogeneous occupational groupings dealing with common problems, and C-groups

[7] K. D. Benne. "History of the T Group in the Laboratory Setting," in Bradford, Gibb, and Benne, *op. cit.,* 80–135.

(community), which dealt with problems of the laboratory itself. The common tendency, however, was for these groups to become T-groups as well.

The use of community groups brings up another point that shows the central position of group formation in itself. The early laboratory had included community meetings in which problems of the whole management staff were discussed. These meetings were gradually disbanded, and control was kept by the staff. In this way the possibility of the importance of larger units than the group was played down. Consequently, concern with social problems became secondary, as it was not directly relevant to the group experience itself.

In discussions with trainers and trainees of that period, as well as from the study of Benne's definitive account, we get the impression that the T-group developed despite everybody's efforts: core trainers and many trainees were interested in back-home application; many of the social psychologists wanted mainly conceptual development; and clinicians pushed toward therapy. Out of all that, the T-group developed as the heart of the enterprise, a group devoted mainly to its own problems, to the discussion of the progress of the group itself and of the effects of the members on each other. It is apparent that this social invention corresponded to a deep-felt need on the part of all concerned. Thus, pure experience won out over goal-directed effort.

It must not be supposed, however, that this development resulted from calculated planning or acrimonious conflict. On the contrary, the different developments occurred in a mood of discovery: each new departure was felt to be exciting experimentation, and the whole atmosphere was one of participation in a bold venture for the future. Stuart Chase, in his book *Roads to Agreement*, described his experience at Bethel in 1950.[8] His chapters on his visit to Bethel vibrate with excitement. The open power plays within the groups, the exposure of personal interactions which are usually covered up by social conventions, the different group arrangements suiting the ideology of the leaders, the management of his own talk to ensure maximum participation, all these descriptions combine to make the reader feel that something is happening which can engage the emotions and loyalties of the members. Chase saw the possibilities inherent in the groups for education for emotional growth and imagination, improvement of teaching techniques through discussion,

[8] S. Chase. *Roads to Agreement.* New York: Harper, 1951, 83–99.

new methods of group therapy, and general improvement of people's lives. He also saw the danger of sensitivity training becoming a cult, because of the jargon and the need for a mystic solution to all the ills of the world. He notes that cult and scientific method have never mixed, and hopes for scientific modesty in future development. He ends another chapter, however, with the plea, "Give us another five years,"[9] the old cry of the hopeful leaders of social movements. Within five years the movement had started to solidify.

THE DORMANT PERIOD

In the early 1950's, the format of the National Training Laboratory started to jell. The period of adventure was over for the time being, and a definite system was adopted. Thelen, one of the early leaders, describes the shift in this way:

There was a crossroads about 1953 at Bethel, where really the die was cast. Here were the two major alternatives: (1) it could be as it started in 1947, a kind of a place where people who had different ideas could come together and try out and compare notes and further the art. And so this would have been my image that I was pushing for in '53, it would have been more like the Air War College . . . a place where you would comb the country to find guys handling groups in quite different ways, and then you would bring them together in one spot, and you could compare them. (2) The other image was that we've got a pretty good thing here. There are about 200 million people in this country, all of whom are potentially beneficiaries of this, and so to save our country they need more skill and training and so on. This first is the idealistic angle. And, of course, the other angle was financial. Our financial problems would be solved if we buy this one, and they would be only just beginning if we buy the other one. But at any rate, whatever the reason was, one noticed over the years ahead that the reflection, it wasn't explicit, that the implicit buying of this second position, one of the most interesting bits of evidence, for example, was the first three or four Bethels I was at, the staff would meet like for four days, distributed over two or three meetings, beginning three months ahead to plan T-groups and talk about them and talk about other parts of the lab and so on. But then it got so after this plan, the only changes that were made were brought in by people who were brought in to be T-group trainers, because we thought they would be good T-group trainers, and nobody had any idea what they would do.[10]

[9] *Ibid.*, 82.
[10] H. Thelen. Personal interview.

Here we see the point of view of a member of the exploring group. Social movements need a phase of consolidation between the time of early tentative development and the time of expansion and visibility. For sensitivity training, the period of the 1950's was such a time.

Several circumstances conspired to create this phase. One was the condition of society. This was the period of the silent generation, of muting domestic conflicts and reforms, not a time of continuous experimentation, or acceptance of a change-oriented movement. It also meant that funds were drying up. This general conservatism corresponded to the tendency within the National Training Laboratory to stick to the T-group form that had developed. Benne describes the problem of the years after 1956 as reintegrating the T-group into the rest of the laboratory program.[11] The T-group had become a social fact by itself.

The organization of the laboratory strengthened this development. By now, trainers could be "second generation," that is, people who had gone through as trainees and stayed with the laboratory until they were accepted as trainers. These new trainers had been inducted into the laboratory as it existed, in contrast to the original "first-generation" staff, who came to the laboratory directly as trainers from other interests. This new group was conscious of a tradition they might oppose in some particulars, but must accept as a general framework. The laboratory settled, therefore, into a routine and became self-motivated. The ideology was not supplemented by accepted mechanisms, and the movement became more formalized. Compensating for the addition of the new second-generation trainers, some of the original group, many of whom had been interested in conceptual-experimental work, tended to withdraw from active participation.

The quiet surface of the movement did not, however, imply stagnation. Other branches of sensitivity training were becoming important at this time. One major development was the growth of the laboratories of the West. One of the original staff members of Bethel, Paul Sheats, left after the first year to go to UCLA, and there started the Western Training Laboratory in Group Development. Sheats was mainly an educator who wanted to disseminate knowledge about behavioral science to the adult population, and had little theoretical and ideological commitment. Nevertheless, he recruited staff from business schools and other institutions who were different

[11] *Op. cit.*

from the Bethel staff of the time. Among them were J. R. T. Bugental and Robert Tannenbaum, who were concerned with values and the meaning of group training for the whole society. Bugental became one of the founders of "Humanistic Psychology." Here is Tannenbaum's description of the period:

> The Eastern development, the East Coast development, of course, grew out of Kurt's [Lewin] work, and was heavily group-dynamics oriented. When we began our work on the West Coast, after about the first year or two, it very quickly got oriented much more toward individual dynamics than group dynamics. And there was a period in around the middle '50's when there was quite a struggle going on between east and west around the individual and the group emphasis. Lee's [Bradford] genius played a key role in working through this struggle; and he was open to influence. And I think *we* were open to influence, and we began even by the middle '50's trading staff and so on; we began influencing others. But as I see it now, there is much more of the individual emphasis in sensitivity training now than there is the original group emphasis, although it's a matter of figure and ground rather than either/or. Now to me, this whole development, its significance, its meaning, is very heavily in the values area. I think that many things are happening culturally, societally, organizationally, and really personally, that coincide with this particular development and make this development highly relevant.[12]

Somewhat later the National Training Laboratory included both the Eastern and Western branches.

Thus, this period allowed the laboratory and its main technique, the T-group, to develop and become an established institution. New influences were absorbed without much difficulty. Bethel and what it represented assumed a definite form. This form is well described by Gay Luce, a science writer who visited Bethel in 1956:

> Each delegate is assigned to a T-group. Every morning for two hours he and about 16 others meet with a faculty leader and two researchers, who will record in minute detail who says what, to whom, how often, in what tone of voice, with what gestures. It is the beginning of no-privacy.
>
> What do they do? They are told "become a group." No agenda. No objective goal. The sixteen or so strangers will hassel [sic] like blind men defining an elephant. The leader will behave like a psychoanalyst. The group must study itself. Delegates rate one another: who they like or dislike, who likes them, who is an able leader, etc.

[12] R. Tannenbaum. Personal interview.

These tests are repeated. They're known as sociometrics. Delegates learn how they have been rated. They begin to see how others perceive them. A shock! Emotions are loosed. Encouraged. Soon delegates openly criticize one another, as they try to formulate and understand the group's interaction. In theory sessions they will hear about "hidden agendas," for example. Aware of secret motives, they will begin to question one another in the T-group, begin to confess feelings and secret motivations. They will analyze role-playing from the afternoon A-groups, in which the entire laboratory will act out a community conflict. The T-group soon has a lot of common experience, bull-sessions beginning with breakfast and meetings until the hours when the eyes close and one murmurs without listening. Activities accelerate, until Bethel has a frenzied, unceasing busyness. (The director, it's been said, used to drive off campus and pant for a while.) The T-group is the core.

You've been reading Bethelese for a paragraph or so. This is a language, part military, part business, part medicine, part physics, part psychology, part slang, part English. It has the prestige of a scientific sound, occasionally masking common sense with a complex sound. NTL sophisticates, like good cooks, know when the jargon is best omitted.[13]

DEVELOPMENTS IN EUROPE

During the same years, the movement increased its influence outside the boundaries of the United States. This influence was not one-sided. At least in England, similar ideas had sprung up independently in the Tavistock Institute. The influence of Tavistock had been felt in the formative period of NTL. We have already mentioned the early and enduring connection between the two centers. This was followed by an exchange of personnel, and Elliot Jacques, the technical secretary of the Institute who had been prominent in one of Tavistock's early industrial projects, the "Glacier" Project,[14] visited Bethel while some American staff members participated in seminars at Tavistock in 1949.

From 1948 to 1952, W. R. Bion, one of the main theorists at Tavistock, published a series of articles in *Human Relations* which proved to be very influential.[15] In these articles, Bion developed the theory of the workgroup in which the members' resources are di-

[13] Gay Gaer Luce. Unpublished manuscript.

[14] E. Jacques. *The Changing Culture of a Factory.* London: Tavistock, 1951.

[15] These essays were later collected and expanded in W. R. Bion, *Experiences in Groups.* New York: Basic Books, 1961.

rected toward a definite goal by means of an assumption group where certain interpersonal relations are played out. The main assumptions are dependency relations between the members and the leader or his surrogate, fight-flight or aggression and withdrawal, and pairing or explaining interest between members of the group. Only if these problems are solved and put in balance can the group proceed to its tasks. The articles aroused much interest, and some of the trainers at Bethel were quite impressed by the theory. H. Thelen and the group around him in Chicago tried to expand on Bion's work, and instituted both training and research based on his theory. The research was thus undertaken independent of the National Training Laboratory mainstream and was connected with education in the community. Some Bethel participants were recruited by the Chicago group, however, adding strength to the therapy orientation.

The trainers at Tavistock faced the same problems as the Bethel trainers. Although training was well received by the participants and many felt that the experience had been beneficial, little effect could be shown outside the sessions. The solution Tavistock adopted was opposite to the one adopted by NTL. The Tavistock staff concentrated on the particular problems of the organization with which they were working and brought these problems into the training as early as possible. In this approach they were guided by the medical model which Tavistock's background dictated. Looking at the client—be it the total organization or some individual in it—as a patient who had a definite discomfort, they gave first priority to alleviating the specific pain. Thus, a training program was like a prescription for the specific patient and his particular symptoms; it should lead as fast as possible to the peculiar situation of the client. This orientation prevented the generalized methods and exercises of American counterparts and led to a series of particular relationships between Tavistock and its clients. In consequence, although contact between NTL and Tavistock persisted, the operations of the two centers diverged. Tavistock procedures were introduced into the United States independently in 1964 by Margaret Rioch.

The European centers of sensitivity training did little to propagate the movement on a large scale. The impetus on the Continent and even in Britain itself came from direct contact with American sources. Some of this influence occurred through repatriation of professionals who had studied in the United States. Thus, Anne Schutzenberger returned in 1952 to France after studying at the Research Center for Group Dynamics and attending Bethel sessions. She also received training in psychodrama, and when she instituted an intensive group training program in Paris it was based partly on Moreno's psychodrama (see Chapter 6) and partly on group dynamics.[16]

The main avenue of European spread has been the active missionary efforts of the American centers prompted by the immediate need for increased industrial productivity in the Marshall Plan era. Under the aegis of this program, productivity teams were sent to Europe, and among them were advocates of group training techniques. The first team was quite unsuccessful, because many aspects of sensitivity training were not adaptable to European traditions, and minor points provided a great deal of irritation. This setback was partially counteracted by the visit of several European social and industrial psychologists to the United States. They observed different programs and established close relations with academic and applied groups. Thus, in France, the Low Countries, and Scandinavia, centers for sensitivity training developed.

These circumstances, occurring as they did during the dormant period of the American sensitivity training movement, enabled the Europeans to pursue independent development, and T-group work in Europe has remained connected with industrial and organizational efforts. Two associations of trainers, the European Society of Social Psychologists and the European Institute of International Studies for Group and Organizational Development (EIT), coordinate the efforts of the leading trainers in these countries. These organizations also exert a certain control by restricting membership and conferring professional standing which seems to be of some importance.

The principal departure of European trainers has been in the direction of work on the organization as well as on the individual. This effort is somewhat parallel to OD (organizational development) in the United States, but antedates it and has different results. The main thrust is more ideological, and is an attempt toward self-government of organizations, or "autogestion" (see also Chapter 11). The ideal model is participating group action, where leadership, management, and organization become superfluous. Thus group work is integrated with this effort at organizational reconstruction or even a reorganization of society.

An advantage of European work in this field is its capacity to accept different threads of the American movement without becom-

[16] She is given credit for introducing both T-groups and psychodrama to France. Her book on psychodrama was published in 1966; Anne A. Schutzenberger. *Précis de Psychodrame*. Paris: Presse Universitaire. A projected volume of T-groups, *Observation et Psychotherapie de Groupe et en Formation,* is still available only in mimeographed form.

ing involved in the whole divergent organization. Thus, in the early period, the influences of Moreno's divergent psychodrama and classical T-groups were absorbed into the same system. A great influence on many trainers was Carl Rogers' visit to France in 1962. Rogers' ideology of nondirective training, combined with his work on encounter, fitted in very well with current trends, and Rogers has provided the leading theoretical influence in the field at least as far as psychology is concerned. However, even Rogers did not influence the European movement to move in an experiential direction; Western European, and especially French, work in this field has stayed closely tied to industry, business and personnel management.

It may be that Europeans are better able to accept pleasure for pleasure's sake without a self-improvement justification. The language of the personal growth centers has been taken over by purely recreational enterprises and not by centers which give some self-improvement rationale. The French Club Méditerranée advertises its resorts in a language identical to that of encounter groups. "Our life, our actions, all year round are *mechanical*. Vacations open the door to a spontaneous life . . . it is meant to be *experienced*, as the chance to multiply human contacts under nature's equality, to discover a new type of society."[17]

EXPLOSION

The impetus for change and expansion came from the West Coast. It is best personalized by Michael Murphy.[18] Murphy was a student at Stanford in the early 1950's, studying religion and philosophy. Later he visited an *ashram* in India, absorbing Hindu religious thought (as he said, "before it became fashionable"). Finding himself at loose ends for a while after his return, he and his college roommate decided to start a center for self-expression and for investigation of ideas they had found in India and in some marginal communities in California. One of the precipitating events was their attendance at a symposium, Man and Civilization and Control of the Mind, at the University of California San Francisco Medical Center in 1968. Among the speakers was Aldous Huxley; his talk on Human Potentialities[19] inspired them to start a series of sessions. Murphy

[17] Club Méditerranée, advertising folder.

[18] Personal discussion with M. Murphy.

[19] This talk has been reprinted in the report of the symposium. Aldous Huxley. "Human Potentialities," in S. M. Farber and R. H. L. Wilson (eds.), *Control of the Mind.* New York: McGraw-Hill, 1961.

had inherited a farm in the Big Sur Hot Springs area from his grand-father, and there they founded the Esalen Center (named after the Indians who had lived there). The first session was held in 1962—"The Expanding Vision." This was a seminar series given by Huxley, Alan Watts, and others of similar orientation. What did expand was Esalen itself: within a few years it conducted sessions the year round, had a resident staff, full-time interns, and a research pro-gram.

This time, the West Coast movement could not be absorbed easily by the National Training Laboratory, in spite of attempts to achieve a link. Although the founding of Esalen was independent of the central office, connections were quickly established. The Esalen group recruited staff members from NTL, especially members of the West Coast branch who had been close to the ideas that came to fruition at Esalen. At least one of the basic ideas of the Esalen system was very similar to the general T-group theory—a series of group sessions without agenda, directed toward interaction and reaction among the members as the main topic. The Esalen-type group, how-ever, does not aim at training people for group activity. The watch-words are personal growth, expansion of human potentiality, and encounter. Also group activities are only one part of the Esalen pro-gram. Other Esalen sessions could be devoted to different techniques such as art, dance, Chinese gymnastics, and religious problems. Murphy acknowledges the legitimate ancestry of Bethel, saying that Esalen was a sort of bastard child. After all, he adds, the organiza-tion of the National Training Laboratory did not exclusively use the ideas of the 1920's, so Esalen was not likely to rely on the 1940's.

In fact, the National Training Laboratory adopted some of the Esalen techniques. Beginning and advanced human relations work-shops directed by people who had been active on the West Coast use some of the extreme encounter techniques. Trainees in the advanced lab, who are known only by pseudonyms, have violent fights and love scenes. Their training area is off-limits to the rest of the laboratory, and treated like an inner sanctum. Their presence, however, seems to affect or infect the whole place, and a visitor feels a heightened sensuality pervading Bethel.

In this sense the Esalen movement has become part of the gen-eral sensitivity training movement. But there is some tension be-tween the different centers, and as a rule each goes its own way. Some people within the National Training Laboratory look at Esalen as a dangerous venture or worse. Even some who favor it feel that it is good to dissociate oneself from it. In this way Esalen can expand while NTL accepts consultantships from more conservative and staid industrial and government organizations. The Esalen movement with its human potential centers has remained separate from the National Training Laboratory.

Other new developments came from California. The Western Behavioral Science Institute (WBSI) was established in La Jolla. It soon became a center for encounter groups, primarily through the influence of Carl Rogers, who had a leading part in its establishment. Rogers had been one of the main theorists and practitioners of counseling psychology.[20] His basic assumption was that there is a healthy core in each person which may be obstructed through unhealthy experiences or behavior patterns. The function of the counselor is to give the client a chance to express himself freely, by remaining as passive and supportive as possible ("nondirective counseling"). In later years, Rogers worked out the ideological implications of this counseling theory. These consisted of a deep-seated conviction that each person has his own intrinsic value and that his individuality should be respected. The nondirective counselor, therefore, would not force his own therapeutic convictions on the client, but would only help him to reach his own potential. It can be seen how easily this point of view fits with the ideal of human potential. It was Rogers who popularized the term "sensitivity training" and directed the efforts of the Behavioral Science Institute toward it. The whole direction of the Center is similar to other encounter group centers, but there is more emphasis on application and dissemination. Rogers obtained a research grant in 1966 to apply sensitivity training to a whole school system in Los Angeles. Other work included consultation with the city of San Diego and the production of tapes with which a group could conduct its own encounter session by following taped instruction.[21]

If WBSI occupied the border region of academic life, another

[20] C. Rogers. *Client-Centered Therapy in Current Practice, Implications and Theory.* Boston: Houghton Mifflin, 1951.

[21] Rogers' change from academic counseling toward a more inspirational message is shown in his two later books, *On Becoming a Person* (Boston: Houghton Mifflin, 1961) and with Barry Stevens, *Person to Person: Problems of Being Human* (Lafayette, Calif.: Real People Press, 1967). The flavor of this last book can be gotten from the complete biographical identification of the co-author, "Barry Stevens: High school drop out, 1918, because what she wanted to know, she couldn't learn in school."

West Coast development crossed the border of therapy and remedial action. This was the Synanon movement, whose main purpose was to treat drug addicts.[22] Synanon is a complete residential community with the patients taking responsibility for running the place and for the socialization of new members. The main feature of Synanon is the "game," or "haircut," a group interaction with stress on working out hostilities ("synanon" is a corruption of "seminar"). The idea of Synanon was supposedly established independently by the addicts and alcoholics themselves. Although Synanon is still mainly maintained for addicts, it now attracts people searching for the group experience as such. While the regular inmates of Synanon try to substitute the group experience for their need for drugs, the regular client of sensitivity training centers comes to Synanon as a way of getting strong experiences and uninhibited response.

At the same time, another aspect of the sensitivity training movement became prominent in the field when the Tavistock group entered the United States. In spite of the friendly relations between NTL and Tavistock, little was known about the development of the Tavistock work, especially their work with group development. The introduction of Tavistock to the United States was mainly the work of one clinical psychologist, Margaret Rioch:

> I went in 1963 to one of the Tavistock conferences in England which are held at the University of Leicester every Spring. I went because a British friend of mine said this is a unique kind of thing, and if you are a psychologist you ought to know about this sort of work. And I went, and was very deeply impressed by what I learned about the way people behave in groups, and by the dedication and discipline of the staff, and so I thought it would be the thing for us to have. As an American, I thought I better go see what we had in America too before I did anything much about it. I did then go to Bethel that summer to one of the National Training Laboratory's summer events, and was convinced that the Tavistock method is different and has a different emphasis and that, therefore, we would not be actually duplicating anything by trying to transplant this into the United States. So then, in 1964, I thought it isn't enough just for me to have this idea and try to convince other people that it would be a good thing to set up here, but some other Americans ought to go and see. So the British people, the Tavistock people, set up a special conference in the summer so that Americans could go, and about twenty-five Americans did go. And there was enough interest and enthusiasm that I thought it was justified to set it up here; and

[22] L. Yablonsky. *Synanon, the Tunnel Back.* New York: Macmillan, 1965.

then we did, together with the Yale Department of Psychiatry. And I think that in that newsletter you have the history of the American conferences and so we went ahead and did it. I am by training really an individual psychotherapist, and this is an extension and new field to me, but one which seems to me so terribly important for people to take a larger view than just the individual and his individual relationships, but to take the view of what he does in a group, and what the group does to him, and what some of the processes are that go on in groups of various sizes and among groups. As you may know, and I think I have said, we don't call what we do sensitivity training. People may or may not become more sensitive, but that's not our emphasis, and we don't call it that.[23]

There are still very few Tavistock training centers in the United States; the main activity is a summer session in Amherst, Massachusetts, with other smaller workshops being conducted at the Washington School of Psychiatry, Johns Hopkins, and subsidiary centers. As their aim is primarily to help in understanding group activity for professionals, their clientele is very restricted, and consists of persons who in turn have influence within the movement.

While all these activities were going on, the National Training Laboratory was not idle. Besides staying in contact with the new developments, the leaders of the laboratory formalized and expanded their procedures. The National Training Laboratory became a formal branch of the National Education Association, with its own governing structure, and Leland Bradford as director. A formal network was established with members and associates who had to pass rigorous standards, pay membership fees of a few hundred dollars, and were then available for special jobs if institutes asked for them. The training laboratory also bought a former small private hospital which the local psychiatrist had been using at Bethel to use as part of a training center to supplement the rented quarters at Gould Academy. As a further sign of national acceptability, the first thorough description of the history and practices of the T-group was published in 1964, almost twenty years after the start of the movement.[24] This volume is dedicated to the T-group in its essential form, without considering the different activities of the West Coast or Tavistock groups.

Thus NTL asserted its identity, and the 1960's saw a great expansion of activities. This was in large part due to a reorientation of

[23] Personal interview.
[24] Bradford, Gibb, and Benne, *op. cit.*

the target population. This time, the NTL staff members were ready to approach the power groups. As an innovation, in 1964 the Presidents' Labs were inaugurated to which company presidents and similar officials were invited. Thus, corporation policy could be directly affected. NTL also undertook projects in foreign aid and organizational help to foreign service, Peace Corps, and large poverty organizations such as Mobilization for Youth. This activity paid off increasingly in the scope of NTL. Within five years its budget increased tenfold to an annual level of over $3 million. Income and activity within the network increased correspondingly.

NTL also expanded its foreign activity, again as part of foreign aid programs, but also as part of aid to underdeveloped countries. In direct contrast to Agency for International Development, programs were developed as adjuncts to industrialization, in an attempt to avoid the pitfalls of authoritarian economic development. Other NTL-inspired ventures included those of a team from the University of Michigan to adapt Israeli kibbutzim (cooperatives) from agricultural toward industrial work, and work by NTL-trained Puerto Rican psychologists to introduce sensitivity training to Latin America. These were diffusions of the NTL method based on American support, and did not lead to independent development as in Europe.

From the multitude of weekend encounter groups to classes in social science, from churches to industry, from therapy to productivity, sensitivity training had arrived.

AT THE CROSSROADS

By the end of the 1960's sensitivity training had arrived as a cultural force. We can ascribe this cultural explosion to several factors. The development of group centers paralleled similar developments in society, so much so that it is futile to speak of simple cause and effect. Certainly the social climate of the 1960's was hospitable to sensitivity training, encounter groups, and all the offshoots. In some instances we can see mutual influence. The civil rights movements used group methods such as role-playing and confrontation groups, and the roots of sensitivity training lay originally in intergroup relations work. Art forms such as living theater consciously used encounter group techniques for training and for audience involvement. Indeed, the new style of confrontation of political and social action implies group techniques in political action, artistic performance, and religious ritual.

Further, many of the basic tensions of society which sparked this social movement increased during the 1960's. A whole generation was growing up who had seen neither depression nor economic want, who could crisscross the country in search of excitement, and who viewed life as having some deeper meaning than material wealth and scientific understanding could give them. Use of the language of science in spite of distrust in rational solutions paved the way for experimentation with group experience as a way to reach beyond the common experience of the society.

The sensitivity training movement was thus spurred on by social unrest while at the same time providing some of the techniques and opportunities for expression of this unrest. Sensitivity training is, however, not only a way of obtaining strong emotional experience. Some of the practitioners, especially in the Esalen branch, could see in the movement a straining away from social alienation; others could see it only as a tool for solution of human relations problems, useful for anybody who was willing to employ it; still others felt uneasy at an interpersonal exercise that could not attack the social problems of the time. In the last years of the decade, the very success of the movement brought fundamental questions of this kind to the fore. Each organization had to decide on its own future.

Partly through these tensions and partly through individual circumstances, changes and crises became explicit within the different organizations. The problem can be clearly seen in the "General Motors of Sensitivity Training,"[25] the National Training Laboratory. Trying to remain the center of the whole movement, it attempted to stay abreast of all developments, absorbing each new aim as it came along. It may be difficult to remember that the original impetus to sensitivity training came from a concern about social problems. Out of the several early experiments on group training, the T-group was developed as the central mechanism. While much of the verbal emphasis was on change and even on social change, the actual effort was exerted toward individual training in small face-to-face groups. This technique had particular appeal to the high echelons of management. In certain cases, current social problems of the time did manage to impinge on the workings of the laboratory. At the Bethel laboratory of 1968, a Black Caucus of delegates convened and issued demands for high representation of blacks among delegates, training staff, and clerical staff, direct concern with ghetto problems, and qualification of trainers who would work with minorities. The

[25] W. Schott. Review of *Please Touch* and *Encounter* in *New York Times Book Review*, June 28, 1970, 8.

response was a meeting between delegates of the caucus and members of the NTL board, in which a program of intensified recruiting and review of professional qualifications for work in the slums was worked out. The details of the demands or the program are not particularly remarkable, and they are analogous to the processes going on in legions of institutions at the time. What is remarkable is that no group techniques were used in the whole procedure; the negotiations were carried on in the same way as in organizations that were not experts on group technique.

The same current problems have turned up at many centers of laboratory training. In several discussions, questions of discrimination against blacks and women came up.[26] In both cases there were said to be good reasons for *de facto* discrimination: there are few blacks who have the background in behavioral sciences necessary for inclusion in the NTL network. Also, many management clients of NTL prefer male trainers at least for their primarily male executive staff. This is the same problem faced within any occupation; the existing patterns are designed to maintain the status quo, and some different approach will have to be used to break through this mold. In general, these changes occur through pressure by the disadvantaged group, with confrontation and negotiation. The paradox in a training group such as NTL is that as an organization they are committed to change and their business is to advise other organizations on change problems. But they react very similarly to other organizations when the problems concern them.

The National Training Laboratory had to look at its position in great detail as Leland Bradford's retirement approached and the search for a successor began. This was a good time to reassess the stance of the organization. Expansion of budget had brought in its wake an expansion of staff and administration, and there was a definite tendency for established procedures to become accepted as permanent. This included reliance on group processes, especially the T-groups, limitation of action to situations in which their procedures could be effective, and increasing control of the organization by an in-group in cooperation with a board that included important business sponsors and clients. The definition of the NTL purpose was

[26] An interesting example came up in the New England Conclave of Applied Behavioral Sciences in March, 1970. Several small discussion groups concerned themselves with discussion and the women's group came up with a bill of particulars. The black group reported that they "met for lunch for a short period and after lunch for a longer period of time." The moderator thanked them "for the report in the spirit of openness."

given as either "experience-based learning" or "application of behavioral science knowledge to social problems," but it was clear that this did not include some experiences and some parts of behavioral science, such as mass communication.

In early 1969 the choice for director fell on Warren Bennis who had been active in industrial training and educational administration and had written extensively on research in the field as well as on some of the philosophy underlying the whole movement. At that time he was vice president in charge of educational administration at the State University of New York at Buffalo. Bennis hesitated a long time before deciding whether or not to accept the position.[27] He felt that reorganization of purpose was called for: social change was to be the primary aim, with group technique used or not used depending on the situation; emphasis would be given to the current scenes of social change and problems; the board would be reconstituted to de-emphasize business connections; finally, a major effort would be made to build a university-like institute near Washington (the grounds had already been secured) to train change agents systematically and for sustained performance. Bennis pledged himself to raise the necessary funds.

The negotiations lasted for several months, and finally, in December, 1969, Bennis decided that NTL was not sufficiently committed to a new program to make it advisable for him to take the directorship. His refusal caused some bitterness within the organization. The issues he raised remained important, however. In the interim, Bradford remained in his position, obviating any immediate decision on succession. Some of Bennis's proposals were actually carried out: some reconstitution of the board was undertaken, and further plans were made for the institute. The basic issues of direction and organization had been brought out and had to be considered. Marginal members of the network questioned the centralization of power in a few people with the practical consequence that these few people were assigned to remunerative workshops. Recurrent staff reorganization and questioning of current procedures show this to be a period of transition.

In the fall of 1970, Vladimir Dupre, who had been active in NTL laboratories in the Middle West, was chosen as director. He started a reassessment of organization and budget that would uncover, and presumably alleviate, many of the tensions that had developed in the decade of enormous growth.

[27] Warren Bennis. Personal interview.

A reorganization separated the service facilities according to client, such as community and business, into separate organizations. Completely distinct from these service functions was a training organization for trainers which also would develop an accreditation procedure, comparable to certification by other professional organizations like psychologists or social workers.

A crisis also developed in the Western Behavioral Science Institute.[28] Here two distinct factions were formed, the scientists and the humanists. In a certain sense it was again a conflict between means and ends. One faction, the scientists, was primarily interested in application and dissemination and wanted to stay with existing methods and theory, to look for support from government and other resources, and in short, to act like a research and consulting organization. The other group, the humanists, wanted to stay away from a commitment to established procedure in order to experiment with unorthodox techniques, but without the shackles as well as the prestige of the scientific method. It was found to be impossible to accomplish both goals in the same institution, and the humanists left WBSI to form the Center for the Study of the Person (CSP). After the split, the latter group seemed more active, sponsoring a summer program for group training, for instance, and also giving fledgling trainers responsibility over encounter weekends for which the participants came from the general Los Angeles–San Diego community. This activity made the Center well-known in the area, while little action was forthcoming from the people remaining at WBSI. The split demonstrated clearly the underlying tensions in the movement. The CSP kept the religious fervor of other institutions, while WBSI retained the form and language of applied science.

Esalen also changed abruptly. Murphy explained it as follows:

> First of all, the big change at Big Sur is that we are phasing into a situation which, by Fall, 1970, we will be running one-month, four-month-long, and seven-day programs only. The two-day and five-day programs will all be moved to San Francisco. The idea is that at Big Sur we are going to have a center for training and for exploratory work and for research work in depth, where people can come and consolidate and refine their approaches, where professionals can work on their approaches in more depth, and where people who come will have more time to assimilate what happens to them. One of the reasons for that is that people come away from these weekends with a big high on, and they don't get a chance to integrate them, the insights, and the new attitudes and behaviors

[28] *San Diego Magazine*, June, 1969.

sufficiently, so these longer term programs will hopefully give people a chance to do that. Now, if you come for a month-long, or see now, there's a four-month-long residency program, that is the most in depth. That involves a mixture of approaches: encounter, Gestalt therapy, our body and sensory awareness approaches, meditation, and many other approaches. And we are gradually developing a kind of unified curriculum. We are learning how to do it. We have been learning for three or four years how to build a curriculum up out of these various elements. And in the four-month-long period they will be getting that. Now the last two months of that program will be more focused on training. People will be able to lead groups and be critiqued by the leaders and by their fellow group members. It will be a training program. But that training program is going to be designed to the particular desires and needs of the participants. There will be a lot of self-design in the training part of that four-month residence program. The present plans call for two parallel tracks in that four-month program: one with the approaches emphasizing more the body. You would have more of the Tai Chi Chuan, the sensory awakening, the bio-energetics, the structural re-integration kinds of things. The other half is going to emphasize more the purely interpersonal-intrapersonal with the emphasis being more on encounter, Gestalt therapy and all, meditation. But both of these tracks will have a lot of overlap. It is merely a matter of emphasis. So that there is a slightly different major, you might say. Now, the month-long programs will be of all sorts and kinds, just like our program now. Now the people who are in the month-long and four-month-long will work in two shifts a week in the grounds, in the kitchen, sixteen hours a week, and that way we are reducing the size of our staff. Our working staff down there was eighty; it is now down to thirty-five, and that is the highest it will ever be. We might even get it down to thirty. That's the people who are actually working staff.[29]

It can be seen that here the effort is being made to develop a permanent, self-sustaining activity instead of the changes and growth in many directions of characteristic previous periods. The need for additional funds is also becoming urgent. In the spring of 1970 and 1971 the Esalen staff and Friends of Esalen went East to put on a benefit performance for the new Esalen program in New York, and others were planned for Los Angeles.

These three developments of NTL, WBSI, and Esalen show the kinds of questions being asked after a period of unexpected growth. Is a new maturation in sight in which the movement will be consoli-

[29] M. Murphy. Personal interview.

dated around a few basic ideas? Is there a trend toward development as a religious or political force which may go in unexpected directions? What are the relations to society and to the issues of the times? These questions are being discussed in the different organizations. Choices will have to be made; new alignments and directions are possible. The movement is entering a new phase.

Chapter 5

Internal Logic and Mythology

"Thought would destroy their paradise."[1]

We are now ready to explore the central beliefs of this movement. A look at its history has shown us a variety of sources from which it derived its purposes, and a number of different practitioners and practices associated with the movement. It is practically impossible to define the sensitivity training movement either by its practices, theories, or methods. Nevertheless, there is an affinity among the different groups of practitioners, although they may be moving in different directions. This harmony in sensitivity training is conveyed primarily by a common experience and its interpretation.

This central experience is the discovery of strong emotional action through group process. Interacting in a group, putting attention on process, reacting to the other person—all lead to extremely strong emotion, a feeling of change, and intense satisfaction on the part of the group member. The experience is in part justified as being part of a belief system and in part as relying on scientific theory. Thus we have to look at the justifying factors in two ways: in this chapter we shall deal with the mythology of sensitivity training, that is, with its belief system as a social movement using the external approach; in the next chapters we shall deal with behavioral science theories.

The search for groups in which intense emotional experience can be enjoyed is a sign of disturbance in many societies, occurring

[1] T. Gray. "On a Distant Prospect of Eton College."

at times of deep social unrest, and especially during the rise of new religions. Thus the group experience of the early Christians is clearly a similar phenomenon, as were the underground Masses of the Reformation. Paul Goodman, a leading social critic, has called this period in history, our time, the Second Reformation.[2] In more recent times, political movements started the same way, in small political cells or circles. In all these cases, however, the group experience alone has not been the justification, whether to attain religious salvation, some healing process, or salvation through secular means. Religious organizations have received attention by issuing eschatological warnings that the end of the world is near, and that, therefore, attention to the here and now is more vital than to one's future. Secular movements have sought for similar effects by pointing to the imminence of revolution or some upheaval of the present social system.

Sensitivity training is novel in accepting the group experience as having value in itself, without recourse to any ultimate aims. Correspondingly, the group experience has become the center of the movement. In earlier times, intense emotional experiences could always be explained as a working of the agency which gave the movement its own flavor, be it religious or political. In these instances the development of the science of pragmatism de-emphasized the experience itself while emphasizing the ultimate goals.

The catchword for the sensitivity training movement is "here and now." The term was invented by Moreno in his work on psychodrama,[3] one of the techniques which is basic to much of the work in sensitivity training. In his book *Microcosm*, Philip Slater has contrasted the here-and-now orientation within a group with three other ways in which a group could promote group process: extra-group data, general principles, and personal histories. Classroom teaching concentrates on the relation between extra-group data and general principles.[4] Therapy stresses principally the relation between events in the group and personal history. Academic work may also use the general group process, usually as a way to explain general principles. The uniqueness of sensitivity training is that it uses the present experience only, not as a wedge to get into people's past the way therapy does, and not as a wedge to interpretation as teaching methods

[2] P. Goodman. *The New Reformation*. New York: Random House, 1970.

[3] J. Moreno. "The Concept of the Here and Now, Hic et Nunc: Small Groups and Their Relation to Action Research," *Group Psychotherapy*, 22, 1969, 139–141.

[4] P. Slater. *Microcosm*. New York: Wiley, 1966.

do. Concentrating on outside events, interpretation, and verbal discussion is seen as an escape from the present experience and from the essential work of the group.

This new kind of group activity found in sensitivity training needs a justification to become acceptable for its prospective members. Thus we find a mythology of the here and now which is separate from any social psychological theory developed for the professional audience. This myth of the here and now ties in with the tensions within society that we have noted in Chapter 3: the growth of a large prosperous mobile middle-class left without any central belief or controlled ways to get excitement. It rejects history, even personal history, and any enduring structure. It also rejects symbolization. In effect, one of the main techniques of sensitivity training is to make symbols concrete and active. Thus the statement "I hate you" will be quickly acted out in a fight, the statement "I love you" in an embrace, unhappiness in crying, and so on. The implication of this attitude is a complete denial of some recent developments in human history of the importance of abstraction and symbolism.

The cult of the experience is justified by deprecating symbolic statements, especially higher abstractions, and extolling strong sensual experiences, especially the more direct ones. This value shift is carried out in three ways: from symbols to concrete expression, from intellect to emotions, and from the mind to the body. One part of the here-and-now myth, therefore, is the rejection of a language of symbols in favor of direct experience and action; thus, group exercises, which sometimes look like children's games, are really given a deep meaning. One of the more famous of the exercises, called "trust fall," consists of a person falling backward, confident that his partner is going to catch him. Under the conditions of the group, it is highly unlikely that the partner is not going to catch him. While it is true that to an outsider this may look like a ritual, apparently it assumes deep meaning within the group, so that people really feel that this is the only way to express trust. Similar ways of making abstract concepts concrete are embodied in the myth and ritual of many societies. In all cases, participants realize that the concrete form is known to be a substitute or an explanation of the abstract concept. In the mythology of sensitivity training we learn that concreteness is the high road to understanding. Thus one of the early practitioners of sensitivity training in industry, Douglas McGregor, coined the expression "gut learning" as the only kind of learning that has any meaning and will hold. If we do not have to look beyond the present, any record keeping or symbolization of language would be unnecessary. Language is useful only for recurring situations, and to refer to things absent in the present situation.

Allied with this rejection of symbolism is the rejection of the function that makes symbolism possible, the intellect. Attention is directed toward the exalting of emotion or the direct sensual experience. Group experiences become stronger if their meaning is not mediated by thought but accepted directly. This technique of concentrating on feeling and senses has been for a long time the technique of mysticism and of allied techniques. Here again we must stress the fact that in sensitivity training no ulterior aims can be acknowledged, no ideology gives meaning to the experience, and, therefore, the experience has to be celebrated for itself. Thus we find an emphasis on concentration on sensual experience. Exercises comprise simple concentration on one sense organ, such as one's sight, feeling, or hearing. This emphasis extends to whole programs of education based on sensual experience or emotional education or, as it has been called, education for ecstasy.

Using dualistic terminology, we find an emphasis on the body as contrasted to the mind. Bodily exercises have been used, especially by religious groups, for a long time. In fact, some California encounter groups make extensive use of Far Eastern and Indian dance, gymnastics, and physical exercises as an aid in their programs. Other physical exercises have been tried which are based on more modern concepts, from gymnastics to psychoanalysis.

Charlotte Selver, Ida Rolfe, and Alexander Lowen are the more prominent advocates of this somatic aspect. Selver and Rolfe are physiotherapists who have developed complete methods of practice, movement, and exercise intended to lead to a regeneration of the whole person.[5] Lowen is more in the Reichian tradition of psychoanalysis. Like this student and friend of Freud, he poses the liberation of the body, especially the sexual organs, as an equal and even fundamental problem to that of social change.[6] Lowen has developed an integrated psychosomatic "bio-energetic" approach which is in-

[5] Neither has written a comprehensive exposition of her theory or techniques. A vivid reportage of both of them is given by R. Gustaitis, *Turning On.* New York: Macmillan, 1969, Chaps. 14 and 15. Selver has published several articles showing the ideas, and Rolfe and her followers are publishing the *Journal of Structural Integration.* Two somewhat uncritical illustrated articles by Sam Keene on Rolfe's technique appeared in *Psychology Today* (*4*, October, 1970, 56–62): "Sing the Body Electric" and "My New Carnality."

[6] A. Lowen. *Love and Orgasm.* New York: Macmillan, 1965; and *The Betrayal of the Body.* New York: Macmillan, 1967.

tended to release the hidden energy of the body, especially of the lower part. Procedures of sensory awareness or awakening have become the most popular parts of encounter groups and form the subjects of the best-selling publications, notably among them Bernard Gunther's *Sensory Awareness below Your Mind* and *What to Do until the Messiah Comes.* He describes the rationale for this aspect of Esalen as follows:

> I guess largely I feel that most people in our culture tend to carry around a lot of chronic tension, and that they tend to respond largely on the basis of *habit* behavior and often goal-motivated behavior. And what I call sensory awakening is a method to get people to quiet their verbal activity, to let go their tension and focus their awareness on various parts of the body or various activities or feelings in the body. And of experiencing the *moment*, experiencing what it is they are actually doing as opposed to any kind of concept or conditioned kind of habit behavior.[7]

Sensitivity training represents a reaction to the development of intellectual history. Claude Levi-Strauss has recently distinguished between the savage mind and the modern mind.[8] The savage mind proposes a completely coherent picture of the world in a concrete manner. What the modern mind would consider a symbol is for the savage mind a real fact. He claims that what is metaphor for the modern mind is metonymy for the savage. The modern mind has developed science by deliberately refusing to assume that different realms of experience, such as animals, stars, trees, human actions, and feelings, can be classified in the same way. For the modern mind, these different realms are investigated separately, using purely pragmatic methodology. Mythological thinking, which in a way is what Levi-Strauss means by the savage mind, tries to put everything into a coherent system. The modern mind, represented by the experimentalists, perceives a fact and uses a symbolization of it for easier manipulation, quite conscious that it is only a symbol.

The last four hundred years have gradually seen the increase of the importance of the modern over the savage outlook. While day-by-day activities were always regulated by principles of practicality, they were interpolated into a completely coherent world view. The

---

[7] Personal interview. Cf. B. Gunther, *Sensory Awareness below Your Mind.* New York: Collier, 1968; and *What to Do until the Messiah Comes.* New York: Collier, 1971.

[8] C. Levi-Strauss. *The Savage Mind.* Chicago: University of Chicago Press, 1966.

scientific outlook and its philosophical underpinnings have stressed mainly instrumental value, problem solving, emphasis on the intellect, and a free, almost playful use of symbols. Since the rise of science, there has always been a reaction against the values implicit in science. There are several forms which this reaction can take. One is the belief in ultimate nonrational values, the emphasis on ends over means, and the rejection of certain scientific facts in order to fit into a preconceived world view. This is a conservative, anti-intellectual way which traditional religion has used in its step-by-step fight against new developments in science from Galileo to Darwin to Freud. As these three examples show, scientific thought has usually prevailed, and much of the approach of science has become ingrained in many people. Science may frustrate some aspects of human life. But this frustration does not lead readily to a return to ideas which have preceded scientific development.

Another way to reject the "modern mind" (in Levi-Strauss's sense) is to use some of the procedures and language of science in a mythological sense. The central belief of sensitivity training, the use of behavioral science concepts to go from symbol to event, from cognition to emotion, and from mind to body, may be the first comprehensive attempt of this kind.

The progression of behavioral science to a social movement in sensitivity training illuminates one of the paradoxes of the pragmatic outlook. Pragmatism is the philosophy most attuned to the scientific method. It judges a procedure by its outcomes, by whether or not it works. It rejects explicitly the need to integrate each act and idea into an overarching framework. It is satisfied if an idea is useful for a reasonable time. Thus, pragmatics concentrate on choosing means that can be judged in this way, and are suspicious of ultimate ends that may only arrive in the distant future and be used as a justification for all kinds of mischief in the meantime. The philosophy of sensitivity training follows this logic in its origins from philosophy based on James and Dewey, as well as in continuous resistance to questions about the ultimate aims of the procedures.[9]

The pragmatic orientation of rejecting ultimate aims can easily slip into a perspective of shorter and shorter time spans. A T-group workshop can be accepted for its short-range objective of leaving the participants with good feelings without worry about ultimate aims.

[9] The original philosopher of the movement, Kenneth Benne, came out of this tradition. He provides the link to current philosophy in his challenging collection of essays, *Education for Tragedy*. Lexington: University of Kentucky Press, 1967.

But the same can be said about each session, each interaction, each experience. Thus, denial of ultimate ends may lead beyond a rational short-term time perspective to a cult of the instantaneous and sensual experience. Sigmund Koch described the resulting model of human nature in this way:

> The Group Movement is the most extreme excursion thus far of man's talent for reducing, distorting, evading, and vulgarizing his own reality. It is also the most poignant exercise of that talent, for it seeks and promises to do the very reverse. It is adept at the second remove image-making maneuver of evading human reality within the very process of seeking to reembrace it. It seeks to court spontaneity and authenticity by artifice; to combat instrumentalism instrumentally; to provide access to experience by reducing it to a neuter-pap commodity; to engineer autonomy by group pressure; to liberate individuality by group shaping.[10]

Sensitivity training can be seen as a reaction against the scientific outlook by an emphasis on direct, immediate experience. It can be seen as the logical end-point of the transition from the extremely long-range outlook of religion to the middle-range time perspective of science, to the immediacy of the here and now.

Fiction may be best adapted to making explicit the philosophy basic to a movement, a myth only implied in scientific writings and actions. We shall conclude the chapter by looking at the novels featured in some of the bookshops in human potential centers. The leaders of the movement seem to feel that these novels express the relevant ideas of sensitivity training.

Probably the most widely accepted novel of the new consciousness is Robert Heinlein's *Stranger in a Strange Land*.[11] This is fittingly a science fiction novel, the experience of a human brought up as a Martian viewing Earth men. Heinlein himself describes the story as part adventure, part satire, and part a description of a new religion. The adventure does not need to concern us here. The satire is a deliberate attempt to examine every major action of Western culture, to question these actions, throw doubt on them, and if possible to make antitheses of each action appear a possible and perhaps desirable thing rather than unthinkable. This aspect of the story fits in with the general acceptance of change and rejection of permanent institutional frameworks in the sensitivity training movement. The

[10] S. Koch. "The Image of Man in Encounter Group Theory." Unpublished manuscript (*Journal of Humanistic Psychology*, in press).

[11] R. Heinlein. *Stranger in a Strange Land*. New York: Putnam, 1963.

religion proposed and the community based on it are probably the most important parts of the story for our purposes. This community is founded by the Martian and consists of a kind of mystical togetherness, in which groups or communes become a whole. The members live in sexual and, in the long run, spiritual union. As the Martian happens to be by inheritance one of the richest men in the world, economic problems do not exist for the group. Thus, the development of their religious community can be self-contained, and they can spend their time considering their experiences in great detail. What they do experience is, essentially, each other. After their initiation the members of the religion possess a peculiar power, which derives in great part from a concentration on the here and now. This is backed by a belief in transmigration of souls so that each person has an infinity of time to live and does not have to worry about intermediate distances or time spans (an interesting identification of short and long time perspectives). Other characteristics of sensitivity training are present in the novel: the religion is propagated through language training, that is, through teaching Martian, which seems to be a language without symbolization. Thus, a concentration on the here and now, on sensuality, on strong group bonds, and on the rejection of symbols becomes the basis of the religion. We should not be surprised that the novel found much appeal in the sensitivity movement.

The ironic aspect of this case is that Heinlein actually has quite a politically and socially conservative stance, being a conservative Republican, and when asked to give a seminar at Esalen, rejected the idea saying that it is not necessary to believe in the Martian religion to write a novel about it. In fact, one part of his reservation comes out clearly in the book: this is that the group cannot be advocated for the whole society; it is a program for the wealthy and for an elite class. Another implication is that the Martian culture, although it is stronger at the moment than the Earth culture, would eventually be overcome by humans, because Martians, not being concerned with intermediate problems, let the time of their superiority slip.[12]

Other novels prominent in the libraries of sensitivity training are those of Hermann Hesse and Hannah Green's *I Never Promised You a Rose Garden*. Of Hesse's novels, *Siddhartha* seems to be the most popular in encounter centers.[13] It is again the story of a super-

[12] R. Gustaitis. *Turning On*. New York: Macmillan, 1969, 79. For Heinlein's political views and his own evaluation of his book, see A. Panshin, *Heinlein in Dimension*. Chicago: Advent, 1968.

[13] H. Hesse. *Siddhartha*. Berlin: S. Fischer, 1935.

human character, this time an Indian Brahmin. He seeks perfection in ritual, individual discipline, various callings, even in the company of the Buddha, but is never satisfied. He is always perfect within the situation but cannot endure any commitment. Like Heinlein's Martian, he can make a success out of mundane life, but prefers to turn to a new existence. Siddhartha is shown as the man who is perfect because he can involve himself totally at the moment in anything, although he will commit himself to nothing.

I Never Promised You a Rose Garden stands in contrast to the other two books.[14] Here the protagonist is not successful; on the contrary, she is a psychotic teen-ager being treated in a mental hospital. She represents the underside of the mythology—the acceptance of one's own world in preference to the everyday construction of society. The heroine lives in her own world with its own language and gods; she created this world in response to a situation into which she had unique insight but with which she could not cope. This novel shows her readiness to accept new experience, any experience that might have some value. In a fictional way it represents the ideas of R. D. Laing and Alan Watts, other inspirations of the movement, who interpret psychosis as the attempt to communicate an essentially ineffable insight.[15]

The mythology thus exalts emotion, experience, the senses to the point of espousal of excess, even psychosis. Anything is better than the routine, nonsensual kind of ordinary mundane existence. This ideology runs into conflict with the actual background of the clients and their sometimes fleeting recreational needs. The published reports of observers noted both the pervading mythology and the reluctance to accept it as a way of life.

Perhaps the best example of the relation of the mythology to the reality of the encounter group is given by the experience of Ken Kesey. His novel, *One Flew over the Cuckoo's Nest*,[16] sets a schizophrenic and a psychopathic patient as heroes against the unfeeling and overpowering administration. The strength of the book, sections of which were written under the influence of narcotics, lies in the empathy with the main characters. In his life, as well as in this novel, Kesey has promoted irrationality, the search for transcendence, new systems, and a new religion. Kesey assembled a band of followers

[14] H. Green. *I Never Promised You a Rose Garden*. New York: Holt, 1964.

[15] R. D. Laing. *The Divided Self. A Study of Madness*. Chicago: Quadrangle, 1960. A. W. Watts. *The Wisdom of Insecurity*. New York: Pantheon, 1951; and *Psychotherapy East and West*. New York: Pantheon, 1961.

[16] K. Kesey. *One Flew over the Cuckoo's Nest*. New York: Viking, 1962.

around him, the Merry Pranksters, and was invited to Esalen. This one-week session is still one of the traumatic experiences of the Center. People do not like to talk about it, but Tom Wolfe's description of it in *The Electric Kool-Aid Acid Test* is a glimmer of what happened.

In Ken Kesey and his Merry Pranksters the middle-class Esalen residents were faced with the extreme of their own position. "The clientele at Esalen had come a long way in a few weeks and many were beginning to peek over the edge of The Rut. And what they saw . . . it could be scary out there in Freedomland. The Pranksters were friendly, but they glowed in the dark. They pranked about like maniacs in the serene Hot Springs. Precious few signed up for a trip with Ken Kesey, even in seminar form."[17]

This confrontation shows the limitations of group dynamics, the sensitivity training mythology. There is a strong belief in the immediate, in senses, in extremes, in breaking the bounds. In fact, there is also a new ritual, a new boundary, and really a new aspect of respectability. From the point of view of the Merry Pranksters who had taken the myth to its ultimate conclusion, Esalen "was a place where educated middle-class adults came in the summer to get out of the Rut and wiggle their fannies a bit."[18] The mythology is tempered by the very conditions that produced it. Apart from the impact of mechanization and the escape from it, there is also a strong streak of conformity, of people who are living in a society that makes it possible for them to pay the fees to support sensitivity training centers. The tensions within this basic belief, therefore, bring about some of the inconsistencies within the movement, but also some of its vitality.

[17] T. Wolfe. *The Electric Kool-Aid Acid Test.* New York: Farrar, Straus, 1968, 119.
[18] *Ibid.*

Part III

THE SCIENTIFIC BASE

Chapter 6

Precursors

"Once upon a time, . . . while our Ford was still on earth . . .—or our Freud as, for some inscrutable reason, he chose to call himself whenever he spoke of psychological matters—. . . ."[1]

The sensitivity training movement is conditioned by its historical antecedents. As a social phenomenon, it depends on the stresses of society which produced it, on its leadership and membership, and on the nature of its belief system. Viewing it as an intellectual scientific enterprise, taking the internal approach, we must consider the ideas explicitly professed, their antecedents, and their current status as social psychological theory.

This dual nature of sensitivity training becomes clear if we consider the question of why sensitivity training arose when it did. In interviews with many leaders in the movement, two answers have generally been given. One is in terms of the needs of society, the alienation or the mechanization of society in the aftermath of the Second World War with its result in unprecedented social reconstruction, affluence, and mobility. Another answer centers on the increase in the knowledge of social psychology, and the techniques that had developed. Both of these sets of conditions were important for sensitivity training to occur. The first answer is sufficient to explain why a movement like sensitivity training arose within society. This answer was discussed in Chapters 3 and 5. The second set of

[1] A. Huxley. *Brave New World.* Garden City, N.Y.: Doubleday, 1932, 25, 44.

conditions is necessary for a more complete and specific understanding of the features of sensitivity training, however. It will be discussed in this and the following chapter.

PSYCHOTHERAPY

Freud

The theories of individual behavior are the oldest sources. They represent the early efforts to understand the theory and practice of change. Freud's discovery of the unconscious and of the irrational forces guiding human nature is important in understanding the later developments of the intensive group movement. Despite the attraction of psychiatrists and clinicians to sensitivity training and its diffusion in different kinds of group therapy, however, the direct Freudian influence is small. In part, Freud's philosophy is quite opposed to that of sensitivity training. Although Freud admitted the strength of unconscious drives and called for their acceptance by society, he also felt strongly that their control in society was necessary. Especially in his later writings, Freud saw suppression of some kind as the price of civilization, and that unleashing the force of both libido and aggression, the death instinct, could be infinitely dangerous to society.[2] All the branches of sensitivity training are much more favorable to the acceptance of unconscious drives.

A connection with sensitivity training is made by some of Freud's followers, especially the more socially oriented. The strongest Freudian influence occurred in the general atmosphere transmitted through the whole culture. The fact that a person does not necessarily mean what he says, that acts and words or mistakes in words can be seen as a revelation of the person, that a person may be acting-out in therapy an unresolved problem, and that this acting-out will occur in an interpersonal context, have become part of the culture, especially of social science. Another general influence of Freudian theory is the frank acceptance of both sexuality and aggression in current society. Nevertheless, most sensitivity trainers would distinguish themselves from Freudians in that they would not accept all attractions as sexual and would not want to equate aggression with the death instinct. Their philosophy would accept aggression as an important concomitant of positive affect. This is the important distinction between Freudian theory and the work in sensitivity training. It

[2] S. Freud. *Civilization and Its Discontents.* Garden City, N.Y.: Doubleday, 1930.

can be stated with confidence, however, that only in our secular culture which has been ingrained with psychoanalytic philosophy could sensitivity training have arisen. Although theories in sensitivity training may agree or disagree with Freudian theory, they all recognize the importance of his findings and theory.

Freud's new perspective on the individual psyche had great impact on social mores, but he wrote little directly on social psychology and group interaction. One of his books on leadership and growth, *Totem and Taboo,* expounds his theory of the original horde, consisting of a male, children, women, and the growing sons, and its transformation into modern society.[3] The leading male of the horde has control of all the women; at some point, out of jealousy, the brothers will kill the male, that is, the father. Then they will eat the father to share the guilt and power, which is the origin of the totemic feast. This is the original misdeed, the original sin which led to religious explanations and thus to social control through religious ritual. This description of the origin of religion and of society has been accepted by some as the description of group development. Slater, in *Microcosm,* has shown analogies between Freud's description of the primal horde and group development in a session in social psychology run on T-group principles (cf. Chapter 12).[4] He found that at a certain stage relatively soon after the inception of the group there was rebellion against the leader, or some way of symbolically excluding him, such as symbolically killing him, after which the group could proceed on a more even keel. Group leaders claimed that the initial killing of the leader and some kind of feast which often follows it is one of the most prominent regularities of group formation. It has been questioned whether the group members described by Slater might have read *Totem and Taboo* or have been familiar enough with its ideas from other sources to be somehow influenced to re-enact the scene. Be this as it may, this example shows the influence of Freudian ideas and psychoanalytic theory on both group members and group leaders.

Besides being an unquestioned scientific innovator, Freud also was one of the first persons who could build a philosophy of life out of a new view of science. The example of *Totem and Taboo* shows how Freudian influence has become pervasive, so much so that it is hard to say whether we can observe the influence of his theories on actual behavior. This is particularly true of the group of people who

[3] S. Freud. *Totem and Taboo.* London: Kegan Paul, Trench, Trubner, n.d.
[4] P. Slater. *Microcosm.* New York: Wiley, 1966.

are especially susceptible to sensitivity training. The influence of Freud in sensitivity training may lie more in the emotional acceptance of different ideas. Freud and other leading psychoanalysts are rather infrequently mentioned in the literature of sensitivity training. Many of the leaders see themselves as possessing alternatives to Freudian approaches. There is a great contempt for therapy in some of the human potential centers, and a definite attempt not to drag up early memories or anything outside the group in practically all of sensitivity training. The older and more mature psychoanalytic movement is recognized as a standard to measure oneself against, or as an old idea to be overcome; if one may use Freudian terms, a father figure to be slain. This seems to be a main function of the Freudian influence on sensitivity training.

Reich

A more direct psychoanalytic influence was exerted by some of Freud's less orthodox followers. One of these was Wilhelm Reich. Reich altered classical psychoanalytic theory and method in two ways: by stressing the necessity of sexual enjoyment for a full life, and by widening the therapy of narrowly defined neurotic symptoms to a notion of character disorders.[5] The first way emphasizes bodily, sensual, and sexual expression, and the regime of physical exercise in encounter centers is partly based on the work of one of Reich's students, Alexander Lowen. The protest against society rationalized in bodily release can also be traced to this source. Reich's second innovation, the study of character, is the precursor of the diagnosis of behavior within the group as revealing a person's character, his difficulties, and his potentialities. Reich's concentration on the whole character of man led him also to an interest in social conditions, especially the influence of social repression on the family and on personal and sexual development. Here, too, we can see origins for the claims of sensitivity training to bring about social change and release physical and mental creativity.

In his later years, Reich became more literal in his theories of sexual power, defining it as a substance, orgone, present in the atmosphere which could be captured in special boxes. In the early 1950's these boxes became popular in many circles, and Reich attracted a considerable following. The customers of the orgone boxes came from the social and cultural background that ten years later supplied the core of the clientele of encounter centers.

[5] W. Reich. *Character Analysis*. New York: Farrar, Straus, 1949.

Klein

Another influence of psychoanalysis on the movement was through the English branch, especially through Melanie Klein, who directly and indirectly trained many of the leaders in Tavistock. One characteristic of her technique was a lack of emphasis on childhood experiences and concentration on feelings during the therapy session: the origin of the here-and-now orientation of Tavistock Institute. Her brand of group therapy was influential in the development of the Tavistock theory.[6]

Bion, one of the original theorists, considers the group as a family or an organism which has to stay in balance with reasonable leadership in order to function.[7] The type of constellation he sees in any group corresponds to a kind of biological unit like a family, with a father (leadership), a function for procreation (pairing), and a function for releasing tension within the group (aggression). Only as long as leadership, pairing, and aggression are in a certain kind of balance is the group able to function efficiently. Bion also thinks that the same balance is necessary for the individual, and that diseases, for instance, are in part a function of imbalance of these factors. It is hard to say in general whether the analogy of the group to the person is a direct heritage of Freud.

These two influences from psychoanalytic thought, those of Reich and Klein, have led to extreme differences in their techniques of sensitivity training. The Kleinian influence in Tavistock and the Reichian in American personal growth centers are considered to be extreme opposites in leadership style. They are also opposite in the relation between theory and social movement. Reich's influence in encounter centers has led to popularization and recruitment to a social movement. Klein's influence at Tavistock has led to a restriction to professional activity and to the treatment of specific problems.

Moreno

We cannot leave a discussion of the psychiatric precursors of sensitivity training without treating Jacob Moreno. He was an early psychotherapist, rival to Freud, who developed his own unorthodox concepts and novel techniques. He and his followers have always stayed apart from the orthodox movements in psychoanalysis and in

[6] M. Klein. *Contributions to Psychoanalysis, 1921–1945.* London: Hogarth, 1948; *Developments in Psychoanalysis.* London: Hogarth, 1932; *Our Adult World.* London: Heineman, 1962. Cf. also M. Segal. *Introduction to the Work of Melanie Klein.* New York: Basic Books, 1964.

[7] W. Bion. *Experiences in Groups.* New York: Basic Books, 1961.

sensitivity training, but he has influenced them and has been active as a link between psychiatric treatment and small group techniques.[8]

In 1912 Moreno had already developed a concept of encounter similar to that which is used in sensitivity training.[9] Shortly afterward, he developed a psychodramatic technique that was used for therapy, or as Moreno put it, as an alternative to classical psychoanalytic technique. Psychodrama developed as an expansion of the general therapist-patient situation. Moreno felt that traditional psychiatry was too artificial and bare, and that the patient would be in danger of not generalizing what he learned in one situation to any others. Moreno wanted to go one step further and bring a social situation into the psychiatrist's office. This he did by adding new characters to the psychotherapeutic interview, representing people who were involved in the person's life: usually the father and the mother; love objects; and also one character who represented the patient himself, what he really felt and could not or did not want to express, or what the therapist wanted to say that the patient really felt. Psychodrama, therefore, is quite a formalized technique as distinguished from role-playing which is part of sensitivity training. In the ideal situation, it consists of a special stage on three levels, comprising three concentric circles; the inner and middle circles represent the most secret thoughts, and the lower circle the mask which a person wears for society. This technique can be adapted as well to dramatic performance as to therapy. In fact, some plays of the 1920's, such as Eugene O'Neill's *The Great God Brown*, use similar techniques. Moreno is also reputed to have trained some stars of early motion pictures before they were discovered, such as Peter Lorre and Elizabeth Bergner. We may note the similarities of his technique to the contemporary Stanislavsky technique or Method acting (cf. Chapter 13).

Psychodramatic method is also intimately connected with psychodramatic theory which has striking similarities to, and differences from, the theory and mythology of sensitivity training. In common with many sensitivity trainers, Moreno alternates between being a psychiatrist and a scientist, even claiming the mantle of the prophet. One of his early books, *The Words of the Father*, in effect seems to be the words of God, and is principally distinguished by the quantity of words printed entirely in capital letters.

[8] Moreno gives the history of his work in the introduction to *Who Shall Survive?* Beacon, N.Y.: 2nd ed.; Beacon House, 1953.

[9] *Einladung zu einer Begegnung* (Invitation to an Encounter). Vienna, 1916.

Some of Moreno's work and techniques have become common-place among social psychologists, especially the method of sociometry and the technique of role-playing which developed from psychodrama. For Moreno, however, the two techniques of sociometry and psychodrama form an inseparable whole, and are really only two aspects of the application of the same theory. His theory concentrates on two characteristics of the person, which he calls "tele" and "spontaneity."[10] Tele is interpersonal attraction within a group, or an individual's attraction to other people. Thus, tele is measured by the sociometric test, that is, by asking a person with whom he likes to participate in certain activities. For Moreno, one criterion of the sociometric test is that it has to be real: not only can the question be asked, but corresponding action must be taken. For instance, a person cannot be asked whom he wants to play games with unless these games will actually be executed and in the groupings the subject has requested. Thus, sociometric tests both measure tele and make it effective in the social situation. For Moreno, therefore, sociometry results in reconstruction of society according to the principles that the members of the society themselves want.

Within this reconstructed society, then, spontaneity can be expressed. Spontaneity is a trait people may possess in varying degrees, but like any skill it can be developed within a person. A society developed along sociometric lines would be the ideal society in which to express spontaneity. In this sense psychodrama is a formal method of testing. Psychodrama also includes a method of developing spontaneity by getting a person into a situation in which he has to act-out certain feelings or actions. At the same time as his spontaneity increases, his problems can more easily be demonstrated to the psychiatrist and be influenced by him. Here psychodrama becomes a psychiatric technique, including specific rules of procedure, of initiating therapy, choice of techniques at different stages of process, and procedure of termination. A patient going through this technique is like any psychiatric patient, and the therapist is responsible for the whole process. On the other hand, the therapists themselves go through a definite course of training, working themselves up from alter egos to protagonists, to assistant directors, and finally to therapists. This technical training also includes an indoctrination to theory.

Psychodrama seems to be more like therapy than like sensitivity

[10] J. Moreno. *Who Shall Survive?* and *Psychodrama*, Vols. I and II. Beacon, N.Y.: Beacon House, 1946 and 1959.

training. However, its ideas have been adapted to sensitivity training. Although the methods sketched are those used for hospitalized patients, Moreno himself has used psychodrama as a short-term technique for laymen. For instance, in New York a psychodrama theater is open to guests, and anyone in the audience may become a participant in the drama. The resulting philosophy is also similar to that of sensitivity training. It aims at the reconstruction of society from the individual outward, considering social constraints and structure as repressive factors that inhibit the pure sociometric and spontaneous development of society and the person. This corresponds to the basic philosophy of sensitivity training too, which also sees the regeneration of society starting within the individual. As sociometry is more formalized and older, some of the difficulties inherent in this approach can be seen. Institutions using the sociometric test in earnest have often been suspected of using it as a backhanded way for introducing segregation, which would be the outcome of many sociometric tests. In fact the outlawed "freedom of choice" plan of Southern school districts is in effect a sociometric test.

Thus, both in specific techniques and in general underlying philosophy, Moreno must be counted as one of the precursors of sensitivity training. By his own effort, he has tried to bridge the gulf between psychoanalysis and social psychology, and therefore has been able to use many of the psychoanalytic concepts in groups. His exact position is difficult to assess, partly because some of his flights into fancy seem to negate his more conventional scientific work. He certainly has developed some of the techniques and prepared the theory for much of what goes on today in encounter groups and sensitivity training. That he initiated the terms "encounter" and "role-playing" does not mean that anything which goes by this name is really traceable to him. It is clear, however, that he has had some direct influence on people connected with sensitivity training. His work in the United States began in the early 1930's in Saint Elizabeths Hospital, Washington, D.C., where the first American psychodramatic stage was built, and many people have had at least some contact with it. Some of the people working in group dynamics, especially Ronald Lippitt, had close contact with Moreno and were familiar with psychodramatic techniques. In another way, he also influenced some of the resettlement programs during the New Deal period. Farm resettlement was conducted in part according to sociometric principles with Moreno's help.[11] It should be remembered that Leland Bradford also

[11] C. Loomis. "Sociometrics and the Study of New Rural Communities," *Sociometry*, 2, 1939, 56–76.

acquired his ideas about self-propelled groups during the same time, working on related problems.

The psychodramatic school is today somewhat separate from the work in sensitivity training. The whole formal theory stands outside the general mainstream of the field and is less open to influences from other branches. On the other hand, psychodrama, sociometry, the cult of spontaneity, the notion of encounter, the term "here and now," and the acceptance of psychotic states as valid states of the individual—all seem to be derived from Moreno's work. We shall review the present state of Moreno's work in Chapter 10.

SOCIAL PSYCHOLOGY

Lewin

The theorist most recognized as having given his ideas to sensitivity training from a social psychological point of view is Kurt Lewin.[12] We have discussed him before as one of the prime movers of the National Training Laboratory. Lewin's work had been connected with both the group and the individual, but his field theory was applied directly to the use of groups and analogies did not need to be made from an originally individual-centered theory. If people say that T-groups and sensitivity training developed because the time was right and psychological theory had advanced to the optimum point, they usually mean it is because of the work of Kurt Lewin.

Lewin's influence on the development of sensitivity training has been discussed already as part of the history of the T-group movement. Under his direct influence the movement was started. Here we will mainly discuss his previous theoretical and applied work in relation to the growth of sensitivity training.

Lewin's work, especially toward the end of his life, had two primary concerns. One was an abstract, mathematically oriented theory to encompass both the individual and the group. The second was a concern with applied topics, a great readiness to jump into application, and especially toward the end, a strong belief in the group as an important unit.

Lewin's psychological theory has some affinity with early Gestalt psychology, which is concerned with the arrangement of objects and their relationship, as well as with immediate perception. Con-

---

[12] For references on Lewin's works, see Chap. 1, footnote 5.

trary to most Gestalt psychologists, though, Lewin was interested more in action and decision as opposed to the emphasis on perception of most of his colleagues. In his procedure, he used basically sociological concepts to understand the person; thus he talked about different regions inside the person: a leadership region, an executive region, tension between different regions, and permeability of boundaries. In a certain way, therefore, he viewed one person as a model of society. In social psychology, the concepts he had used for the study of the person fitted extremely well when talking about groups. His main concern in groups was the question of what action a person would take. Given a goal, a person might have to choose a path to that goal taking into account that varying group atmospheres and different people's power over him might force him to take a different path.

He was also interested in the relationships between the different parts of the whole group. Looking at subgroups as regions within a larger field, he then could study the interrelation between the different parts of the field, such as communication between them, influence one group can use to change another, or power relationships of one part of the group over another. He also discussed the relationship of part of the group to the whole group. Again he looked at forces that might hold a person within the group and those that might induce him to leave it. The resultant effect of staying within the group has been called cohesion of the group itself, which may either refer to the whole group or to the attraction of members to the group.

Lewin's theories provided a conceptual base for handling groups as units and for seeing the individual as part of a group. Beginning in 1935 he used his theory for experimentation and later in practical situations, such as in changing food habits during the Second World War and solving conflicts within industries and between ethnic groups. The applied side of the theory was always very important, leading him to say, "Nothing is so practical as a good theory." Some of his earlier work had already foreshadowed interest in sensitivity training, or in some of the uses to which it has been put. Thus he sponsored work showing that group discussion and the commitment of members to a decision would change people more than the best lecture on the same topic. Although there is some doubt about the general validity of those studies today, they were influential in providing support for T-groups or any kind of groups that would produce change.

At the time of the start of the sensitivity training movement, and partly based on his experience at the Connecticut workshop, he formulated a general theory of change.[13] This theory stated that people usually act or think in an equilibrium. There is some allowance for deviation from the equilibrium point, but the farther the deviation goes, the more there is pressure to return to the central point again, analogous to a pendulum or a spring. He also felt that group environment reinforces this so-called quasi-stationary equilibrium. Thus, if one removes individuals from a group and convinces them to change their course of action, they will return to their previous condition upon returning to their old group. In a similar way, one can pull out a spring, but the moment that one lets it go, it will return to the original position. Therefore, in order to change a person and make the change permanent, one must change the whole group situation; first disturb it or make it flexible, then change the structure of the group and reset it for a different equilibrium. Then a change would be permanent. He calls these three stages "unfreezing," "change," and "refreezing." The first workshops and industrial experiments were conducted on the basis of this formulation. The Connecticut workshop, for instance, was an attempt to make people more efficient in intergroup relations, and also, if necessary, to change their standards. The first Bethel workshop was also designed to produce changes in people's behavior and to increase the general efficiency of leaders and members of groups.

Thus, the events which occurred at the start of sensitivity training fitted with Lewin's theory. They illustrated a new mechanism in unfreezing a group, and the strong experiences and emotion that accompanied the feedback could be seen as a sign of accomplishing this change. Whether Lewin would have accepted this emphasis on experience and feedback is a question that cannot be answered because of his untimely death. His theory was designed for a here-and-now orientation, as he stressed the field situation at a given time, as distinct from, for instance, psychoanalytic theory, which emphasizes the importance of the past.[14]

After Lewin's death, two branches of group dynamics founded by him could be distinguished, one which adhered to the more theoretical formulations such as communication, influence, cohesion, group structure, and power; and the other which ventured into industrial applications and finally led to sensitivity training.

[13] "Frontiers in Group Dynamics I: Concept, Method and Theory in Social Science; Social Equilibrium," *Human Relations, 1*, 1947, 5–40.

[14] R. Barker, T. Dembo, and K. Lewin. "Frustration and Regression: An Experiment with Young Children," University of Iowa Studies in Child Welfare, Vol. 18. New York, 1941.

HUMAN RELATIONS AND COUNSELING

Hawthorne Studies

In the applied fields of human relations in which sensitivity training became influential, new theories had arisen that foreshadowed the principles of sensitivity training. One was the new look in management, and the other, nondirective counseling.

New theories of management arose in the late 1920's and early 1930's as a reaction to the overly rational scientific approach to management. The old approach tried to analyze industrial progress in technological as well as human terms in order to make it more efficient. The limits and drawbacks of this management technique were first shown clearly in the Hawthorne (Westinghouse) studies.[15] These studies, in the scientific management tradition, tried to investigate the effects of different amounts of light on performance. It was found that of more importance than the actual amount of light was the fact the workers considered themselves important because they were being studied; any experimental change led to an increase in production.

Attention was then shifted to the motivation of the worker. Special groups were set up and procedures developed in cooperation with the workers themselves. It was found that the workers felt they were being taken seriously. Under these conditions they were alert to the interests of the company as well as to their own, and understood the principles of management and were able to suggest improvements. The effect was a reorganization of the company, the institution of a counseling system, and a turning away from the rigid methods of personnel management. The new school of human relations stressed mainly the motivations of the workers, their integration into the business, and a concern for problems of the workers as human beings. Later theorists, such as Argyris, have pointed to the unavoidable conflict between individual needs and organizational requirements; in fact, most human relations programs, including the one in the Hawthorne plant itself, have been discontinued. Nevertheless, the original optimism of the new discoveries led to theories which stated that management could be improved by releasing the worker to express himself.[16]

---

[15] F. Roethlisberger and W. Dickson. *Management and the Worker*. Cambridge, Mass.: Harvard University Press, 1939.

[16] A review of the Hawthorne studies is given by H. Landsberger, *Hawthorne Revisited*. Ithaca, New York: New York School of Industrial and Labor

McGregor

One of the early theorists in this field was Douglas McGregor, who had been a personnel manager himself and was later head of the Industrial Relations section of MIT; he had been instrumental in bringing Lewin to MIT, and in fact, the Research Center for Group Dynamics was part of the Industrial Relations section. McGregor's ideas exerted a direct influence on the start of the National Training Laboratory and can be taken here as representative of the developing human relations schools. He formalized the distinction between the scientific management and the human relations approach under the names of Theory X and Theory Y. Theory X (the scientific management approach) looked at man as basically a passive being who must be forced by promises and threats to perform work; the organization must therefore be adapted to provide this kind of motivation for the worker. Theory Y (human relations approach) views the worker as self-propelled, trying to realize his potentialities within the work scene. McGregor agrees at this point with Maslow's hierarchy of needs (see Chapter 3) and also that D-needs (the basic biological needs) are not motivators for work when they have been at least minimally satisfied. The new task of management, therefore, is to organize the working situation in such a way that workers direct themselves in the most efficient and satisfying ways of functioning within the enterprise.[17]

McGregor also felt that this philosophy of management could not be taught by the usual verbal instruction. He was very hospitable to new, emotional techniques of teaching, such as role-playing, discussion groups, and unguided problem solving, all of which were techniques also adopted originally at Bethel. The human relations approach to management thus paved the way for the treatment of large-scale organizational problems in small groups.

Nondirective Counseling

In the same way as the human relations approach was an intellectual precursor of sensitivity training applied to industry, so counseling was a way to make the transition from psychotherapy to discussion groups. Carl Rogers developed nondirective counseling as a treatment for people who were troubled with a problem that in-

---

Relations, 1965; for an attack from a radical point of view see A. Hampden-Turner, *Radical Man*. Cambridge: Schenckman, 1970, Chap. VIII.

[17] D. McGregor. *The Human Side of Enterprise*. New York: McGraw-Hill, 1960.

capacitated them, but was not great enough for them to be considered sick. Rogers felt that a great proportion of his patients, above-average college students with minor problems, were best helped by giving them a chance to express themselves in a warm, supportive climate provided by the counselor.[18] The counselor, by accepting the patient at his own evaluation and expressing himself mainly by repeating the client's own words or giving a noncommittal grunt, could get the patient himself to realize that either his problems were not as crucial as he had thought, or that he could find a solution to them by himself. It is, of course, impossible for a therapist to stay completely neutral. The client himself wants a response and is extremely skilled at picking up any cues from the counselor that he is doing the right thing. Frank has compared this technique to the work of operant conditioning.[19] It can be shown that any reaction of the counselor will be interpreted by the patient either as approval or disapproval. Any idea that leads to a favorable and interested reaction of the counselor will be repeated more and more by the client.

The underlying theory, like that of human relations management, conceives of an essentially healthy man stymied by social restraints. A situation that makes it possible for a person to express himself will be sufficient to reach unforeseen climaxes in insight and self-expression. This theory precludes a more or less active role on the part of the therapist or group leader, and can give justification to encounter groups formed without respect to any pathology in the participants. It becomes a useful theory for obscuring the line between therapy and sensitivity groups.

[18] C. Rogers. *Client-Centered Therapy in Current Practice, Implications and Theory.* Boston: Houghton Mifflin, 1951.

[19] J. Frank. *Persuasion and Healing.* Baltimore, Md.: Johns Hopkins, 1961.

Chapter 7

Current Concepts and Methods

"There are three stages in your integration. There is learning, there is understanding, and there is acceptance."[1]

Techniques of sensitivity training evoke a strong emotional experience in the participants; the relatively simple rules of emotional feedback and concentration on the here and now lead to intense experiences that seem to give insight into new ways of life, at least for the duration of the group session and a short time afterward. Experiences of this kind have been known in other contexts. Nevertheless, sensitivity training is unique in that it cherishes the technique and the experience for their own sakes.

We have discussed the conditions in the society and culture that have led to the rise of sensitivity training. The leaders and group members need a justification for their experience. In the spirit of the times, it should be couched in the framework of social science. In the last chapter we discussed some of the scientific background on which theories of sensitivity training could be built. Now we can turn to current theoretical explanations.[2]

The basic problem within sensitivity training theory is the relationship of the individual to the group. The Lewinian tradition provided a guide for the work of the National Training Laboratory. In

[1] G. Orwell. *Nineteen Eighty-Four*. New York: Harcourt, 1949, 264.

[2] This chapter owes much to participation in a Conference on Intensive Group Techniques organized by the Foundations' Fund for Research in Psychiatry, in Puerto Rico, June, 1969, especially the paper by Michael Kahn, "The Return of the Repressed," and the discussion by Herzl Spiro.

Lewinian theory, individuals and groups are isomorphic; that is, the same concepts are valid for the analysis of either. An individual or a group is conceived as a region consisting of subregions whose inter-relationships become important in understanding its structure. Sub-regions in the individual represent central beliefs and ideas, the cognitive structure; subregions in the group represent statuses and roles. Groups and men can therefore work in harmony: man is ideally fitted to group life, at least life in certain groups. Here the theory meshes with McGregor's formulation of Y-theory or similar theories by Rensis Likert and Chris Argyris. These theories claim that some types of groups are ideally suited for man's complete development. It is the task of T-groups to provide this kind of group environment.[3]

Two main principles of Lewin's theory form the basis for the progress of the T-group as conducted by NTL. One is the theory of encapsulation within a group, that the changes in the individual have to be part of his group membership. The other is the theory of channeling and feedback.[4] This theory, developed as it was at the end of the war, has a quasi-military ring to it, analyzing effective action in four stages: reconnaissance, action, intelligence, and evaluation. After the cycle the feedback loop starts over. In group life, this means trying out of a new idea (reconnaissance), perhaps in role-playing or in a staged situation, then the action itself in conformity with the idea, feedback of the action for analysis by the group (intelligence), seeing what has been done and who has performed well or badly (evaluation), then new role-playing again (reconnaissance), and so on. The combination of these two principles gives us the basic theory of the T-group.

The problem of the T-group then becomes one of having this activity performed in such a way that change occurs, but stays anchored within the group. There should be a planned activity dependent on the group. As a result of it, individuals should become more cohesive group members and should be able to act more efficiently as individuals. These two ideas may seem contradictory, but such a contradiction was exactly the purpose of the T-group theory. It was achieved by creating an initial ambiguous situation. If the first stage of the situation is so confusing that people lose all cues for expected

[3] D. McGregor. *The Human Side of Enterprise*. New York: McGraw-Hill, 1960. R. Likert. *New Patterns of Management*. New York: McGraw-Hill, 1961. C. Argyris. *Interpersonal Competence and Organizational Effectiveness*. Homewood, Ill.: Dorsey, 1962.

[4] K. Lewin. "Frontiers in Group Dynamics II: Channels of Group Life and Social Planning and Action Research," *Human Relations, 1,* 1947, 143–153.

behavior, the only basis of action is to establish a new identity within the group. All possible attempts are made to increase the ambiguity of the initial situation. Outside status is eliminated, and this is why the original T-group was a group of strangers. Some people have likened this initial ambiguous situation to an existential encounter, the primordial dread of the unknown, and the real stripping of the individual's soul for a new experience.[5] It may be doubted that at the present time the initial situation has remained ambiguous. If only from previous reading, people know in general what to expect in a T-group. Somewhat paradoxically, they come in knowing that they do not know what to expect, and are quite ready and eager to be confused and to be put into an ambiguous situation. To a certain degree, however, even experienced T-group participants feel some shock in the initial encounter, a situation with no ostensible aim outside the group, and are each new time threatened by the unclarity.

This situation is indispensable for beginning T-group or sensitivity training, from which then the process of reconnaissance, action, and feedback can proceed. The rest of the procedure follows easily within this framework. New attempts to establish relationships are explored, new progress is tried out, tentative decisions can be made, and what has happened in the tryout is then discussed. One of the important questions is the role of the trainer himself. From one point of view, the progress of the group depends in part on eliminating the trainer, getting rid of group dependence on the person who originally controls the group, and relegating him more to the role of a member who might have certain expert knowledge. We have discussed in the last chapter an elaborate theory of this process formulated on a combination of group dynamics and Freud's *Totem and Taboo*.

In effect, of course, a trainer in any situation is more than a dispensable initiator; if he were not, then the emphasis on training trainers and on professional competence would not be so important, and the quality of trainers and differences between styles of training would also not be crucial. The trainer has a responsibility that goes beyond expert knowledge, to use the action of the group to fulfill the purposes of the training. Although his role might be quite passive, he has to know when he must intervene to keep the group within the experience that sensitivity training is supposed to provide. The trainer, therefore, has the responsibility to set limits on the activities

[5] For example, A. Hampden-Turner, *Radical Man*. Cambridge, Mass.: Schenckman, 1970, 157.

of the group, so that it does not get too emotional and does not try to escape from the present situation by discussing some outside problem. He must push toward the correct interpretations and, in general, keep the group going. If one looks through all the literature about the role of the trainer and of the group, it is clearly the trainer who provides the link between the general National Training Laboratory theory and the actions of the members. The illusion of democracy in a group of this kind is equivalent to the illusion that the trainer really relinquishes his role. A good trainer makes the group feel that he comes out of the group, but at the same time he leads it toward the relevant experiences and provides the relevant indoctrination of the Bethel atmosphere.

Finally, there is the question of the stability of the change, of the transfer of the training from this group to other groups. This relates closely to the question of the effectiveness of the training itself. Lewin's theory states that training based on the group is stable as long as it is related to the same group atmosphere. If a person goes back to the situation from which he came prior to the change, however, he loses his new anchorage in the training group and has no base for effective change. Several ways have been proposed to escape this dilemma. One is for several people from the same organization to attend the workshop. In this case, the person has a new group anchorage in the people who have come with him to the workshop and, therefore, the possibility of preservation of change. Another current theory is that change will occur most readily in a situation where the individual is dominant or has little resistance to overcome. For example, he will be more effective in changing within his family than in his work situation. Over the years, the claims of the group dynamics movement for permanent change in behavior have declined. The current claim is for a general change of attitude and way of life, perhaps an ability to listen more sympathetically, rather than for specific changes or an increase in group efficiency.

In observing discussions and role-playing in the back-home situation, one sees a great cynicism among people who have not been through the experience and who are not able to understand the great values such training has had. Belief in the transfer of learning gives way to more general claims of the creation of a new culture, a social movement instead of a goal-directed procedure.

Theoretical and methodological development in NTL has been centered on the group and change. Lewin's original ideas about the use of the group to disrupt old patterns and create a new, effective equilibrium were mainly designed for situations where the group is used as a vehicle for initiating and consolidating change. Rather than going in the direction of enjoyment of the group experience, much of the theory of NTL has evolved into finding a means to produce change and to train people who can initiate change in individuals, in organizations, and in society at large. Probably the most theoretically active center of NTL theory, and even of the whole movement, is the Human Relations Center at Boston University. This Center is directed by Kenneth Benne and Robert Chin, who have done very incisive work in the theory of groups and their use for change.[6] Chin has distinguished the different techniques men have used to produce change in other men. They are coercion, reason, emotion, and education. The sensitivity training approach is partly a rejection of coercion, but on the other hand, it is also a rejection of an exclusively rational and educational approach. It becomes, therefore, almost therapeutic in the sense of engaging the deep parts of the personality. Engagement of the whole person, which can be done best in separation from his usual surroundings and in a group atmosphere, is difficult. The questions that have concerned the leaders in developing their theory and practice have been about the kind of group best designed to promote this kind of change and affectivity; in addition, the way a group like this develops, grows, and proceeds through several stages, and finally the way that group experience can be generalized to other experiences. In answer to the first question: What kind of group is good for producing change in the person, we find the model of McGregor's Y-theory. It is a group in which the leader holds a passive but directive role. In theory, at least, he is the kind of person who ought to work himself out of a job. He gets the group started, and in the first session provides some directions for the things the group should do and should not do. He clearly should not provide an agenda, and should present no particular aim, but should keep the focus of the group on feelings, feedback, and understanding the dynamics of the relationships within the present situation. It is hoped that at some point the leader will become unnecessary, and the group can take over, reorganizing and giving their leader a position as member of the group.

The main characteristics of a mature group are the openness of people's expressions of their feelings about each other and the seriousness with which they work on different exercises that may be determined by the leader or decided on by the group itself. Thus,

---

[6] Much of this has been published in W. G. Bennis, K. D. Benne, and R. Chin (eds.), *The Planning of Change.* New York: 2nd ed.; Holt, 1970.

T-groups approach the ideal of the Y-theory. In contrast to the personal growth groups (Esalen), the exercises are usually not performed for the benefit of one person, but for the benefit of group action. Some task may be set, depending on the composition of the group. In T-groups there is probably more play-acting than in any of the other kinds of groups. Groups will imitate communities or consulting firms, and then try to help others or try to organize their own community. For example, they might be given the task of gaining entry into an organization through contact with the manager. Then a scene is set up in which some of the members try to see a secretary, get an appointment with the manager, and talk to the manager or one of his associates about the plans.

The aim is to make the group an efficient working group, with the members able to criticize each other freely and to work together. All kinds of mechanisms and techniques are used for this purpose. If available, videotapes are made of the groups in action, and people can watch themselves and the rest of the group interact. In other situations, recordings or observations are made. The important thing is a lack of self-consciousness in discussing what one did, what the other person did, and why one did what one was supposed to do. It is not unusual for a fifteen-minute action to become the basis of discussion for an hour or more. It is sometimes hard to distinguish this activity from a sort of glorified gossip session, but this may be part of its charm and attraction to the group. The group members gain a deep sense of identification with their group. In laboratories where the participants are divided into several groups, each group very quickly develops a definite character or personality. This kind of activity is close to the basic idea of the original T-group, and even the original experience from which the whole movement derived.

It cannot be overstated, however, that the NTL emphasis is to view people as members of the group, with their learning dependent on their interaction with other people within the group. The group's activities away from problem solving and toward the expression of emotion, affection, and aggression, and involvement with each other, lead to the ideal group of the theorist and personnel manager, as well as to the kind of group that can be the courier of change within its members. Change is emphasized within the training group itself, where the individual members are being changed, and in giving skills to become change agents which the members might have when they come out. The emphasis on change, instead of on stability, corresponds to the movement's opposition to the continuity of social structure. Besides, it is felt that there are enough institutions to maintain stability, and it is important to create institutions that can promote change.

In dealing with the problems of individuals and society, then, the NTL point of view assumes a basic harmony between the two. It tries to adapt both toward each other in order to make both open to change. In this way it tries to rationalize the intense experience in the training groups and make it a socially controllable affect. When a conflict arises between these aims and actual outcomes, the trend has always been to hold to the experience itself. This has limited the adaptation of the technique for greater effectiveness in specific situations or facing frankly the possibility of unavoidable and tragic contrast between the individual and the group. Faced with these problems, NTL has accepted techniques designed purely for individual experience when they were developed in the personal growth centers, but it has not been willing to take a clinical or professional approach to problems of permanent effects. It has stayed as true as possible to its original theories and practices, but faced with choice, has turned more toward remaining a social movement than becoming a rigorous technique. Two solutions to this dilemma are the extreme personal growth center approach, a social movement associated with Esalen, and the extreme problem-centered approach associated with Tavistock.

The personal growth movement as represented by Esalen has opted for the use of intensive group techniques only for the sake of the individual. The theory on which this solution is based must be explicated from different applications, instead of from an analysis of existing theory. The personal growth centers are really too new to have been able to codify techniques and basic assumptions, especially as their whole emphasis is on doing and experiencing first and thinking afterward. The movement also abounds with people who would be very averse to making theoretical formulations, and who are happiest being charismatic leaders or gurus. Their attempt to make this charisma explicit has been up to now a failure. The more classical writings of people like Rogers, Schutz, Maslow, and even Aldous Huxley make it possible to construct a framework that may approximate the basic ideas on which encounter groups are run.[7]

If one were to construct a central model on which this whole movement is based, it would have to be the model of a prisoner in a

[7] C. Rogers. *On Becoming a Person.* Boston: Houghton Mifflin, 1961. A. Maslow. *Toward a Psychology of Being.* Princeton, N.J.: Van Nostrand, 1962. W. Schutz. *Joy.* New York: Grove Press, 1968; and *Here Comes Everybody.* New York: Harper, 1971.

cage. Underlying most of the thought is the idea of man (or whatever the essential man is) as being imprisoned by different layers of circumstances which do not allow him to reach his full potentialities. Allied to this image is also the supposition that, if he could escape, everything would be good, and he would only use his potentialities for creative and beneficial results. The different kinds of suppression which make this impossible for man at the present time can be represented as several layers of obstacles. One is simply the body, or more precisely, the nervous system. Aldous Huxley has made the point that the senses and thinking severely limit the experiences of the world a person can really have.[8] Thus, man is encased in a cage with only a few openings from which he can get only a selected view of reality and of his own feelings. Huxley's answer to getting beyond this point was an escape through direct mystical experience, and later also through use of drugs such as mescaline. It may be that Huxley's own extreme consciousness of the limitations of sensory experience was a result of his own very traumatic bout with blindness with which he had to contend for most of his life. However, this same theory is echoed to some extent today in McLuhan's emphasis on the medium, although he puts it into more positive terms, such as that man is what media make him. From these sources we can find part of the basis for the emphasis on sensory awareness training, namely, the search for experiences that might get man through to a direct consciousness, independent of the senses. The group experience might be a way of breaking through the sensory barrier. Also, other techniques such as meditation and other sacred experiences, as well as drugs, are not rejected out of hand.

Another part of the prison, essentially the same as the sensory part, is the misuse of the whole machinery of the body. The relationship here is not seen in a dualistic way as in the religious view of the willing mind and the weak flesh. As a matter of fact, there is no rejection of the body in the ascetic sense. On the contrary, the experiences of the bodily self are accepted as part of the real self. The objective here is that the potential use of the body is really a great portion of possible experience which the self must come to terms with in reaching its full potentialities. One of the greatest taboos at Esalen is speaking about *the* body, *the* hand, *the* head. One can speak only of *my* body, *my* hand, *my* head. A great amount of Esalen's training includes using neglected parts of the body more, and con-

[8] A. Huxley. "Human Potentialities," in S. M. Farber and R. H. L. Wilson, *Control of the Mind.* New York: McGraw-Hill, 1961.

centrating on different bodily experiences. The start of most Esalen sessions consists of working up the different muscle patterns within the body, or excluding some of the senses in order to make others more important. A variety of gymnastic exercises accompanies every session or encounter group, and the movement has attracted many people whose main interest has been in gymnastics. Here the theoretical influence of Wilhelm Reich is probably the strongest. Although presumably the exercises are part of a tightly knit system of psychophysiological therapy, they have been used by themselves, and also tried quite successfully in training athletic teams. This is similar to the development of Moreno's psychodrama toward the training of actors. The use of the body in all its capacities is an essential part of all human-potential training, and fits very well with the rejection of symbolism. For instance, the metaphor of being centered, of having a center of one's life which in a sense corresponds to identity, is used in encounter groups in a very literal way. Participants are taught a stance in which the center of gravity is relatively stable by spreading the legs slightly and leaning forward. Similar stances to these have been used in many sports, especially when stability is necessary, such as in skiing or fencing.

The physical expression of psychological concepts reaches its definite statement in William Schutz's *Joy*. Schutz developed a system of interpersonal relations within the tradition of small-group experimentation. He constructed a measuring instrument which enabled him to conclude that the three main dimensions found in interpersonal relations are inclusion, affection, and dominance, as well as their opposite active expressions, yielding the three pairs of exclusion-inclusion, dominance-submission, and affection-aggression. This work of Schutz has been part of standard sociological theory and has been used in experiments and in analysis of dyads and groups. When Schutz later became involved with the Esalen movement, he constructed exercises which in the anti-symbolic tradition of the movement translated these concepts into action. Thus there are exercises to promote inclusion, affection, dominance, and combinations such as trust. Exercises on inclusion, for instance, would include persons trying to break into a circle formed by the rest of the members of the group, or trying to break out of it. An exercise on affection would consist of one member being lifted by the rest of the group members and stroked and fondled. Exercises on dominance are in effect varieties of general physical contests. In general interpersonal interactions, of course, these kinds of relations between members are more formalized and not worked out physically. The physical acting-out and working-out of these drives presumably help break the mold in which the person is captured in interpersonal relationships, and make him creative and free to act with other people. These exercises, of course, very closely resemble children's games, and could be explained by the fact that what we are doing is regaining our lost childish innocence.

Another kind of restraint on man is shown in Rogers' theory, which he had developed originally in his counseling work. It follows the old mental health approach of a person being bound by bad habits, irrational fears, and other restraints from his past, which make it impossible for him to work to his full capacity. In later years at the Western Behavioral Science Institute, Rogers developed the idea of a new kind of life, of a new civilization based on short encounters and the ability to have deep feelings with people whom one sees only rarely.[9] Thus, immediate spontaneity, to use Moreno's term, is exalted. Interaction with people whom one has just met can overcome any previous experience, any previous constraint on the person. Encounter groups, efforts to relate quickly and deeply to people whom one has met in the last half hour, are ways of releasing the person from any of the chains of the past. This theory of immediate relationships, the philosophy of immediate contact, of getting beyond any social constraints, is the next step in the liberation of the person from his past constraints.

The final theoretical barrier consists of the social constraints and social forms that are hindering the person. This would make the movement hospitable to radical movements, the so-called counterculture, as a chance for the construction of a new life and a new society. There is little in the official literature of the movement, as far as it can be called official, which really treats active ways of changing the total society. The general effect has been to ignore society, to concentrate on laboratory sessions, and perhaps to imply either that a new society can be constructed from regenerated individuals, or that a periodic immersing of the individual in the different situations of human-potential centers will make them impervious to the restrictions of society. Rogers, in trying to reconstitute a whole school district, has been working on a real social reconstruction, but he has put little theory into the social part of the work, and has concentrated mainly on encounter groups in different parts of the system, such as among students, faculty, and administrators. Perhaps the most out-

---

[9] C. Rogers. "Interpersonal Relationships U.S.A. 2000," *Journal of Applied Behavioral Science, 4,* 1968, 208–269.

spoken spokesman of the movement who has treated social questions has been the writer and philosopher Alan Watts. Watts advocates the acceptance of all deviate parts of society as important and as more genuine than the conventional ones.[10] The image of the shackled soul is very strong in him, and he accepts the fact that madness, or what we call madness, might get us closer to the truth than conventional thinking. But he also advocates a society that tolerates and respects all kinds of different activities which people now consider deviate.

In general, the social efforts of people in the field have been directed toward gaining acceptance for a variety of experiences including those which they themselves induce and toward really trying to show how the individual can live without society. There is a general feeling that the individual can live without social forms and that social forms are not natural, but there has been no consistent attack on them or ideas about how to change them.

In contrast to the two American developments, NTL and personal growth centers, the English version, the Tavistock approach, stays closely problem-oriented. Although Tavistock trainers have varied backgrounds and use different techniques, one can discern a common orientation. The psychiatrists and psychologists have had psychoanalytic training and the other social scientists have had sufficient contact with this doctrine to be deeply influenced.

The common psychoanalytic background of the trainers has had several consequences. One is Tavistock's clinical orientation which has resulted in the concentration on actual problems. Intervention by Tavistock occurs only when some complaint is presented which warrants treatment, and the problems of the client remain important throughout the whole process. Books written by Tavistock members, even if their titles indicate general topics, treat specific social and organizational problems. For instance, A. V. Rice's book, which had a wide theoretical impact, is called *The Enterprise and Its Environment*.[11] It deals, however, with a calico mill in India and its specific problems, including the differences in organizational theory necessary for textile and for chemical plants. The usefulness of training has been of prime importance in the whole development of Tavistock work. In opposition to the American trend, which has been to rely less and less on specific results and aim for a diffuse influence

---

[10] A. Watts. "Divine Madness" (tape recording). San Rafael, Calif.: Big Sur Recordings, 1969.

[11] A. Rice. *The Enterprise and Its Environment*. London: Tavistock, 1963.

on society, Tavistock trainers have tried to solve their dilemma by pulling the back-home problems into the training program itself. Exercises are not geared toward general processes but deal with precisely those problems that brought the participants to the program in the first place.

Another consequence of the psychoanalytic orientation has been an emphasis on rational understanding. Although psychoanalysis acknowledges the irrational, emotional factor in man—indeed, it was the first theory to do so—the goal for the trainer as well as for the trainee is seen to be a deepened understanding of one's own behavior and of one's fellow man. Thus emotional outbursts, loosening of inhibitions, and new ways of acting and feeling are only means to the end of better understanding, and are not valuable for their own sake. This may be likened in a medical situation to unpleasant or dangerous, but necessary, drugs needed to cure the patient, but not advisable to be used or abused without professional license. This attitude puts responsibility on the professional to use intensive group techniques only under limited, justifiable conditions.

Psychoanalytic theory is basically concerned with the individual rather than the group. This legacy has had a paradoxical effect on Tavistock theory which is based on an elaborate theory of individual functioning. Tavistock trainers had to look for a way to direct their ideas toward social units. The result has been a general adoption of systems theory: looking at the individual in his interpersonal environment, the group within the formal organization and the enterprise within the social environment. At each stage the system adapts to the needs of the situation: the individual drives, needs, and perceptions will depend on the kind of group a person is interacting with; the shape of an industrial enterprise will depend on its economic function, the kind of supplies it needs, and the nature of its economic contributions to the society. The psychoanalytic voice has led Tavistock theorists to the most thorough acceptance of social factors in the whole field of sensitivity training.

Because of Tavistock's unusual problem orientation, the actual group sessions are varied and adapted to the immediate need. There are, however, some general principles of group conduct which distinguish Tavistock groups from other sensitivity training groups. Some groups are conducted not to deal with the problems of specific organizations, but for training professionals in understanding group functions, and these have a more generalized format and exhibit more the essence of the technique. In contrast to almost any other sensitivity training method, Tavistock laboratories and conferences are programmed, and the schedule is posted from the beginning for all members to see.[12] A list of intragroup, intergroup, and large-group exercises are scheduled at a certain time, and the trainers will appear at that time and be there for the scheduled period, as a sign of their responsibility in the whole process. There does not seem to be any pretense that the trainer is dispensable. Beyond this point, however, the exercises are very free. People are told within a group to try to get something done. Between group exercises, they are told they can negotiate with each other, observe each other, and are given a place where they can send their delegates and enter into negotiations or agreements. Their consultants or leaders are there to point out what is happening, what the group is trying to do, and what kind of principles are occurring in the group. If they are not so occupied, they frequently sit apart from the group, even far away in a corner. The purpose is frankly a learning experience. Members are supposed to learn what happens in groups, to understand how groups function, and how they can use this knowledge in their own work. Apparently the events that do happen are not too different from those happening in other types of sensitivity training groups. Tavistock groups seem to have a very great impact on the participants, however. From casual observation, I would say that even professionals require longer to get over the experience in one of these groups than in any other kind of group, and participants hold some resentment as well as deference toward the leaders they have had for a long time. This is, of course, similar to the relationship a patient has with his ex-therapist.

The interventions a leader makes are tinged with psychoanalytic theory and are frankly exaggerated, using mythology or very strong language. Interpretations are frequently based on Melanie Klein's psychoanalytic technique and are couched in poetic mythological terms. People talk about murdering and eating each other, not about irritating each other. Thus the stress on the primitive urges occurring in most civilized societies and underlying even the most superficial group situations is made clear.

The main purpose of these groups is to find out what happens under the surface of any social interaction. An oversimplification of the contrast between Tavistock groups and NTL groups is that Tavistock groups emphasize the evil in man and NTL the good. Margaret Rioch, the U.S. protagonist of Tavistock, expressed this view very clearly in a letter, including her reservations on such oversimplification. I quote:

[12] M. Rioch. Personal interview.

As long as one thinks in terms of good and evil, it is, of course, nonsense to think that man is one or the other.

I think what I was trying to get at was something like this. Our Conference staffs are generally deeply aware of the tragic and paradoxical elements in group life. And out of this awareness we tend to stress the tragic and paradoxical aspects of the events which occur in the conferences. One example of this is the way in which an admirable and good intention toward one person or group can bring about untoward effects either in that person or others. Another is the way in which a small event can be blown up and misinterpreted if it fits the need of the group to do so. We are especially interested to make clear how each person bears a responsibility in one way or another for the events of which he is a part. Since the world at present seems to us to be not a very pretty place, we find ourselves more often than not pointing out the complicity of all of us in this unrosy picture.

One of our colleagues said once, again in a grossly oversimplified *bon mot*, that the NTL is concerned with love and we are concerned with death. Well, I should say that we are not 100% grim and we even laugh occasionally, but still there is something in it.[13]

Problem-centeredness, professionalism, and appreciation of the tragic in life make Tavistock-influenced sensitivity training more a part of the traditional social scene than a popular movement. Tavistock has published a series of monographs on work in coal mines, textile and chemical plants, prisons, housing projects, and other areas, but it has not given rise to the spate of books describing the experiences of participants which the other centers have. This contrast shows that the sensitivity training movement rests on some base of social science, but that in some circumstances it can become a social movement where scientific background becomes irrelevant. We recognize this as the crucial feature of sensitivity training regarded as a part of society.

[13] Personal communication.

Part IV

PRACTICES AND APPLICATIONS

Chapter 8

Landscape

"The tortured complexities of the human spirit are, as we all know, extremely interesting. People will talk endlessly about themselves. With very little encouragement, they will talk just as much about their friends. They will even pay good money to plumb the depths of the human condition in total strangers—as witness, the Living Theater, the cinéma vérité, and the nonfiction novel. Such explorations are variously regarded as: palliative, recreational, liberating, or compulsory. Whatever the rationale, many people relish the process of peeling layer after layer to come to essence."[1]

In previous sections we have discussed the historical, ideological, and conceptual context in which the intensive group experience was assimilated. We can now describe the various uses to which it has been put and the different forms to which it has been adapted.

It is important to understand the organization of the field before attempting to describe and evaluate the many ways in which sensitivity training has been used and has interpenetrated with other institutions of the society. We can locate sensitivity training by constructing a map of society in which different social institutions and activities are arranged according to their concerns, strengths, functions, and degree of involvement. Within this landscape, sensitivity training occupies a certain region which may shade along its borderlines into other institutions that are really not part of the movement, although they may partake of some of its features and also use in-

---

[1] E. Lathen. *Pick-Up Sticks.* New York: Simon and Schuster, 1970.

tensive group experience. We shall locate and distinguish the different varieties of sensitivity training by using three dimensions: (1) experience for itself or as an instrument, (2) strong or weak impact, and (3) the individual vs. the group orientation.

The main criterion for an interpretation of the experiences seems to be whether they occur within the context of another program and have a definite aim, such as in personnel management, or as part of a definite program of psychotherapy, or whether they are intense, emotional experiences viewed as having value in themselves, similar to an artistic or mystic experience. One way of expressing this difference in interpretation is to distinguish between self-expression and change. Both are terms used frequently within the movement. The experience of a group encounter might lead to self-expression and transcendence. On the other hand, it might lead to personal or social change. Change is a highly value-laden word within the movement. The profound experience of group sensitivity training may give people a feeling of change. Many of the techniques used have been sold as methods of changing people, and change has become quite valuable in itself. Thus, discussions about change agents and changes in systems will replace more theoretical lectures in some sensitivity training programs.

Beyond the experience itself, change is the primary aim of group sensitivity training, but on the other hand, self-expression is the goal of the experience itself. The distinction between change and self-expression is important in the interpretation of the experience. In the context of other programs, such as psychotherapy, management, or instruction, the intense emotional experience can be used to produce a desired change. But the goal of these programs is not the experience, but change. On the other hand, if the experience is valued because of the intensive feelings it produces, then no further justification is necessary. The stress on self-expression itself will increase the feeling tone, the emotion connected with the expression, and this will lead to very strong feelings and to cultish behavior. There is no further effect. This division, experience vs. change, points to the consequences of the experience.

Second is the quantitative dimension, the strength of the emotional experience, whether it is very strong and intense, or so weak that it approaches rational persuasion. The strength of the experience is important subjectively in what it means to the person, whether it becomes part of his whole life, or whether it is just a weekend experience that may be undergone for other purposes. Strong experiences occur typically in intense sessions like those at Esalen, which last for days or weeks and involve the person as a whole. These are also the experiences people return to, and which make them gradually come to identify themselves as people involved with the group movement. On the other hand, less-deep experiences can be those which are tools for a certain purpose, such as dealing better with groups or learning social psychology, or those taken as a casual refreshment.

Finally, the experience induced by sensitivity training occurs at the intersection of the purely personal and the interpersonal. At best, the experience is an intensely personal, satisfying one. The participant feels that he can transcend the limitations of his ability and feelings and that he can use powers and sensations previously closed to him. He cannot achieve this experience by himself, however. It has to be done in a group context. Thus, the other group members either temporarily or permanently take on great importance for him. This is the relationship between the personal and interpersonal to which all the internal theories of the movement are directed. The theorist must explain how interactions with other persons, unexpected feedback, expression of emotions, and interacting on the feeling level have an effect on a person and modify his behavior. There is no perfect balance between individual and group action. Groups may be directed toward the individual or toward the group level. Individual experiences may be used in the functioning of a group, or the group may be used for the further development of the individual. The immediate experience is modified; either individual feelings are subordinated to the welfare of the group or society, or the group situation may be used to make individuals react more strongly, to express themselves more fully and to concentrate their attention on personal feelings. Thus, one of the dividing lines which split both theory and practice in the sensitivity training field has been the emphasis on individual versus group development.

The three aspects of sensitivity training, goals, strength, and level of input, give eight possible combinations. Besides, there are activities in society similar to each of the eight types which are not sensitivity training, for example, psychotherapy may or may not be an aspect of sensitivity training. Inclusion of these "neighboring" activities shows to what parts of society sensitivity training is related and, so to say, locates our map of sensitivity training in the landscape of society.

The accompanying chart shows the eight possibilities of sensitivity training according to this scheme. They are labeled *A* through *H*. With each of these types we can connect similar activities that do not involve sensitivity training. These cells are designated by the letters *A'* to *H'*. The boundary lines of the field of sensitivity training are not very definite and are continually shifting, especially as long as sensitivity training is expanding, for instance, in the field of therapy. Similarly, within sensitivity training the divisions are not based on fact, and some particular applications may include several squares of the table, but the separation into different types of sensitivity training is useful in understanding the field.

TENTATIVE ASSIGNMENT OF EXPERIENCES TO THE SCHEME

	Experience-Directed		*Goal-Directed*	
	Strong	*Weak*	*Strong*	*Weak*
Individuals	A' (Mysticism)	C' (Resorts)	E' (Psychotherapy)	G' (Education)
	(Psych-Resorts)		E (Therapeutic Methods)	G (Training)
	A (Encounter)	C (Recreation)		
	B	D	F (Indoctrination)	H (Management)
Group	B' (Ritual)	D' (Art)	F" (Cell-Groups)	(Personnel Management) H' (Organizational Development)

The different aspects are not independent of each other. It is most likely that the experience-directed (autotelic) session will be also intensive and the instrumental program will have a weak impact. These two extremes represent the most common sensitivity training programs.

The strong autotelic experience (cells *A* and *B*) is the one that has given the sensitivity training movement its present-day prominence. It is the experience generated by the encounter centers and similar groups which has so impressed the participants. There is evidence of the strong feelings generated at encounter centers in the titles of the books that have recently been written about them, such as *Turning On, Please Touch,* and *What the Hell Are They Trying to Prove, Martha?*[2] Each of these books looks at the experience of self-expression itself and does not discuss any further aims. In fact, the centers are not trying to prove anything. The glowing description of the experience itself is justification enough.

The other extreme, the case of weak impact and instrumental aim (cells *G* and *H*), is of a more practical, intellectual type. It includes the techniques that are part of a definite program, either personnel management, training, teaching, or organizational development. Here the experience is sometimes so limited that the leaders will talk about organizational development and rational theories and downgrade the importance of the strong experience itself. Sometimes people in this field reject personal encounter groups and the somewhat mystical experiential ideas that come out of them and stay closer to other techniques of change and of producing results for the client.

These two extreme wings are part of the same movement and can be evaluated in several ways. The original T-group experience is seen best as a purposeful event. Persons interested mainly in change and not in the experience itself say that the T-group used as an instrument has proved itself to be the best technique for producing the desired change. However, most of them still believe in experiential training and in producing direct encounters as a mechanism for change. Though the lack of proved results is somewhat discouraging, they still cling to the value of the direct experience. Conversely, even the groups most concerned with self-expression still cling to the value of change. Although they justify their technique principally by the value of the experience itself and not that of change, they readily claim that some of the techniques used by their centers are able to produce change. Thus it is curious to notice that even the most extreme encounter centers will use very different techniques for producing change. Practitioners who have generally expressed contempt for encounter groups and have advocated behavior therapy, or other

[2] R. Gustaitis. *Turning On.* New York: Macmillan, 1969. J. Howard. *Please Touch.* New York: McGraw-Hill, 1970. D. Alchen. *What the Hell Are They Trying to Prove, Martha?* New York: John Day, 1970. Others are M. Shepard and M. Lee, *Marathon 16.* New York: Putnam, 1970; B. L. Austin, *Sad Nun at Synanon.* New York: Grossman, 1970; and fictionalized accounts such as John Mann, *Encounter.* New York: Grossman, 1970; J. Sohl, *The Lemon Eaters.* New York: Simon and Schuster, 1967; and movies such as *Bob and Carol and Ted and Alice.*

quite mechanistically oriented techniques, are invited to give lectures and demonstrations. The integration of the movement comes therefore from the fact that even expressive religious-type groups will accept different techniques for change, while the most pragmatic, non-experiential groups stick to the experience of interaction and encounter. In effect, many of the people who work in the more pragmatic groups use in different contexts some of the strong nonverbal techniques.

It is only one step from the extremes within the realm of sensitivity training to other activities in the society which no longer can be called sensitivity training. Intense groups can become purely expressive. Individual experiences can lead to forms where the encounter group is no longer necessary, such as mystical experiences, chants, and meditation which have attracted a clientele from the same group of people who go to encounter group meetings. Some of these activities are undertaken at the centers themselves.

For those people who need mechanical or chemical aids for getting strong experiences, the drug culture has provided the means for doing so. The connection between mysticism and drugs has always been close, and the use of psychedelic drugs is again an extreme that goes beyond the culture of the encounter group but is closely related to it. At this level, encounter groups, mysticism, and drugs are all reaching for analogous experiences in different ways. This is the region we have labeled *A'*.

The same extreme, if kept in the group context, leads to another kind of religious activity: ritual (*B'*). Certain of the exercises, especially the nonverbal ones, have become ritualized responses within a group, and they function as the game or conventionalized behavior by which participants assume the group solidarity. Some of the people who are strongly involved in this group culture feel that a session of any kind is not complete without some of the exercises, gymnastics, or other techniques used in encounter groups. These techniques are guaranteed, for those who are used to them, to get the experiences they seek. They also help the group maintain its identity. Thus ritual, which is the social expression of the meaning of religion, also becomes a group expression, and certain acts become important in themselves and lead to a strong feeling and intensive group experience. Religious and other organizations use ritual in their own contexts, and the religiously oriented members of encounter groups sometimes gloss over the distinction between encounter groups and the original meaning of ritual. Thus, at some sessions, such as in the Center for the Study of the Person, an unorthodox Mass is celebrated which employs some features of encounter groups as well as some features of the Catholic ritual.

Thus strong autotelic programs shade over into the use of some institutional features of religion, and encounter groups may provide much of the satisfaction of religion to people who cannot accept the missives and beliefs of current religions. They may even look for a more esoteric kind of religion, such as Eastern mysticism, Zen, or Yoga. Thus *A'* and *B'* correspond to two aspects of religion: mysticism and ritual.

On the other end of the spectrum, group experience shades into more mundane activities. The weak role-directed experience has been used in industry, education, and other institutions. If it is group oriented, it will overlap into areas where society feels group action is necessary. It may shade into the intense camaraderie of military organizations. One of the earliest examples of self and mutual criticism, the feedback of group dynamics, occurred in Carlson's raiders, a commando group in the Pacific during the Second World War.[3] It may also shade into other group activities in industry, such as team-building activities and organizational development. Creation of experience may mean merely having sessions where people can talk out problems more easily than in normal conferences; this is a common activity for many people. This may shade into many general activities of personnel management or organizational development (*H'*).

The weak experience as it applies to individuals becomes similar to general education techniques (*G'*). Group experiences can be used to make people change their behavior and accept new ideas in a quicker and more personal way than general lecture methods can do. Decreasing the strength of the experience more and more and increasing the theoretical or symbolic input gradually result in using discussion methods in teaching or including more sensory experiences in the general curriculum. Thus, in its most attenuated mode, sensitivity training becomes a general teaching technique.

In its extreme contrasts, sensitivity training lies on the social map between the personal or ritualistic expression of individual religion, the search for ultimate meaning in life resulting in strong experiences, and on the other hand, the pragmatic methods of education, skilled training, and giving people skills for better production or better learning. This is the general field in society that sensitivity has

[3] M. Blankford. *The Big Yankee: The Life of Carlson of the Raiders.* Boston: Little, Brown, 1947.

marked out for itself. Appropriate to a scientific age with little trust in religion, sensitivity training imbues the functions of religion with some of the ideas of social science, of science in general, and of organizational techniques, thus giving new meaning to two of the aspects of religion isolated by Glock and Stark, namely, the experiential and the ritualistic. On the other hand, it gives education and training within society a stronger emotional and more sacred character.

The two remaining sets of types are the weak autotelic experiences and the use of encounter groups for strong experience as part of a program. Weak autotelic experiences are really an attenuation of the strong mystical religious experiences which come when group interaction and the emotions accompanying it are focused on as ends in themselves. Most of the processes take place within the framework of a vague interpersonal relationship which is neither clearly individual nor group oriented and thus straddles the third dimension. They include both cells C and D. Individual development centers have a kind of weak effect; the main outcome is not a deep quasi-religious but a more recreational kind of experience. People meet in pleasant surroundings, have scheduled interactions with each other, and other scheduled activities—gymnastics, baths, massage, fun and games in general—and go home feeling newborn. Thus this kind of activity shades into recreational activities which are not based on the distinctive working of the strong group experience (C'). The activities in a regular resort, cruise, or the special new kind of resorts such as Club Méditerranée or Club Internationale, are not really very different, and some of them consciously use the language of encounter groups to attract customers. The whole philosophy of the here and now, of sensory enjoyment, can easily shade over to simple hedonism, the new cult of joy; *Playboy,* the organ of the new hedonism, notes with great approval the sport of sensitivity training's nude encounters and other of the more extreme sensual kinds of activities in the human growth centers.[4]

The infusion of ritual and the ritual experience into group encounter is also shown in the affinity of sensitivity training to artistic endeavor. This is shown in the relation between cells D and D'. Art has developed partly out of religious ritual, especially drama. Sensitivity training partly signals the return of art to its origins. The borderline region here is the attempt on the part of art and drama to overcome the division between artists and audience, and also to

[4] R. Kaiser. "Letting Go," *Playboy, 16,* 1969, 80–82+.

make creativity at least look more spontaneous and less circum-scribed than usual. In many ways, artistic endeavor today tries to be both uninhibited and spontaneous, as well as responsive to the audi-ence. Theater performances sometimes approach sensitivity train-ing, and it is not always clear to the audience if the performances are really carefully staged and rehearsed. New ideas in theater, such as the Happening, are sometimes intermediate stages between un-planned group encounters and presented performances, with the audience participating. In the same way, visual effects are some-times created by having some electronic device responsive to the audience. Even musical performance sometimes involves the whole audience. It is difficult to say how much sensitivity training has in-fluenced art, and how much both are representative of the same trend. Certainly trends in art such as mechanical sculpture, psycho-drama, and fingerpainting predated the conscious production of in-tensive group effect, but they clearly helped in this development and in turn were affected by it. On the other hand, the whole movement of modern art and many of its ramifications are influenced by the sensitivity training movement, although a great part of it is, of course, independent of sensitivity training. The group effects, the group interaction, reappear in different artistic productions at the present time, so that we can put it into the borderline region (D').

A final group in sensitivity training's armamentarium is the use of strong experiences for a particular end (E and F). It may be at this point where the most danger and the strongest controversy about the use of the techniques lie. Strong intensive group experiences can have a great influence on people and may lead to some change. It might be that the applications of these experiences for certain changes may lead to undesirable direct effects and especially also to unknown side-effects.

Let us consider first the techniques of individual change which can become operative through strong group experiences (cell E). These fall under the general topic of psychotherapy; the relationship between psychotherapy and sensitivity training is hard to delineate. In effect, psychotherapy is the use of strong interpersonal interaction to change a person. Individual psychotherapy is a two-person rela-tionship, but in group psychotherapy interactions within the group are considered important. Here again the distinction between ther-apy with and without sensitivity training is sometimes hard to make. In each case, forces are involved within the group, and the effect of insight or sudden change will come through some group experience. In psychotherapy, however, change comes about through insight into a person's previous acts as well, and the whole experience is interpreted with a view to individual self-understanding. Sensitivity training, with the emphasis on the here and now, frequently rejects any bringing in of experiences outside the group as an escape from the present situation. The more emphasis is put on the experience itself, on the ongoing interaction, the more the group psychotherapy situation is a simple sensitivity training experience.

The question of the relationship between sensitivity training (E) and traditional psychotherapy (E') is therefore quite complex. The deep emotional experience may be sometimes threatening and frightening, but generally it is intense enough to leave a feeling of strong achievement, accomplishment, and frequently enjoyment in its wake. The trainers usually shy away from digging into a person's past, although some of it is unavoidable. They certainly have no plans for a person's future beyond the session itself or beyond the workshop; therefore, if a change really occurs, it may leave the person quite defenseless and without anybody to help him. In fact, there has not been much evidence of enduring change of a deep nature, but for disturbed persons who are attracted to a center of this kind, a relatively minor change may be sufficient to lead to permanent harm. On the other hand, in skilled hands the use of the strong experience might be a valuable adjunct to traditional psychotherapeutic technique, and many patients themselves seek encounter sessions when they are dissatisfied with the slow progress of psychotherapy in order to get some shock that might make them more open to the influence of their therapist. It can be seen that the combination of sensitivity training and traditional psychotherapy can be manifold. The mere existence of sensitivity training provides a stimulus for the therapist, a kind of competition, and it might be interesting to learn whether therapists have been influenced by the fact that the patient might go to an encounter center if he cannot get quick results through therapy.

Finally, there is a particular type of group which employs a strong change-directed experience (cell F). An extremely strong kind of encounter group is sometimes used in promoting social change. This technique, too, did not originate with the rise of sensitivity training. Many revolutionary groups have started as cells the size of the sensitivity groups, ten to fifteen members who work together at some encounters, adapt their actions to each other, and become a workable unit. Among groups of this kind were the early Christians whose techniques show a startling similarity to present-day groups. Others were groups in the various religious reforms movements, the Calvinist shock troops, the Jesuits, and the later religious cells of the Methodists, Quakers, and other sects. Social change, motivated by political action, saw the creation of the different radical student groups, Carbonaris or the Italian revolutionaries, and later diverse anarchist and other cell groups.

In all these groups, however, the aim of the movement, be it salvation, social change, or revolution, was paramount, and the technique of group interaction was re-invented each time as an adjunct to the larger goal. What is new in the use of sensitivity training is that the technique of inducing strong group experiences comes first, and the justification of its use comes later. Sensitivity training has therefore been adapted by some groups for their own training, and the broad diffusion of sensitivity training could become a useful tool in the hands of many different groups who want to achieve political power or effect social change. As far as can be seen, this has not occurred thus far. One of the most deliberate uses which have been made of it is the consciousness-raising technique of the Women's Liberation Movement. However, one does not have to be an alarmist to have seen in the mass exercises of encounter groups the possibilities of fascism or other mass movements not bound by social structures and social restraints. The borderline here is quite uncertain, and we are left with the interesting question of whether a movement that espouses change for itself and gives techniques for change can be harnessed to any ideology, or whether it needs a specific ideology to be effective.

Between religion and instruction, between art, healing, and politics, is the place of sensitivity training in the social spectrum. It fills the gap left by a technological society that has given men control over their environment to an inordinate degree but has been less successful in understanding man, the questions of religion, exploration, making life beautiful, and interpersonal relationships, whether they are disturbed, as in psychotherapy, whether they are needed for management, whether they are needed in the struggle for power. The source of danger is clearly within man, and sensitivity training has given man a strong experience and the ability to evoke it practically at will, which might give him the feeling that he can control these problems.

We shall in the next few chapters turn to an examination of the various types of sensitivity training in detail. We shall start by describing the autotelic experience in the encounter centers (cells

A–D), and then the use of sensitivity training in three specific programs, psychotherapy (E), management (H) and training (G). A
remaining use (F), the use of sensitivity training for social change,
will be treated later in a general discussion of the social implications
of sensitivity training.

Chapter 9

Psych-Resorts

"Last year, she and some friends decided that 'the cocktail party is out' and gave a series of parties that, she said, incorporated the encounter group into the social situation."[1]

Sensitivity training can be pure experience. This experience has been interpreted and rationalized for various purposes and thus made palatable to the modern mind. If we want to find its basic attraction, we must look at sensitivity training where it offers the experience most freely, where it promotes intensive group action openly as a new way of life to be enjoyed. This insight can be found in the personal growth centers now in the foreground of the popular appeal of the movement.

The function of these centers in current society is to provide recreation, perhaps re-creation in the original sense of the word, as a leisure-time activity. The proliferation of encounter centers, always with very interesting Greek or Indian names, and principally set up for weekend or week-long sessions, has been widespread because many people view the encounter experience as a new leisure-time activity. It is a peculiar leisure-time experience which provides a feeling of accomplishment and of refuge for people who face important problems. Most of the centers have interesting programs of all kinds, combining group experiences with gymnastic dance, various art forms, philosophically oriented lectures, family problems seminars, and whatever. People view the encounter experience as

[1] *New York Times,* Feb. 18, 1971, 39.

recreation because of the beautiful setting of most of the centers, the variety of programs, and the publicity the centers have received in books, magazine articles, movies, newspapers, and television. Most of these centers do not promise any dramatic results from a visit. They mainly advertise the experience and the stimulation that a particular program can provide.

The by-now-famed encounter group weekends probably show the autotelic group experience in its purest form. Its different varieties cover cells *A, B, C,* and *D* on the chart in Chapter 8. A description at this point of a typical weekend may prove effective in showing in summary all the different applications of sensitivity training and the essence of the movement.

Let us spy on a typical weekend session, starting on Friday evening and lasting until Sunday afternoon.[2] People begin to arrive at the Center, an attractive resort area, late Friday afternoon. They are assigned to rough but comfortable accommodations which provide some of the atmosphere of a college dormitory, summer camp, and resort motel. After the evening meal, people gather one by one in their assigned rooms, looking around somewhat uncomfortably at those who will share this "unique, intense" experience with them. At this point, or after some introductory exercises, the groups are divided so that each of the training groups consists of twelve to fifteen people divided as evenly as possible by sex. At the appointed hour, each staff member assembles his group in a circle, giving rather sketchy introductory explanations of what is going to be done. He also points out the rules of the session, the ways to encourage people to participate in the proceedings, the additional opportunities as well as the limits. There may, of course, also be some administrative matters such as food, lodging, or fees to discuss. After this, the real work (or play) begins. The group leader—sometimes it is hard not to call him the social director—starts an exercise to get people into action. The purpose of the exercise is to give everybody some idea about the other people in the group by having everybody present something about himself, some deep concern, without having the group become a therapy session. The exercise may take the form of a party game, such as introducing oneself with an alliterative name—"Silent Sam" or "Mournful Minnie"—or it may be a more physical game, such as body exercises or a mixer of the "spin the bottle" type. Purely physical exercises might include dividing the group into pairs or triplets

---

[2] Descriptions not otherwise credited are derived from the author's personal experience.

who stay close together with closed eyes and try to learn about each other through the sense of touch. Participants who have heard some general publicity or heard personal friends talk about the strong sensual, sexually tinted experiences will look for sexual thrills, and usually get them. This kind of initial warm-up exercise produces the effect of getting people to move away from the usual modes of behavior, and to become interested in the self-presentations of the other people in the group.

The next step is to prepare the participants for interaction in the group. Again this may be done through exercises, such as giving everybody a few minutes' interaction with everybody else to explore each other physically and mentally. This will be succeeded by staged interaction between people who have hit it off particularly well or particularly badly. Some of these interactions, of course, may occur spontaneously. The activity of the group then should begin to center either on one person or a constellation of two or three. Since people have come in great part in order to bring up some of their own problems, it isn't too difficult to find somebody in a group of ten to fifteen who is willing and even eager to bring up his difficulties. The personal problem that a person brings up can then be discussed at length and breadth, acted out, interpreted, and spun out according to all the techniques the Center has at its disposal.

Probably the person who is first to volunteer to reveal more of himself than necessary is also a person with some urgent difficulty he wants to discuss. Although the general rule in encounter centers is that a person can have all the attention he demands as long as he demands it, he cannot stay in the limelight forever. There are other persons who want to be the center of attention too, or they would not have come to the session. The limit of a person's time on center stage may be determined partly by the amount of authority the leader chooses to exert. The leader might end the group's concern for one individual with an exercise like one of those which have been publicized and which most participants who have heard about the place are expecting. Most of these exercises have been described in encounter group literature, such as William Schutz's book *Joy*.[3] Many consist of the literal acting-out of some need or feeling. Thus, a person who is felt to be in need of nurturance may be lifted up by the rest of the group and stroked, and in this way gets both the feeling of trust in the people, who of course are not going to let him fall down, thus experiencing "group support," and some feeling that everybody

[3] W. Schutz. *Joy*. New York: Grove Press, 1968.

treats him nicely, that people like him. It is unlikely, of course, that any of the other participants will refuse to help in exercises of this kind. Other exercises might be more negative, such as everybody's saying something bad about the person, or the person being asked to say something bad about everybody else. After these exercises are over, participants start to feel that the needy person got help for what seemed to ail him, and that he can now become the audience for somebody else. Thus the way is open for a transition to another person.

Usually, especially in the early stages of the session, the transition is quite natural. One person might have become particularly involved in the first participant's problem. He might have played the role of a family member or an antagonist. Alternatively, his problem might follow naturally from the first one, and he might begin occupying the center of the stage. For example, Person A, a very young-looking girl, was talking about her problems with her mother who had mistreated her as a child and was still destructive, and the difficulty which she now had in excluding her mother from her home. The girl was crying about her guilt, her inability to face older women or other women in general. In acting-out this scene, it became natural that role-playing and other games were conducted mainly with one of the older women in the group, a child psychiatrist who felt put upon by younger people who were acting-out their problems on her in her professional life as well as in her private life. This antagonism became part of the group scene. The interest of the group was transferred from the young girl to the older woman, who in any case was not willing to stay in the background for too long. This way, the stage could be reset for an exercise with the second person which continued until another person became involved in the problem and was able to wrest the center of the stage from the psychiatrist.

The first evening session continues in this way until a majority, or at least a substantial minority, of the participants have had a chance to act out their problems and hear them discussed by the group. As the hour becomes late, about one or two o'clock, people become tired, and the discussion starts to peter out. The participants go back to their lodgings or they may spend some time with each other, or may enjoy some of the special features of the Center, such as the hot-spring baths at Esalen.

The next day, Saturday, is the main day of the weekend session. Meetings start in the morning and continue until late in the evening or, as in a marathon, as far into the next morning as the members are physically able to go. The general technique remains the same, but now there is a chance for more intensive and longer activities as well as the operation of group pressure to include everybody as a protagonist. During the evening intermission the participants have had a chance to think about the general working of the group and what has happened. They can assess their reaction to the different members and figure out from whom they have heard and from whom they have not heard. The group as such begins to have an individuality. People talk about what they have accomplished, what they would like to accomplish, and certain rituals that are becoming part of the group.

Exercises such as body lifting or "trust falls" (falling backward into the arms of another group member) were used the evening before, and other members feel that they deserve similar treatment and ask for it. Thus, in one group, one of the members waited until the end of the session, and then asked for the nurturance or semi-nurturance experiences that everybody else had had for himself. A certain amount of greed for affection and for any kind of experience can, therefore, be accommodated. On the other hand, if a person is obviously outside the culture of encounter groups, he will be tolerated, not attacked or included as much as other people would be. Thus, in one session, there was an older woman who had really come in order to bring her daughter, and who neither wanted anything from the group nor could meet the group on its own terms. For instance, when one of the members talked about the abandonment and physical enjoyment of dance, she would talk about dance games, or general mixers that were being used in her circle of friends or Golden Age club. Other members would listen politely, and then go on to talk about something else. In effect, she provided a common-sense outlook when the discussion became too abstruse and cultish; when she was not around for a while, everybody agreed that she really didn't belong, and that a little of her went a long way, although within the group, despite its valuing of spontaneity, nobody had the heart to tell her.

The group becomes ritualized, and people start to know what they can expect from each other. Thus, gradually, stronger emotions are being shown, and people who were holding back for a while are ready to emote at the slightest provocation. Stimulus and response are sometimes quite incongruous to each other. An exercise of rhythmic clapping (different people trying to clap different rhythms) suddenly caused one of the members to jump up, fall down on the floor, and give a very emotional appeal about his loneliness, his lack of understanding people, and especially his relation to his wife. It was quite obvious that he had been waiting for an occasion of this kind, and the slight heightening of emotion which rhythmic behavior can produce gave him a chance to release his feelings.

There are a variety of activities, but a certain sequence is observed which depends partly on the Center, partly on the leaders, and partly on the composition of the group. Such a sequence might begin with some of the exercises for which the places are famous, such as beating pillows or other physical exercises, or some game such as imagining oneself as a flower or with another name. Activities of this kind raise expectations that something is going to happen, and under these conditions something is bound to happen to someone. This event then becomes the content, and other people start bringing in related experiences, or react to the way the person expresses his own problems, until the sequence of effects is wound up again. A new exercise might start a new routine of the same kind. Toward the end of this day, particular groupings might have been formed; thus, one couple or three people might sit together at all times, having side-interactions while the main performance goes on on center stage. Friendship at this point, like everything else, assumes the height of importance, and thus a slight change in seating arrangements might assume cosmic proportions for the group, might make some people very happy or might be discussed as if they were beginnings and endings of lifelong love relations or friendships.

Efforts will also be made to give everybody a chance, or make it everybody's duty to put something of his problems into the group. This occurs in two ways: the leader feels some responsibility to give everybody a chance to act-out his own problems—after all, they all paid for the weekend, and should bring back something for which they have come, and some people are not so eager to push themselves forward as others. But there is more to it than just avoiding dissatisfied customers. The group is starting to establish rules, and one rule in an encounter center is that one has to put in some performance of oneself in order to be accepted as a member of the group and so share its affects. People who are too shy or uninterested in the proceedings will not be accepted for affective relationships. Crying is a ticket for membership.

Pulling in the deviates or unwilling participants might be accomplished in many different ways. If a person participates actively in a discussion or disagrees strongly, he will be pulled into the group simply by the fact that this disagreement can be acted-out physically; in this way a person may find himself in the center of the stage almost without having looked for it. Other techniques directly aid in pulling people in, such as asking them what they want to talk about; or the leader may almost formally start to work with one person, going through a sort of preliminary psychiatric examination— "When do you feel wrong? When do you have problems?"—and so on. This kind of direct approach is taken mainly with people who are quite experienced in groups and know how to handle a direct attack. In later stages, when it becomes clear that some people are not going to assume the stage by themselves, this kind of extending the group to every member becomes quite an activity, and it usually does not end until everybody has been able to give something of his own problems for the inspection and interest of the whole group.

Toward the end of the evening, the physical strains begin to show. The last session of the day, the "marathon period" usually started after dinner, is supposed to be the climax of the whole performance, a special experience. It is started again with general exercises. Physical attractions between participants might be acted-out, which passes the time readily. The session tends to be punctuated by the strong emotional outbursts of the people who were quite willing or overwilling to exhibit their problems, by group attempts to get something out of everybody, and finally by the acting-out of personal relationships. Everything goes on simultaneously and, partly because of fatigue, people are no longer able to concentrate toward the end on the group process.

In a sense, one could say that in many of these groups Bion's principles (see Chapter 6) start to show themselves. As there is no real work for the group, it cannot pull together and become an efficient working group. As a result, all the different attitude groups come out. There is fight or flight: people either fight physically or act-out antagonisms, or alternatively, leave the group for a while, perhaps to sleep or in other ways retire from the activity of the group. At the same time, there will be pairing within the group; some people will split off from the group for this purpose. Finally, the main activity of the group must be carried by the leader who makes sure that everybody has a chance to participate; it becomes a tremendous exercise of dependence and counterdependence. Thus the group, torn in these three directions at the same time, finally reaches a very strong emotional experience.

The next morning is the final morning of the weekend session. It is recognized by everybody as the end and a period of cleaning up. People again have been thinking of what has been missing in the group, what else they might have wanted to say, and what kind of relationship they still want to express. Maybe there was somebody they wanted to get to know better, or somebody they wanted to tell off, or from whom they would have wanted to hear more. The leader has had time to think about what the participants might have wanted from the group, and can now add additional exercises to the group session in order to generate strong warm feelings that have been missing from the group. He might give them some exercise that may have practical value at a later time. After the middle of the morning, there are definite attempts to provide a formal conclusion and a formal meaning, now that the exercises are over. People sometimes feel wrenched away from the group and try to find ways to prolong it or make arrangements to see other members of the group later. In fact, the experience of many groups has been that, as long as they are stranger labs, people rarely meet each other later. There is much affectionate formal leave-taking, though, and as people usually come from all directions, they end up going away to their own separate concerns.

The kind of weekend experience described here leaves an almost uniform impression on the participants. At some point there is a strong expression of emotion caused by a really deep, intensive experience which does not last, but whose memory gives the impression that something very important happened. Despite all the aggression demonstrated during the session, or maybe because of it, there is a warm feeling which is remembered as the main flavor of the experience. There is the flavor of a resort or entertainment to the session. People get together mainly for the purpose of having an intensive, enjoyable experience, and if they work at it, they get it. The rules are different from those of daily life, but they are important and enforced nevertheless.

One has to have some difficult or interesting experience to exhibit to the group, and as the population consists of people of above-average intelligence who are imbued with present-day upper-middle-class culture, they can be trusted to bring out the right problems and to use the right symbolism to express them. Thus, when in one session a participant made a big scene of the fact that he could not cry at his mother's funeral, and went around asking everybody whether they thought the worse of him for it, one cannot help wondering whether the theme of Camus' *The Stranger* (Marseult being executed in effect for the same reason) had not permeated society that much, even if the participant himself had not read it.[4] Thus, the first requirement is the expression of some problem which partakes of the

[4] A. Camus. *The Stranger*. New York: Knopf, 1946.

culture of everybody present, can be understood by them, and brings the person to a feeling of being one with the group.

The second rule of the group is an almost universal acceptance of the rest of the group. It is all right, and part of the convention, to be antagonistic toward one person or several people, and these antagonisms can be expressed freely and openly, and may lead to an interesting exercise. One cannot react negatively to any revelation that a person may make of himself, however. The participant convinces himself to take his revelation seriously, and to treat group acceptance as a freely given absolution by the rest of the group. It is hard to see, however, what kind of personal revelations a group might really want to reject. I suppose I approached the limit myself when I admitted in a group that I was mainly an observer trying to get research material; but they forgave even that. There are some rumors in encounter centers that people from law enforcement agencies go through some of the centers to obtain inside information which might be useful later. Perhaps admission of being an agent might be the unforgivable sin.

The German poet Heinrich Heine said on his deathbed, "God will forgive me; that's his job." This is the kind of relationship that exists between each member in an encounter group and the audience. During each scene, the remainder of the participants exist just for the purpose of providing support and a background for each person to act-out what he came for in the group. Thus there is a paradox here. The strong emotion between people, which is a trademark of the movement, comes precisely from the fact that each person in the group uses everybody else as pure objects, as tools to get a strong experience in the situation. What people within the group forget is simply that it would not have mattered who was in the group at all, that people are completely interchangeable. The particular personality of the other people is not relevant; there is nothing personal in the relationship, however strongly personally and emotionally it is acted-out. The other people in the group eventually become simply the other participants or tools for this purpose. Probably the unique feature which distinguishes this kind of action from other staged emotional settings is the fact that each person at the same time is willing to perform the same role for the other people in the group. Although one can speak of exploitation, it is the kind of mutual exploitation in which nobody is really losing.

This peculiar interrelationship among the members may be related to the undoubtedly strong experience everybody receives. One of the great discoveries of the movement is the fact that one can throw together almost any kind of people as long as they are roughly from similar backgrounds, and with a few relatively simple techniques, generate strong emotions within the group and a feeling of an important experience within almost all the members. This technique may be based on the combination of impersonality, people thrown together almost at random, and the strong pretense of personal relationships which runs through the whole session. People let each other be used for verbal expression, physical expression, acceptance of all kinds of weaknesses, and for roles in private actions and private fantasies. But there is a mutuality in this kind of relationship which lifts these experiences from other kinds of professional or commercial relationships where this use is only one-sided. The immediate effect of this interaction process becomes an exaggeration of each act, of each word, giving deep meaning to anything that has happened and is happening. The feedback technique, which is a kind of reverberation of an act until it has intense emotional meaning, is very efficient in this kind of situation. If a quite trivial happening which takes about five minutes is talked over in all its possibilities for the next hour, it is bound to assume a portentous significance for practically everybody concerned, and it has become relatively easy for each person to relate it to his own deepest problems, reaching back into his childhood. Thus, each participant is able to get deep meaning and deep concern from everybody else and flashes of insight into the problems which he has brought into the group. This kind of experience is unique in anybody's life, and thus most people will have a positive feeling toward the whole session which may last for quite a while after the session itself is over.

What we have discussed up to now is the essence of the experience. The main features that distinguish it as a positive one may, under the surface, be the same conditions that are also its drawbacks. Each person can use the others as tools for his own problems, but after all is said and done, nobody is responsible for the outcome. Even the leader, who is trying to lead the group through an enjoyable experience without any bad repercussions, has his function ended at the end of the session.

The more frequently voiced criticism relates to the kind of people who, for some reason, cannot stand strong emotion during the session itself. Negative reactions, of course, may occur, and there may be breakdowns of people who cannot abide by the rules, who either cannot experience the strong emotion or who take the concomitant attacks too seriously. Also, there are always some people who are really quite sick, and who think that this kind of experience might help them, but who only get further into their illness through it.

The ominous problem comes after the session. People are led to believe that others care and want to help them to get a new look at their own problems and maybe give some suggestions on how to deal with them. But here it ends. All the ideas discussed, the new ways found for one's life, were a good game within the rules of the encounter group. A person trying to act on them finds no support after he has left the group. There is nobody responsible to give him further advice or help if he has acted on something he had discovered in the group and it does not quite work out. The philosophy of the here and now refers not only to the past, but also to the future. Probably the happiest participants in these weekend encounter groups, or other creativity centers, are those who accept it just for the occasion, who enjoy the experience and use it for recreation. Recreation has, in fact, a deeper meaning if we take it in its original sense of "re-creation." People might want to do something new and different from their usual way of life and get some refreshing experience out of it. This is the general value of leisure-time activities as opposed to any direct effect which may carry on through later life.

It is not surprising, therefore, that one of the main effects of the groups is that people want to experience them again. In one conversation at Esalen, I heard the whole experience being referred to as a "three-hundred-dollar-a-year habit." Compared with other means of getting strong experience, this habit seems relatively cheap and not dangerous. This is probably true for most of the participants. I have also met people who took the advice given them in the meetings, gave up their jobs, broke up their families, and did not know quite what they were supposed to do afterward. Contrary to the situation in therapeutic experiences, there is nobody around to go back to, except maybe a different encounter session. As with many of these enjoyable experiences, some people become completely addicted. There seems to be a group of people like that, especially in California, where the term "groupie" as an analogy to "junkie" is beginning to be used. (The other meaning of "groupie" may eventually extinguish this usage of the term.) "Groupies" live for the weekend experiences and go from one session to another; at the present time, it is possible to go to very many sessions during a year. They start to experience a reality in encounter with strangers. Other people go even further than that, giving up their regular occupations for hang-around jobs in the centers, such as clerical jobs, cooks, masseurs, etc. These people, as part of their job, usually have the right to participate in some sessions, and it is sometimes pathetic to see how they try to keep the leaders on the path of the true dogma of the Center by repeating slogans if the leaders omit them, or how they cannot bear the sessions to end. Again one can feel that probably these people needed artificial support of some kind and could have done worse than attaching themselves to this movement and this type of experience.

Some of the sessions are designed for weak effect and can be looked at simply as entertainment; many participants in any encounter group take it simply as such. These would fall into cells *C* and *D*, a distinction between individual and group orientations being too tenuous at this level. The location of encounter group centers in beautiful settings, the general vacation atmosphere which prevails, the exaggeration of casual acquaintances into intensely important friends, all these factors show obvious parallels with resort hotels and cruise ships. The easygoing sensuality in these situations enhances the similarity. It is likely that many people are somewhat guilt-ridden about accepting entertainment of this kind and are reassured if it is sold with a serious purpose. Recreation is a valuable part of one's life.

Other encounter centers are stronger medicine. Some try to give participants a unique, quasi-mystical experience, and thus work toward the intensive personal experience (cell *A*). Others try to give the participants group support, a feeling of belongingness to the temporary group at the center, and prepare regular group encounters (cell *B*). The transformation of the centers, especially Esalen, to long-term residential training favors the distinction between the strong and weak impact, the programs which give people a sense of a new life, and weekend or smaller recreational sessions. The variety of session titles shows the wide range of these programs. Besides the old standbys of "Personal Growth," "Intimacy for Couples," and "Sensory Awakening," we find "Creative Meeting (for Unmarrieds)," and "The New Authentic Holiday," for the new-style resort variations; and such imposing titles as "The Body of God," "Myth and Identity," and "The Crack in the Cosmic Egg."

Chapter 10

Healers, Patients, and Groups

"For when a lady is badly sexed
God knows what God is coming next."[1]

The general aim of sensitivity training is change; at least, change is a word that has an almost sacred connotation. In its most beneficial aspects change is healing, and healing depends on the skill of the healer as well as on the belief of the patient.[2] The rise of psychotherapy in this century has mirrored the current scientific ethos, and "therapeutic man"[3] is the product of these times. Many advocates of sensitivity training, and especially its early adherents, shared this healing outlook, and sensitivity training could easily become an adjunct to psychotherapeutic techniques.

In our scheme diagramed in Chapter 8, use of sensitivity training for psychotherapy corresponds to cell E, the use of the techniques with strong impact for individual results. Its borderline with E', psychotherapy in general, especially group psychotherapy, is shifting; this relationship has attracted the critical attention of many psychiatrists, psychologists, and other helping professions.

The origins of many sensitivity training traditions rest in various schools of psychotherapy. Moreno's ideas of encounter, role-playing, and psychodrama (see Chapter 6) were developed as out-

[1] O. Nash. "The Seven Spiritual Ages of Mrs. Marmaduke Moon," in *The Face Is Familiar*. Boston: Little, Brown, 1940.

[2] J. Frank. *Persuasion and Healing*. Baltimore, Md.: Johns Hopkins, 1961.

[3] P. Rieff. *The Triumph of the Therapeutic*. New York: Harper, 1966.

growths of psychotherapy. The influence of Freud on sensitivity training has been strong directly and indirectly through his students. Sensitivity training in England at the Tavistock Institute was mainly initiated by psychiatrists such as Melanie Klein. Encounter groups owe much to the theories of Wilhelm Reich; their modern development came from the work of Carl Rogers and his previous experience in counseling disturbed students. In the history of the T-group itself, there was a point when psychotherapists were invited to Bethel and laboratories became known as psychotherapy for normals.

The connection between the two fields has continued; in recent years, sensitivity training has become quite attractive to people interested in therapy. This attraction has arisen from several sources, from patients as well as practitioners, and especially from students. One of the reasons for this attraction to sensitivity training has been a clear disillusionment with psychotherapy. Psychotherapy has almost become as much a part of the culture as sensitivity training has, or more, and adherents come from the same subgroups of the population. But patients as well as therapists have become dissatisfied with the results, with the length of treatment, with its expense, and with its concentration on only a few patients. Even without direct intent, encounter groups promise many people what they have been looking for in psychotherapy.

There are general principles, however, which serve to distinguish psychotherapy from sensitivity training. The main distinction is the insistence of sensitivity training on encounter-oriented methods stressing the importance of the here and now. Strictly speaking, in sensitivity training all material brought up relates only to the present situation. Group members discuss their present feelings and their reactions to each other; therapeutic exercises relate only to present feelings. The procedures used in the therapeutic situation are similar to some of those discussed in the last chapters, but here they are used as a part of a program of psychotherapy. Several psychotherapeutic schools have made extensive use of sensitivity training techniques.

Gestalt therapy is the branch of psychotherapy closest to the encounter group. Fritz Perls, its originator, found a home at Esalen toward the end of his life, and Esalen has become a main center of Gestalt therapy, using it in connection with other techniques.[4] In

[4] The theory is most comprehensively stated in F. Perls, *Ego Hunger and Aggression.* New York: Random House, 1964. Transcripts are collected in F. Perls, *Gestalt Therapy Verbatim.* Lafayette, Calif.: Real People Press, 1969; and his last self-expressionistic book, *In and Out of the Garbage Pail.* Real

terms of psychotherapy, the theory parallels the technique of encounter groups. Perls' principal influences were Wilhelm Reich and Kurt Goldstein. Through the latter the term "Gestalt" found its way into the therapeutic vocabulary. Goldstein had been a psychologist dealing principally with brain-damaged patients.[5] He showed in careful work how these patients could organize the world around them so they could deal with it in spite of their affliction; they constructed the best possible whole (*Gestalt*) of which they were capable.

Perls combined a theory derived from Goldstein and other Gestalt psychotherapists with some methods derived from Reich. His formulation resulted in a model of a total personality that would be the best possible for that person. Individuals, however, usually cannot cope with this whole personality and reject or lose part of it; thus they have holes in their personalities, diminishing their ability to use their full potential. Gestalt therapy consists of having a person accept the missing parts of his personality. In this context it is irrelevant why the parts are missing; what is important is the immediate reintegration of the personality. Although there is a great range of styles among Gestalt therapists, the main principles hold true for all of them: rejection of personal history by the patient, and of interpretation of it by the therapist (Perls said that interpretation is a therapeutic mistake mainly used to help the ego of the therapist); the lack of any use of the relation between therapist and patient, that is, of transference; the concentration on cues for the "missing" parts of the personality which may be parts of the body shown through involuntary movements, or parts of the character, symbolized as objects in a dream; and the ritual use of earthy language to shock and to fight intellectualization.

True to its own precepts, Gestalt therapy is less impressive in its theory than in its procedure, in the set ritual of its performance. Examining some of the recurrent themes in Gestalt therapy sessions makes this therapy more understandable and shows the way in which encounter groups can be used frankly for therapy. The group is arranged in a circle with two seats left empty; the one next to the therapist will be the seat of the person who is discussed at the moment and whose problems are being worked on (the "hot seat"), and

---

People Press, 1971. A discussion of Gestalt therapy by his followers is J. Fagen and I. L. Shepherd's *Gestalt Therapy Now*. Palo Alto, Calif.: Science Behavior Books, 1970.

[5] K. Goldstein. *The Organism*. New York: American Book, 1939. Perls had studied with Goldstein.

the other will be the seat of the alter ego for this person. The assumption is that this is a therapy session, not a pure encounter; that is, the member-to-member interaction is unimportant. Only the "work" or performance of the member on the hot seat counts, and other members are not to interfere. Interaction is very direct and aggressive on the part of the therapist, who is trying to get as quickly as possible to some of the problems the person is suffering from. While Perls did not write much about his theory, he provided a tremendous number of transcripts of therapy sessions. We can see, therefore, the techniques he and his followers actually use. They use dream technique to a great extent, not interpreting dreams but using the dreams to force the person to express certain feelings and act-out the things he did in the dream, or wished he had done, or that other actors in the dream did.

Perls' theory represents almost literally the image we have presented up to this point underlying the theory of encounter groups. He felt that there are neurotic layers around the person which prevent his acting normally or to full capacity. The work of the encounter group, or the Gestalt therapy session, is to get the person through these different layers and literally to lead to an explosion. Thus, any way in which the therapist can lead the patient to an explosion in the quickest possible time is acceptable. In common with all other theorists of this kind, Perls rejected symbolic action, even language, or any intellectualizing the patient might do.

As most of the patients of Gestalt therapists are intellectuals, or adolescents aspiring to be so, this technique provides a shock to them which may make the more impressionable members devoted followers. As little as Gestalt therapists are eager to give interpretations based on the past, they are also not eager to take any responsibility for the future. Perls was quite explicit in saying that, as the patient came of his own free will and succumbed to the situation, he cannot be responsible for what happens to the patient afterward. Of course, these statements cannot be taken literally. By getting a patient to act toward a person in his past, like a mother or father, as if the person were present, or by using an alter ego to act-out his feelings, the Gestalt therapist is using, in effect, past experiences. In the same way, he at least assumes that the experience will be healthy for the patient and beneficial for his later use. Gestalt therapy seems to be directed to maximization of the strong experiences of group action, based partly on the insight and strength of the leader, physical exercise (working on parts of the body as rejected parts of the personality), and intense role-playing techniques.

Gestalt therapy is essentially the theory or therapy branch of the encounter group movement (especially at Esalen). Other psychotherapy groups also use sensitivity training as part of their work, especially to get the patient into new action patterns. Of course, some theories of the psychotherapist are in direct conflict with the ideas of encounter groups, and therefore classical psychoanalysts, for example, cannot use these ideas. One example of a group therapy technique friendly to encounter groups is transactional therapy. Transactional therapy, as developed by Erich Berne, is also a technique developed partly as a reaction against the long duration of psychotherapy.[6] It has developed quite a tight theory.

Berne sees three types of behavior patterns which any person is capable of; in a sense, three people under the same skin. One is the *parent*, the surrogate of the culture, those habitual behavior patterns one learns from other people that have become sort of a generalized reflex system. The second is the *adult*, the reality-testing component, the part of the person that takes current information and uses it for problem solving. The third is the *child*, the immediate, spontaneous part of the person that provides enjoyment and playfulness. These three concepts, of course, are similar to the traditional psychoanalytic ones of superego, ego, and id, although they are slightly differently defined. The important thing for Berne, however, is that a person functions at a given time on only one of those levels; there is no intrinsic conflict between the three. Some behavior, of course, is appropriate to different situations, and each person can interact with another person at all three levels. Severe personality difficulties arise if people pretend to act on one level and really act on another, especially if they find another person whose own pretensions work with theirs. Berne calls sequences of these acts "games" if there is a payoff or reward at the end. Thus a person might act manifestly as an adult to another person's adult, which means that he acts as if he is discussing some serious problem of immediate concern, but in reality acts as a child to the other's adult; that is, he is just teasing the other person and not honestly looking for a reality-based solution. The person might have learned that he can obtain attention, protection, or some other payoff this way.

For Berne, then, therapy consists of eliminating harmful games and substituting either less harmful ones or harmless pastimes for appropriate behavior. Thus, he discusses with a patient first what

[6] E. Berne. *Transactional Analysis in Psychotherapy*. New York: Grove Press, 1961. A vivid description of the games became a popular book: E. Berne. *Games People Play*. New York: Grove Press, 1964.

kind of payoff is expected, and concludes a contract by allowing the patient to say what kind of behavior and payoff he will accept as a solution for his problem. For instance, the person who exhibits psychopathic behavior might be satisfied if he does not commit any crime for a specified period of time. The therapy technique, individually or in a group, consists of the therapist trying to spot the games, exposing them, and in other ways thwarting the patient from getting the expected payoff from his favorite game. Then he is taught to substitute behavior acceptable both to the patient and to society. This therapy relies on quick changes of behavior and not a deep working on the personality. It sees encounter techniques as methods to discourage people from their favorite games. Transactional centers employ techniques from encounter groups, such as nonverbal communication techniques as well as other exercises, as ways of teaching the patient to play new games. Berne's technique is, therefore, a combination of a purely psychotherapeutic technique with methods of encounter groups. It is an example of a parallel development within psychotherapy, a technique and theory that would be compatible with encounter groups. It uses encounter groups for its own purposes.

Conducting psychotherapy sessions as part of an encounter center and using encounter techniques to produce a quick change in behavior as part of a different theory-based form of psychotherapy represent the two extremes of the connection between encounter groups and psychotherapy. Other schools have found different ways of integrating the two approaches and adapting encounter groups for patients. There is a whole variety of workshops between the two extremes, and sometimes the borderline between encounter in the group experience and in therapy is hard to establish definitely. Examples of such combinations of encounter groups and psychotherapy are the rational psychotherapy of Albert Ellis and Moreno's psychodramatic technique.

Ellis, although he conducts regular psychotherapy also, has perfected a technique which he calls the "rational encounter weekend."[7] This is a kind of marathon session using many of the techniques of encounter groups, but in which the leader or the therapist takes a directive role, interpreting and pushing the patients toward a therapeutic conclusion. It is an attempt to use the loosening-up process inherent in so many experiences of the encounter group, to

---

[7] A. Ellis. "A Weekend of Rational Encounter," in J. Burton (ed.), *Encounter*. San Francisco: Jossey-Bass, 1969, 112–127.

push the participant toward a discussion of his problem and possible therapeutic experiences within the group or at a later time. Among the stresses in the beginning of the session are the so-called high risk-taking procedures, procedures where members find themselves strongly and emotionally involved with other members, both through self-revelation and emotional, sensual, and sexual experiences. The price for having these experiences, as in any encounter group, is detailed self-analysis and discussion of the experience with other members. There is an attempt made for every member to have at least one experience of this kind, and the leader can use the reactions to these revelations and the experience, with some diagnosis, to confront a person with his own needs or evasions or other reactions. The techniques are quite direct, mainly encouraging first volunteers and then other members to act-out their feelings toward other people. This may include a modified version of post office, or other games. The next day, during the later hours of the night, the discussion is said to become problem oriented. The leader then interferes and gives interpretations both in individual cases and in discussing general ideas. There are also conscious attempts to involve every member of the group, including the smoking-out technique for anybody who has not yet brought up his problem. There is no pretense that people have come only for the experience's sake. Some of them are deeply troubled individuals who have come for therapy. Therefore, toward the end, each case is discussed for about a half hour. Ellis sharply distinguishes this kind of technique from the general technique of encounter groups. General encounter groups may be run only for hedonistic purposes, may be anti-intellectual, or may create emotional elites. He tries to combine the techniques and the emotion of the encounter group with the directive, cognitive and behavior modification types of therapy. Ellis', like others, is more a parallel development than an adaptation of encounter groups. For a long time Ellis had been deeply interested in sexual expression and sexual difficulties, especially the dangers of sexual repression, and he has been a prolific writer on this topic. Although he currently writes about encounters and dresses his techniques in the fashionable language and clothing of encounter groups, we can characterize his technique more as a use of some of the techniques and rhetoric of encounter groups for the kind of procedures he has already worked out.

Moreno's technique has an even older ancestry. Moreno can claim, perhaps rightly, that he is the originator of both group therapy and encounter groups. At least he originated the use of the term "encounter" as well as "here and now."[8] His technique of psychodrama is still being used both at his centers in New York City and Beacon, New York, and at hospitals such as St. Elizabeths in Washington, D.C., and in modification in many ways around the world. There are even world congresses of psychodrama that have been meeting every two or three years. Here, psychodramatic groups from different countries give continuous performances, and discussions about different techniques are held. As the name and background of the movement show, most of these productions follow definite scenarios incorporating theories and directions of the procedures of the show. The techniques are quite similar to those of encounter groups, leading the patient to act-out some of the difficulties which have led him to his present state, and in this way facilitating diagnosis and sometimes even treatment. A characteristic point about this branch of sensitivity training is that the scenes themselves are definitely designed around the protagonist, although in some cases the scenes are there first and the people are fitted into them. Moreno's psychodrama follows the first method, with the protagonist, his alter ego, and other people coming into the scene as far as they are needed by the person himself. Moreno's theory also guides a person through the definite crises of life—childhood, adolescence, choice of a mate and an occupation, illnesses, losses, and death—and tries in this way to work through all the problems a person may face in his life by means of a dramatic performance. In a certain way, this is an expansion of regular psychotherapy, through using more dramatic situations than would be possible in the regular psychiatric interview. Other techniques are scenes supposedly representative of problems in a person's life, but they also may resemble childhood games or the training of an actor. Thus, a person may be asked to find some way to get past four guards in order to see an important person, using any techniques—violence, bribery, appeal, flirting, and so on. One of the favorite demonstrations in psychodramatic meetings is a kind of regression to babyhood, where participants are asked to lie down on the stage while elderly women sing cradle songs and use cooing language to put them back into the reassurance of babyhood. This kind of exercise is supposed to be very relaxing.

The dramatic metaphor sometimes makes for spectacular performances; psychodrama has been given in theatrical settings where the audience buys admission tickets. In addition, it implies an organized whole with introduction, climax, and dénouement, making

[8] For the references to Moreno's work, see Chapter 6, footnotes 8–10.

the psychodramatist responsible for a genuine conclusion. In general, though, the psychodrama movement is similar to encounter groups, although individual adherents may be skeptical at the present explosion of the encounter group movement at Esalen.

The combination of different encounter techniques, using a strong artificial personal encounter between people as an adjunct to psychotherapeutic work, is similar to all four of the therapeutic techniques described as Gestalt therapy, transactional therapy, rational encounter, and psychodrama, showing that sensitivity training may be part of a regular psychiatric program as well as an experience done for itself. The four examples show different ways in which sensitivity training can assume some functions of psychotherapy and vice versa. In many respects this is a potentially dangerous issue in which the movement confronts one of the most professionalized and tightly controlled groups in society: medicine. The medically trained psychiatrist or psychoanalyst undergoes a definite course of training before he can assume those roles, and is conscious of definite standards of what he can do in the course of his profession and what he cannot do. These standards have evolved in part to protect the patient and to exert social pressure on individuals who have the power to do much damage as well as to give help. A new development in healing, coming in great part from laymen with very few official credentials, naturally arouses the suspicion not only of the medical profession but also of allied professions such as clinical psychology and social science.

The movement's relation to psychotherapy is an organizational problem as well as an intellectual and moral one, and different schools of sensitivity training have different positions in this respect. Most of the examples of group therapy attempts that we have given up to now have come from the encounter group wing of the movement. This is the part of the movement least fettered by conventional restrictions of society and professions, and most willing to approach experiences over which society in general wants to exercise some control. Many people on the encounter group side are contemptuous of psychotherapy with its cautious, long-range approach. The more established side, the National Training Laboratory, has flirted with psychotherapeutic approaches but has, in general, tried to stay away from psychiatric work. We have noted an early experiment in the 1950's in which clinicians were invited to Bethel. Since then, there have been psychiatrists at the National Training Laboratory but mainly as first aid in case of casualties. An exception are the advanced human relations workshops which include in their repertoire adaptations of Esalen techniques and occupy a similar position between recreation and psychotherapy.

By contrast, Tavistock from its inception has been influenced by psychoanalytic theory and led by psychoanalytically trained professionals. Their group work is, however, an application of psychoanalytic principles to group practice; there is hardly any personal therapy as part of this group program. The therapists who may be involved in the group movement keep this quite separate from their work with patients. Thus, the part of the movement most psychoanalytically oriented does most to keep the clinical work out of sensitivity training. This may look like a paradox, but it can also be seen as a natural consequence of the involvement of experienced professionals.

Thus, it turns out that the main intersection of psychiatry and sensitivity training is the kind of group work represented by Esalen and its offshoots. Discussions about the relationship have taken place mainly within this branch. Group technique has become too ubiquitous for the psychiatric profession to ignore, and even the official organizations have now taken cognizance of it. The American Psychiatric Association established a task force which published a cautious report, and the American Psychological Association established an ethics committee which is dealing with problems arising out of the use of sensitivity training (see Chapter 15).[9] As can be expected, reactions have been quite varied. Probably the majority look at group technique as a fad, like other fads in psychiatric work, which has not yet assumed important or dangerous proportions. The moderate reaction is to acknowledge that some aspects of sensitivity training might be integrated into psychiatric work, if done under medical supervision. At the extremes, some psychiatrists look at group techniques as a distinct danger, something that should be rigorously controlled, and others see in them a new stage of psychiatric knowledge and technique, comparable to the invention of psychoanalysis.

We shall discuss four points at issue: (1) the purpose and aim of sensitivity training as psychotherapy; (2) benefits and risks of the technique; (3) the question of professional control and responsibility; and (4) the effect on the reputation of psychotherapy.

[9] I. Yalom, J. Fidler, J. Frank, J. Mann, M. Parloff, and L. Sata. *American Psychiatric Association Task Force Report on Recent Developments in the Use of Small Groups.* Washington, D.C.: American Psychiatric Association, 1969.

PURPOSE OF ENCOUNTER GROUP TECHNIQUES

One of the difficulties in assessing sensitivity training in relation to psychotherapy is the lack of clarity regarding the aims of encounter group techniques. Sensitivity training and encounter groups do not talk about patients or about cure. They talk about group members and self-realization. Thus, even if the techniques are used in a generalized psychotherapeutic program, one is almost forced to use a criterion of "change" that amounts to any undefined effect at all. On the other hand, if encounter techniques are used in a program with a clear purpose, such as transactional therapy, the effect of the methods can be judged by the contract or purpose of the therapy. But adherents of encounter group techniques may not take these criteria as necessarily valid. In the encounter movement practically everybody is a potential participant; thus, everybody or nobody is a patient, and specific needs for therapy are little considered. The immediate aim is the strong experience which carries immediate subjective conviction of effect; its interpretation as therapy is secondary.

Tensions aroused by using therapy without an aim have led to a novel definition of responsibility. This is centered on the concept of individual responsibility, both for the participant and for the group leader. The latter's responsibility only extends to his own performance—as long as this is genuine and represents the complete capacity of the practitioner it is satisfactory and there is no further responsibility toward the participant. On the other hand, the participant is responsible for himself—he goes into the group of his own free will and is thus responsible for what happens to him there or later.

BENEFITS AND RISKS

The curious definition of the group leader's responsibility makes a discussion of risks, the relation of benefits to danger, precarious. From the point of view of the medical profession, the case could be made as follows. There are few, if any, records of the beneficial effects of encounter groups or cures in a strictly medical sense. Thus it is unclear whether encounter groups ever have therapeutic value, except the testimonials of people who feel good during or after the session. Advocates of encounter groups answer, however, that little is known about the beneficial effects of psychotherapy, for few evaluation studies have been done in this field as well. Of course, there is a considerable body of research on the effect of psychotherapeutic techniques. Besides, psychotherapy certainly is standing on more solid ground, with experience and theory ranging back over several decades and with the accumulated knowledge of many trained practitioners. In addition, patients in psychotherapy come with a definite distress and ask for its relief. This is a different situation from interfering with persons who are functioning adequately in their own setting.

The encounter group is based on little coherent theory, mainly on the touch-and-go kind of technique, and even the practitioners do not claim to know particularly what they are doing. Thus this kind of work is more experimental than clinical, and it might fall into the category of experimenting with human subjects. In fact, most people leading encounter groups would not claim any lasting beneficial effects on the patients or the participants, and thus the question of the danger involved becomes important. The question of breakdowns in encounter groups is controversial, and we have to rest here on a few well-established facts: there have been some breakdowns, suicides, and psychotic episodes in members of encounter groups.

Figures given vary in different studies. A recent, well-controlled study by Lieberman, Yalom, and Miles showed a psychological casualty rate of over 9 percent definitely due to sensitivity training.[10] With certain techniques, the rate was even higher. One of the most disturbing facts coming from the study is that group leaders were unlikely to know whether a casualty had occurred. Thus, most studies that depend mainly on leaders' reports are highly suspect. In short, we still know little about the potential danger of these techniques; but we do know that it is not a negligible problem.

PROFESSIONAL CONTROL

Psychiatrists brought up in the medical tradition feel strongly about selection of leaders who are professionally qualified, responsible to some professional organization, and preferably licensed. The intrusion of a group of leaders, sometimes little more trained than having had one experience in group sessions, must seem to them the

[10] M. Lieberman, I. Yalom, and M. Miles. "The Group Experience Project: A Comparison of Ten Encounter Technologies," in L. Blank, G. Gottsegen, and M. Gottsegen (eds.), *Encounter: Confrontations in Self and Interpersonal Awareness.* New York: Macmillan, 1971.

height of irresponsibility. The whole sensitivity training movement is in a difficult dilemma regarding this problem. Most people in it have some good idea of what are at least the extremes of adequate and inadequate training. Themselves part of a novel occupation trying to reach professional respectability, however, many practitioners feel that it is not quite fair to close the door now on people who might have new ideas. Although some of the organizations, such as NTL, have relatively rigid standards for members of their network, many would resist any restrictions placed on people to run groups in general.

Concern with these problems, especially triggered by threatened damage suits, has brought about new efforts to establish professional standards. NTL has sponsored a committee of individuals in sensitivity training and in the professions concerned to deal with questions of certification and other mechanisms of control and responsibility. This may establish new rules, but shifts in some of the procedures and new kinds of programs are likely to bring up the same problems in the future.

A problem which the psychiatric profession faces is the fact that many students are attracted to encounter techniques. In its compatibility with youth's reaction of breaking out of traditional molds, sensitivity training fits well with today's youth culture, and some of the techniques seem to students, as well as to others, to be the answer to some of the difficulties of psychotherapy. In comparison to the strong feeling tone of the encounter group session, traditional training methods may look somewhat stodgy and old-fashioned. As a matter of fact, some medical and professional schools use some sensitivity training as part of their curriculum. In other situations students go out and try to get their own training in leading groups away from their schools at nearby encounter centers, with the result that their traditional training in psychiatry and clinical psychology may suffer.

In one situation, at the University of Michigan, a conflict arose between faculty and students on this point, and a committee was set up to investigate the situation. The committee found that little harm was done to the students or the patients whom they cared for, at least as far as direct harm could be discerned. The fact that some people are robbed of their defenses without any adequate substitute being supplied may be a more subtle harm which cannot be measured exactly but may have long-range effects. The pressure from the students to supplement their general training in clinical psychology with what was called Project Outreach was so strong that a compromise was recommended whereby the trainers of "outreach" came under nominal supervision of the general clinical psychology faculty.[11]

The uneasy truce which the Michigan solution illustrates is probably characteristic of the general attitude of members of the psychiatric profession toward group techniques. They know the attraction; they also know that group techniques are used now in many situations as a kind of psychological readiness technique. This includes the Peace Corps and its Canadian counterpart, the Company of Young Canadians. Psychiatrists working with the latter group have been extremely skeptical of both the procedures and the results, and some cases of breakdown have been reported.[12] Psychiatrists have frequently been put into the position of having to accept the popularity of these new techniques and to put them under some responsible controls. This situation has made some problems for psychiatrists. A special section of the *American Journal of Psychiatry* on sensitivity training took a skeptical view and included an editorial recommending caution in its use, and treating it as a fad that might go away.[13] The task force appointed by the American Psychiatric Association (mentioned above) was a little more favorable to sensitivity training and raised the possibility of group techniques as a new adjunct to psychiatric work. They also ended by bemoaning the lack of real evidence of positive effect and suggested that research be done on the effectiveness of the technique. Perhaps the nature of the problem is best indicated by the fact that after more than a decade of use and discussion of the effectiveness of group techniques, psychiatric work still has to conclude with the familiar lament, "more research needed."

CONTAGION

A final threat to psychiatry from the development of sensitivity training is the fact that the extreme and questionable groups of sensitivity training and encounter might bring psychiatry into disrepute. For laymen, and especially for people who are skeptical of psychotherapy in general, the distinction between some of the more flashy techniques publicized widely in the press, and some of the

[11] "Report of the Clinical Area: Special Commission on T-Groups." University of Michigan, mimeographed, n.d. (1968–69).

[12] "Stress and Strength at Crystal Cliffs" (Toronto), *Globe Magazine*, Aug. 6, 1966, 5–12.

[13] "Groups," *American Journal of Psychiatry, 126,* 1968, 223–277.

more traditional psychotherapeutic and group therapy techniques, is hard to make. Sometimes people do not want to make them. Thus, attacks by conservative Congressmen, reprints in the *Congressional Record,* and hearings in state legislatures have attacked sensitivity training and encounter groups, but also some forms of group psychotherapy, as an ever-present danger. Psychiatrists are therefore in the position that they might want to separate themselves from any aspects of group encounter. If they help the people who attack sensitivity training madly and furiously, they may help their own enemies. If they do not distinguish themselves from the sensitivity training movement they may be regarded as guilty and responsible for all the excesses that the encounter groups involve.

Chapter 11

The New Entrepreneurs

"He gets ahead because (1) men in power do not expect that things can be done legitimately; (2) these men know fear and guilt; and (3) they are often personally not very bright. It is often hard to say, with any sureness, whether the new entrepreneur lives on his own wits, or upon the lack of wits in others. As for anxiety, however, it is certain that, although he may be prodded by his own, he could get nowhere without its ample presence in his powerful clients."[1]

Can sensitivity training be adapted to the needs of specific organizations? Organizational goals and the aims of sensitivity training would appear to lie at opposite ends of the spectrum. Sensitivity training is a technique which uses a kind of emotional outburst in a group, which may or may not be directed toward change within the individual. The expected changes include more openness, spontaneity, direct encounter with other people, sensitivity to others, and similar changes. Underlying this idea of change is the notion that a group composed of people with these traits is superior to other groups in all circumstances. Organizations, however, are different in their requirements, in their histories, and in their practices, and they may have their own peculiar problems when they realize their need for some new program and turn to sensitivity training. While it may be true that every business, industry, or organization consists ultimately of people, and therefore the problems of people and their interaction are the basis of organizational difficulties, this does not

[1] C. W. Mills. *White Collar*. New York: Oxford University Press, 1951.

mean that all organizational problems are identical. By the same reasoning, the problems could be considered biological or even physical. Organizations often have aims or purposes, such as production of a certain commodity or provision of certain services, which fundamentally have very little to do with the needs of the people within the organization. Interaction within the group might be important for the survival of the organization, but those interactions have to be adapted to this particular purpose. This difference between sensitivity training and organizational needs can be seen at two levels. One is the conflict between two aims: the aim of positive affect within the group and the aim of effective group functioning. The problems of the group may be very particular and special and have little to do with the particular needs of the individual workers or even the small groups they form. It has been the general experience of many organizations which used sensitivity training that sensitivity trainers are too little interested in the specific problems of an organization, while concentrating mainly on the general ones. That is, they cannot adapt their techniques to any specific difficulties an organization may encounter, or to its differences from other organizations. In a more general way, sensitivity training concentrates more on emotional, interpersonal levels, and less on task-oriented levels. It is not uncommon in sensitivity training for a group to be told to be an efficient working group, and groups learn how to interact in a way that gives this appearance. It is hard to see how a group can be an efficient working group without having any particular working goals.

Frequently, the relationship between business organizations and sensitivity training has followed a certain course. The organization is at first skeptical, but agrees for some people to try sensitivity training, perhaps by going to a laboratory. These people return to the organization filled with enthusiasm and apparently better able to control their personal problems or at least giving that appearance. It is difficult, however, to determine whether there have been any measurable differences in organizational functioning. The argument is then made that one of the reasons for the lack of effectiveness within the organization is that one person cannot change the whole organization. Therefore a whole in-house program is started to bring about change in the organization, and the first few sessions excite the interest of the employees. The first people who attended voluntarily feel now like a select group.

After a time, some changes might be made, but then conflict develops in which it is felt that the sensitivity trainers do not have enough concern about the specific problems of the organization. Although they might be helping particular people, they are not particularly helping the organization. Disillusionment sets in. The whole program is quietly abandoned or relegated to some specific minor function, although most people do not feel especially negative about the experience. They still say it was a good idea, but just did not fit into the particular situation of the company at that time, and so on. Some people who attended the training sessions still feel better, are still quite favorable toward sensitivity training, and might still try to promote a few sessions at a later date. In fact, sensitivity training programs have become so widespread that the companies that have used them are too numerous to list; but there are hardly any companies organized completely according to the ideals of their sensitivity trainers.

We find here, in the application to management, similar problems to those which we have found in connection with psychotherapy—lack of definite aims, facile assumptions that everybody has the same type of problems, and lack of organized professional control. In one respect, however, there is a big contrast between the relations of sensitivity training to psychotherapy and to management. The aim of psychotherapy is a drastic and directed change of the individual; sensitivity training may cause insufficient or random effects. In management the effort is directed to the success of the organization and the individuals' involvement is only partial; here, sensitivity training might do more to the individual than is warranted by his working relationship.

The contract that the patient makes with the therapist is to produce a big change within the patient which the therapist will be responsible for guiding. The relationship of a worker or an executive to an organization is almost the opposite. The worker is willing to give some of his abilities to perform a certain task in exchange for a certain compensation. The heart of sensitivity training, the intensive group experience, may fit both conditions. In psychotherapy, the danger is that the patient will take the experience for the change and the therapist will feel no responsibility for the patient or the session. In personnel relationships, the problem is the opposite. A strong group experience may be more than what the worker bargained for, and the exertion of influence on his life and his feelings may be more than the employer had the right to demand in a work relationship.

In both cases, management as well as psychotherapy, we must look to see whether sensitivity training is something more than worthless entertainment and something less than a threat to personal dignity and privacy. The latter problem arises in psychother-apy from a strong effect on the individual, stronger than the client bargained for; in management, the problem goes further: How far can an employer involve his employees for the good of the company?

Some of the most protracted and violent strikes of the early labor movement were caused by the fact that the employer (some-times from well-meaning motives) tried to regulate and control the worker's whole life. This included moral life, amount of drinking, churchgoing hours, etc. Part of the achievement of the union move-ment, besides purely economic gains, was the separation of great parts of the workers' lives from the employers' control. Modern man-agement practices the separation of living conditions from working conditions, personal life from work life, and has tried to eliminate this kind of tension. One of the difficulties in understanding the role of sensitivity training in personnel work is precisely that here man-agement again tries to arrogate to itself the same controls over the worker which it had previously abandoned. This time, it tries to have stronger control mainly of the people at the top of the industrial ladder, executives and white-collar workers.

Unions are organized primarily to obtain extrinsic rewards for their members, such as pay, hours, vacations, job security, or im-proved work procedures. These issues are negotiated through com-promise, solving a more or less intense and protracted conflict. Sen-sitivity training flourishes in nonunionized contexts and has been embraced sometimes by management as an alternative to unioniza-tion. In several cases, however, dissatisfaction brought about by this pretended emotional unanimity led to a quick success by union or-ganizers. Thus, from the point of view of the workers, sensitivity training may be seen as a technique which substitutes emotions for bread-and-butter issues, just as, from the point of view of manage-ment, it substitutes emotions for interest in productivity.

Thus the contractual relationships in business and industry contrast with the emotional involvement in sensitivity training. The sensitivity trainers and personnel managers come to the problem from opposite directions, although seeking a common solution. We find a whole range of possible positions within sensitivity train-ing. There are, on the one extreme, those who only want to use group processes on the general problems of companies and feel that any organization can be improved by the improvement of group inter-action. When somebody attempts to give serious attention to per-sonnel management, these are the people who counter with: "What good does it do if people don't love each other?" Moving toward the middle, one finds people in sensitivity training who are more and more cognizant of the problems of organizations. The NTL approach is a case in point. By background and interest their trainers are generalists, mainly involved in general principles of group interaction. This extends to a distrust of industrial procedures within the organization. In fact, people whose background has been within only one plant are not considered widely enough trained to become associates and members of NTL. They are relegated to a category of special members. Some people in sensitivity training, however, try to expand it to deal with the real problems of organizations. Probably the most prominent approaches today are those of the organizational developers.

As the name implies, OD (organizational development) is an attempt to restructure the organization at the same time as individuals are being trained in personal skills.[2] Thus, it becomes important to involve management in the entire training process and to reorganize the plants in conformity with the new ways of group formation. Probably the foremost example of the use of this technique is the work of Sheldon Davis at the TRW corporation.[3] TRW was mainly involved in aerospace research; it was founded originally by two university professors as a small laboratory and only later expanded by an industrialist, and may therefore have been more open to experimentation than most other businesses. In addition, it builds unique products rather than mass-produced ones, which leads to continuous reorganization and counteracts any tendency to rigid structure. In this corporation it was possible to build up a system of sensitivity training which could be carried over into the actual working situation. Rapid shifts of working groups due to the shifts in production were made easier by sensitivity training programs that concentrated on possible friction between prospective team members. Special sessions for managers, in mountain retreats, were intended to make them adaptable to the demands of the intensive interpersonal relations required. Increasing competition and the cutbacks in the aerospace program have in recent years changed the demands in TRW, and greater routine has become the order of the day. This has subordinated sensitivity training to the requirements of organizational efficiency, and the special programs have been curtailed or

[2] R. Beckhard. *Organizational Development: Strategies and Models*. Reading, Pa.: Addison-Wesley, 1967. W. G. Bennis. *Organizational Development: Its Nature, Origins and Prospects*. Reading, Pa.: Addison-Wesley, 1967.

[3] S. Davis. "An Organic Problem-Solving Method of Organizational Change," *Journal of Applied Behavioral Science*, 3, 1967, 3–21.

discontinued. On the other hand, the company has found sensitivity training and OD to be saleable products and has turned to acting as a consultant to universities, school districts, and cities. An early article about TRW's work was called "It's OK to Cry in the Office."[4] But it is apparently more important to produce something at the office.

Another approach which seems to be more cognizant of the problems of particular industries is that of the English group at Tavistock. Their publications are usually very specific about a certain kind of industry, be it coal, transportation or textile;[5] their workers observe over a long period of time the particular problems of one plant in order to deal with them effectively. Tavistock trainers have also faced critically the question of carryover from training to job performance. Their solution has been to cut down work on general problems and to bring the specific problems of the company and the trainees themselves into the program as early as possible. This makes generalized training programs impractical, but forces adaptation to specific problems. This approach corresponds to the general medical orientation of the trainers of Tavistock Institute. They approach their client as an ailing organization with a certain distress, and their primary task is relieving that distress and preventing its recurrence. Diagnosis and treatment are quite specific.

Other approaches differing from those of the orthodox sensitivity training group are also more cognizant of the task-directed problem. It was apparently over those problems that trainers like Robert Blake broke with the sensitivity training movement. Blake's approach is still quite similar to it; however, his main conceptual tool, the managerial grid, is a scheme concerned with two variables: interpersonal relations and task direction.[6] His main emphasis in training techniques is that both are extremely important and equally valid. The group that is interpersonally related *only*, not task directed, will founder very quickly. His training and exercises are directed toward making people more adept in both fields. He has worked out formal training programs to improve both variables, interpersonal relations as well as task orientation.

[4] J. Poppy. "It's OK to Cry in the Office," *Look*, July 9, 1968, 64–76.

[5] A. Rice. *The Enterprise and Its Environment*. London: Tavistock, 1963. P. Fensham and D. Hooper. *The Dynamics of a Changing Technology*. London: Tavistock, 1964. E. Trist, G. Higgin, H. Murray, and A. Pollock. *Organizational Choice*. London: Tavistock, 1963.

[6] R. Blake and J. Mouton. *Corporate Excellence Through Grid Organizational Development*. Houston: Gulf Publishing, 1968.

Moving on, we find people who have never been part of sensitivity training, who use regular personnel management techniques quite similar to the sensitivity training techniques; but they are using them from the point of view of management and not particularly because they are interested in sensitivity training. What emerges then are people who feel an inherent conflict in the management situation, who try to solve problems as they occur, and who are extremely opposed to the sweeping claims sensitivity training makes. They stress the casualties, the breakdowns, and the lack of real results that sensitivity training has produced in industry. Some of these people have come up from the ranks of labor and have seen the weakness of sensitivity training in actual labor negotiations where there was a real conflict. Others have seen it in management and are more impressed by the dangers and the excessive costs than by the observed results. They, too, are interested in personal relations, but they have never been under the spell of the strong emotional experience which sensitivity training brings.

Somewhat outside this scheme are the European schools which try to combine experimental sensitivity training, restructuring of the organization, and reconstitution of society on the basis of autonomous groups. They use the central concept of "autogestion," where organization or "gestion" is no longer the private property of some (minorities, castes, or upper classes) but has become common property.[7] This point of view rests on an analogy between economics and psychotherapy, namely, that the concepts of private property and public property do not refer solely to property of goods, but that public property refers to the affective life and culture of the whole society. Emotions as property become socialized and conflicts between individuals and organizations are obviated. The mixed parentage of this movement is shown by the references to the term "autogestion" in a glossary: they are to Lenin, Marx, Lewin, and M. Pages (a French follower of Carl Rogers).[8]

The common aim of all these approaches is the motivation of the worker. This is management's legitimate concern, but also part of the worker's own private life-space. The ideal situation is one in which workers want to do the work and are willing to put out their best effort. This happy situation occurs under a conjunction of circumstances, among them, commitment to the goal of the organization, opportunity to express one's own abilities and interests, agree-

[7] G. Lapassade. *Groupes, Organisations, et Institutions.* Paris: Gauthier-Villars, 1970.

[8] *Ibid.,* Glossary, 206.

able personal relations, and appropriate rewards. It is likely that the first two are more important for positive motivation than the last two;[9] however, under modern business conditions, this kind of commitment is hard to obtain, and hence greater emphasis is put on the last two factors. Unions as well as personnel techniques stress the reward, while the human relations movement and later sensitivity training have stressed interpersonal relations. Sensitivity training also uses applications theory in interpersonal relations as a reason for total commitment. The interest conflict within human relations in management can be seen even in its early showpiece, the still controversial Hawthorne experiment. The story is familiar and was discussed in Chapter 6.

We can group the questions we have discussed so far into four problems. The first problem we can call the contrast between goal-directed and interpersonal behavior, or the relation between individual expression and organizational needs. Many people, even some within the sensitivity training movement, have noted this. Workers in a factory, or individuals in any organization, have some needs of expressing themselves, of doing what they want, of working at their own pace, which are necessarily frustrated to some extent by working within an organization. The needs of the organization are necessarily not the needs of all the people working in it, or even of the majority of them. There results a definite contrast between the individual needs and the organizational needs; and for the organization to function, individual needs must necessarily be frustrated, and so individuals will be frustrated within the organization. The function of personnel management, therefore, is to find the *modus vivendi* by which the individuals can receive sufficient satisfaction for the organization to function efficiently. This cannot always be done by establishing intense personal relations. If individuals are committed to the aims of the organization, they are able to tolerate the conflict between organizational and individual aims quite well. By subordinating both to intense interpersonal relations, sensitivity training may perform a disservice to all parties in the conflict. We may note that the language of the trainers is frequently taken from family situations ("sibling labs," "cousin labs"), and that, in families, intense emotional involvement also leads to the strongest conflicts, which are overcome only because of a pre-existing solidarity. This solidarity is missing in work situations, and here the use of interpersonal experiences looks artificial and manipulatory.

[9] F. Herzberg. *Work and the Nature of Man.* New York: World, 1966.

The problem leads back to the motivation of the workers. Are the strongest group experiences, enjoyment of participation within the group, and other advantages of sensitivity training going to help them achieve their financial aims, or are these experiences going to make them forget their economic worries? Are these experiences going to interest them in their jobs? In the same way, the problem arises for managers. Can the advantages of sensitivity training and the joys they derive from that be a substitute for increased profits, or even for the functioning of the enterprise itself?

One of the best descriptions of the ideal state of high morale is given in the following quote:

> There was a tenseness, a quickening of tempo, that was neither youthful nor nervous nor feverish. The mind, the body, the spirit, the whole being seemed free and ready for anything and confident of success. It was not elation so much as it was knowledgeable acceptance of maturity. . . . Good men were better. Men who had seemed mediocre became good. . . . Everybody seemed to realize that everybody else was working his head off. Requests were made, commands given, in quiet voices. Everybody seemed almost miraculously full of tolerance and understanding.[10]

The description is taken from an essay on the U.S. strategic bombing force in the Marianas in the Second World War. The particular conjunction of the task, the wartime morale, and the history of achievement had produced a unique organization. Involvement in the task with the aims and output of the organization is the prime source of high morale and productivity.

Under many conditions, the intense identification of individuals with the aims of the organization will not occur. People work for an organization for different reasons, and invest only parts of themselves into their work. Management's task can be seen as creating conditions for efficient operation even when strong commitment is lacking.

The second problem is the question of whether sensitivity training in this context can be used as a technique, or whether it must imbue the whole philosophy of management. The problems of industrial management, be they purely personnel problems such as turnover, hiring tactics or low morale, or problems of productivity, or those of industrial conflict, are difficult enough to handle, and management has always looked to new techniques for this purpose.

[10] St. C. McKelvay. "A Reporter with the B–29's," *The New Yorker*, 21, June, 1945, 33–36.

This problem involves selecting, testing, counseling, employee relations, and so on. Broadly, on a common-sense basis, most of the techniques used by industry have been quite similar, and are probably mainly determined by the skill of the individual manager. What is sensitivity training in this context? Some people, even proponents of it, say it is merely a technique to let people talk and encourage them to give out their ideas, making it possible for them to speak openly. This may be a general aim which many people could have, whether or not they are sensitivity trainers. What is meant usually, however, by the introduction of T-groups and sensitivity training within a plant, is the use of quite definite techniques, extended sessions of sending officials or employees to diverse training laboratories. These are the situations in which the employees might get the various learning experiences which might make them feel differently about the whole management relationship.

Sensitivity training concentrates mainly on means; it has a pragmatic background, and many of its practitioners will disclaim interest in the ultimate outcome of the training. The guiding principle is that a change in interpersonal relations and attitudes is good in itself, and the aims will take care of themselves. In fact, trainees rarely function any differently in organizations after sensitivity training. The needs and inertia of a functioning organization may be such that some individuals who have found new ways of acting as a result of some training program have little chance to change it. Claims of sensitivity trainers have been scaled down in recent years, and the question of carryover is being more and more neglected.

A new approach to the problem comes from radical thinkers who claim that sensitivity training gives the base for the forms of a new society. This will be discussed in Chapter 16. This may be stating in different ways that the effects of sensitivity training on actual organizations may be felt in Utopia, but not in organizations as we know them. It is now generally conceded that, while sensitivity training is used in hundreds of companies, there are hardly any in which the organization has been changed to conform to the principles implied in the training.

The third problem is the question of voluntary participation. Sensitivity training may not be as great a threat to mental health as it sometimes may appear, but it does have its difficulties, its record of breakdowns, and its adverse effects. The sensitivity training technique itself, by its neglect of privacy and even its hostility to it, by its ideal of self-revelation, by its stress on many activities a person would not want to do normally, is almost completely dependent on volunteer participation. Forced participation would not only vitiate the whole meaning of sensitivity training, but has other consequences for its effects as well.

Volunteer participation in sensitivity training, however, implies self-selection. The techniques of sensitivity training are adopted by a certain part of the population, partly selected by social background, partly by personality, and partly by cultural ideas, and it is most effective for them. Most studies on sensitivity training are in effect vitiated by the fact that it is related to a very special population. Once voluntary participation stops, participants may not be the kind of people for whom this kind of technique was designed, and for whom it has been proved to be agreeable. Groups may, on the contrary, include the type of people who have been able to function with a different philosophy, in a different way of life, and for whom this kind of approach may be actually detrimental. It is known, for instance, that many of the best-documented instances of breakdown have occurred among people who apparently were successful executives whose company felt that they should be sensitivity trained.[11]

Much of the participation of industrial workers and employees in these group sessions is, of course, more or less voluntary. If the corporation participates in a program of this kind, a sufficient number of the employees will be interested and intrigued by this new approach to attend the sessions of their own free will. It becomes, then, a question for the remaining people who originally were not that interested. Let us take now the case in which there is no particular overt pressure exerted. If a sufficient number of people have come back glowing from their new experience, there may be subtle pressure exerted on the rest of the people to see what it is and to find out what pleased the others so much. This corresponds to the method of social spread of the movement; it cannot be charged to coercion. Coercion does occur, however, when people of superior status have gone and encouraged their subordinates to go to the meetings themselves. There is a thin dividing line between ordering a person to go, suggesting it, and the presence of a general belief in an organization that, if the boss has gone and thinks it is a good idea, then maybe it would be a good thing for everybody in his organization to have this experience. Alfred Marrow pointed out that NTL existed on a relatively modest budget of $300,000 until, at his suggestion, the Presidents' Lab was started. Once the presidents of corporations became

---

[11] Cf. Sensitivity Training Panel at the 1967 meeting, Personnel Association for Southern California. Transcript.

involved in sensitivity training (and in this way got the support of top management in many organizations), the budget of NTL increased tenfold.[12] It is hardly likely that this increased participation occurred without any subtle exercise of power.

Thus, the question of voluntary participation leads to two further problems: the question of power in sensitivity training and, technically, the question of group composition. The first is a more ideological problem, the second a technical one. As a small-group technique, sensitivity training has been concerned mainly with the individual in his relation to the immediate environment. It has denied the importance of a distinct social structure, and even the necessity for any social structure. The attraction that the movement has had for many lies exactly in the sense of liberation and enjoyment produced by personality development and letting down all the guards that are usually part of a social situation. In this way, the question of receptivity has been more important than the question of producing actual social change. The question which sensitivity training faces is whether it continues to be a sum of small-scale movements by small groups or whether it uses existing social structures to stress power. Social effectiveness can, of course, be enhanced quickly via the power route.[13] Within organizations the idea was to have change at the working and foreman levels, which is the first line of management. Those were the foci where human relations were supposed to be important and where most of the breakdowns in communications occurred. If one looks at the literature of the human relations movement through its history, it seems that a gradual shift has been taking place. From interest in the human relations of the worker in training and the first-line managers, interest has gone up the range toward white-collar workers and managers, and finally presidents. The idea has taken hold that real change in an organization, as well as in society, cannot be accomplished from the bottom up but from the top down, by working with the power people and through the power structure.

The practical effect of this development has been a gradual change from human relations to organizational development (OD). This constitutes an acknowledgment that strong group experience may be the basis for getting people to sensitivity training sessions, but it is only part of the whole procedure to be undertaken. The same

[12] Personal interview.

[13] F. Steele. "Can T-Group Training Change the Power Structure?" *Personnel Administration, 33,* 1970, 118–153.

people who promote sensitivity training are also the promoters of organizational changes, changes in interaction between people of different departments and different status, as well as significant changes in the structure of the organization. It is becoming increasingly difficult to distinguish between what is sensitivity training and what is not. Sensitivity trainers do quite the same thing as people in personnel management do. Practically everybody today acknowledges the importance of personal feelings, feelings of self-worth and of achievement, in addition to the importance of the strictly instrumental relationship between doing the work and getting paid for one's labor. Thus, a great amount of organization and reorganization work is implied in sensitivity training as well as in traditional management procedures. The differences seem to be sometimes only questions of name and personal status of people who advocate a specific method. Many of the people in OD are also involved in other types of sensitivity training such as therapeutic, recreational, and even nonverbal and emotional work. It would seem that even those people who are strongly advocating organizational development still see the importance of the sensitivity training experience as central to management. Their opponents, however, people from straight personnel relations work, see personnel, that is, organizational, work first, and interpersonal emotions second. These differences can be overstated; the lines are never so clear-cut as the classifications make them seem.

The fourth problem which relates to the special situation of sensitivity training in organizational settings is the composition of the sensitivity training groups. We noted before that a change in attitudes toward group composition occurred in the early years of the National Training Laboratory. The first laboratories were conducted pretty much among strangers, and one of the great virtues attributed to the laboratory was the opening up to a stranger, as well as the interactions between widely varying personalities which a randomly constituted group permitted. Many laboratories, especially those which tried to produce strong emotions, are of course still run according to this principle. NTL itself, when it got more into organizational work, became more interested in getting people together who were not bound by friendship or common interests, but by a specific relationship within the business being consulted. Thus, one could take people from the same corporation department or the same level, or people on different levels working for each other, or people who had no official relationship with each other, or people on the same level but working for different bosses. The names given to these different types of labs were usually those of family relationships, and gave evidence of the stronger emotional ties which bind people in labs than within the organizational setting. Thus, labs of people working for the same boss were called "sibling labs," while labs of people working for different but coordinate bosses were called "cousin labs." With a sensitivity training program tailored to one organization, these original relationships became, of course, very important. Some techniques are used which involve a careful shift over time from stranger labs to other labs, and apply insights learned in an earlier stage to more and more realistic situations. In other kinds of training the relationship is really the most important point, and sensitivity training is used to smooth out particular relationships for a particular job. This kind of work is called team building, and is especially important in organizations with a varying production output where different skills are put together for different tasks.

The advantages of this turning away from "stranger labs" have been important but the new labs are also bothered by some technical problems. One of the essential conditions of sensitivity training is being able to let down barriers, to be free to speak one's mind without repercussions. This becomes a fundamental problem in these kinds of groups. Some of the T-group trainers consider the interaction of the group a professionally privileged relationship (similar to medical) and feel that everybody in the group is bound by general professional ethics. The situation becomes different, of course, if the people in the group continue to interact after the group ends. It is futile to pretend in this situation that people will not remember what has been said within the group situation and will not carry over feelings toward a person from the group situation itself. Although the purpose of the group is free, unrestrained interaction, this very purpose inhibits action in the groups. A trainee feels that he must use a certain caution in interacting with a person who has some power over him even in the most free sensitivity training group. On the other hand, some damage may be done to an executive who was functioning quite well in his own style if he is told in a group that people hate him, that he does lousy work, and that his procedure is all wrong. He might have difficulty in adjusting to this revelation and might not be able to function again effectively in the organization. Some cases of reported breakdowns in sensitivity training have been exactly of this type. It is clearly the least flexible people who will be the most profoundly surprised and attacked. But even in less extreme cases it is not easy to prevent carryover of some resentment for things said in the group to the general working situation.

The problems we have outlined may be reasons for the honeymoon-disillusion cycle of many sensitivity training programs in industry. The price paid may be too high for the visible short-range improvements that come from the program.

There may be, however, a hidden value in sensitivity training applied to organizations. Industrial relations may involve deeper needs than those which can be met by the kind of procedure that, as of today, can be justified by the state of the social sciences and by usual evaluation techniques. Sensitivity training provides some of the trainers with a faith, a sense of mission, which may keep them going in the face of direct frustration. It may also give some of the participants a good feeling, a center for their life, and a new direction. Perhaps the industrial state of today needs more a new religion than a new technique, and for this purpose sensitivity training is as good a candidate as any.

Industrial production in a prosperous society may not give the incentive needed for group motivation. We must remember that the example of the ideal motivation for a work force came from a military situation with strong patriotic fervor. The military is an organization not known for its concern for expressing conflicts, hospitality to basic reforms, or concern for privacy. It may be less the techniques of sensitivity training than the faith and enthusiasm it inspires which could make it useful in promoting organizational high morale and efficiency.

Chapter 12

Teachers and Change Agents

"I'm not saying there will be improvement, but there must be changes."[1]

The final application of sensitivity training we shall discuss corresponds to cell *G* in our chart in Chapter 8, namely, techniques of comparatively weak impact which aim at a change of the individual. These applications may be summarized under the heading of education.

The use of intensive small-group techniques and intensive experiences in education have run the whole range from an auxiliary method to a central philosophy. At one extreme, sensitivity training and group methods are used simply to make people more receptive to some new kind of technique. At the other extreme is a whole new idea of revamping the educational system for more sensory expression and sensory awareness training, instead of symbolic training.

The early precursors of the use of sensitivity training in education can be found along the whole range of experimental developments in group dynamics. Experiments in producing desired changes, such as reducing intergroup tensions or changing food habits, showed the importance of group pressures for the achievement of enduring change (see Chapter 7). From these findings developed the work in experimental social psychology, using the influence of group pressure on attitude and behavior change. This experimental work has shown the importance of a multiplicity of

[1] A. Hitler. Campaign Speech, March, 1933.

variables. Another branch of the group dynamics movement, represented in the development of NTL, was impatient with this slow, continuous procedure and began a wholesale adoption of group methods in education, underpinning them with ideological and experimental support.

The experimental evidence about the effect of intensive group experience on change is mixed. Experimental work using small groups to induce people to change their habits and activities predates some of the actual work of sensitivity training. Experiments showing that food habits were more likely to be permanently changed within a group setting as a group decision than on the basis of the most logical presentation were part of the group dynamics work during the Second World War. The basic idea that a group experience culminating in a decision to do a certain different thing would carry over and become part of a person, even after he leaves the group, is partly the basis of the whole trend of thinking that led to the Connecticut workshop and the establishment of the laboratory at Bethel. The original experiments on food habits showed some advantage to the group-decision method.[2] Much depends on the exact circumstances of the experiment, however. It is true that a good leader in a group decision experiment is better than a bad lecturer, but the reverse is also true. The fact remains that intensive group work which is supposed to lead to definite change involves an inevitable amount of trickery, which is acceptable as part of experimental procedure, but not as a method of conduct in self-directed groups.

In the early period of sensitivity training, however, the idea of making changes through a group experience multiplied in education as well as in the medical and social work fields where education was needed. This philosophy has permeated the whole group-work field to the extent that sensitivity training has become confused with all of group work, although the extent of confusion is probably exaggerated. The basis of sensitivity training still remains the strong experience, the subjective feeling of change, while group work is generally much more goal oriented and wary of strong emotions.

In recent years, with the introduction of many new educational methods, group training has become a method for communication with large groups of individuals who must be won over to new techniques, such as school administrators and teachers. The vividness of the group experience makes what would normally be a dull teaching

[2] K. Lewin. "Forces behind Food Habits and Methods of Change," *Bulletin of National Research Council, 108,* 1943, 35–65.

session an exciting adventure. Also involved may be the selection factor, that people who have been interested in coming have positive feelings toward the idea in the first place. A major drawback, namely, that the vividness of the training situation makes a performance and is appreciated mainly as such, may be overcome if the group methods are only part of a complete program of teaching and consistently applying new methods.

One obvious area of education where sensitivity training may be an appropriate technique is where the subject matter is related to the technique itself. Sensitivity training and group techniques have been used increasingly in teaching social psychology, human relations, and interpersonal relations for various professional groups. The prototype of all these courses is a course called "Social Relations 120" at Harvard. It was started by Hugh Cabot who had his early training in the Harvard Business School, and who has had contact with the Human Relations group there.[3] The technique used in teaching this course consisted of assigning readings and papers, and then letting the group begin discussions on interpersonal relations as well as on the readings. The teacher took no role in the discussion itself, but gave interpretations of the discussion and of the interpersonal relations between the class members at the end of the session. The theory was that teaching in this course would include the traditional outside readings, but inside the class, the interaction itself would serve as an example of the topics taught. One of the teachers in the course, Richard Mann, expressed this aim as seeing great experiences come: the student discovers that what happens in the last fifteen minutes of the class period is exactly what he has read in his textbook on page 373.[4] Thus, conducted well, a course of this kind can become a vivid experience in learning about all kinds of behavioral science.

The varieties of the procedures used in this course can be studied easily, because if nothing else, the course had a tremendous impact on its teachers. No less than three monographs have been published about the original Harvard course, which was directed by R. F. Bales, studies by Mann, Slater, and Mills, as well as a quantity of articles.[5] Conducting a course of this kind, if it is not done as a

[3] R. Mann. *Interpersonal Styles and Group Development*. New York: Wiley, 1967. Mann is Cabot's stepson.

[4] Personal interview.

[5] The books are R. Mann, *Interpersonal Styles and Group Development*. New York: Wiley, 1967; T. Mills, *Group Transformation*. Englewood Cliffs, N.J.: Prentice-Hall, 1964; P. Slater, *Microcosm*. New York: Wiley, 1966. R. F.

series of tricks and gimmicks, puts a tremendous strain on the instructor, in spite of his outwardly passive role. He is responsible for the conduct of the whole class, especially for any harm that may come to the students. The difficulty is to keep the class a learning experience and not to let emotion take over completely. The reputation a course of this kind acquires on campus is that it is very interesting, fun, and also likely to attract some people with personal problems. The role of the teacher becomes in part to talk about the more general problems shown in the scenes just witnessed, to relate them to the topic of the course, and not let the thing degenerate into a party or an emotional orgy. In this situation, especially, it is very hard to screen applicants who are admitted on academic and not personality credentials. There is also a great temptation to pull the group into a complete therapy session. Many teachers might feel that neither is the classroom the place for this nor would it be good for the other people in the group, nor is the teacher particularly equipped as a therapist or willing to take the responsibility for acting as one. There seems to have been very little direct danger, but there are a few incidents reported of student breakdowns. In a similar class at Yale, there appear to have been fewer psychiatric problems among students in the course than among the general run of students.[6]

Courses of this kind are a good source of material about groups and probably the best source of data on the effects of sensitivity training, at least of this procedure. Data have been used in some of the books about the course as a source of theory showing the general nature of group development. Slater, for instance, deduces from the description of the class groups a general group process of deposing the leader, a ritual Freudian killing of the father, and the accompanying totemic feast. Even the fact that at some point in the process students bring in beer or have a party with cookies and liquor is taken as evidence of analogy to the totemic feast. In the same way, Theodore Mills has made films of classes of this kind conducted at Yale which demonstrate the principle of group development interestingly, as events occurring in several of those classes.[7]

One question becomes important here: In these classes the

Bales' exposition, *Personality and Interpersonal Behavior* (New York: Holt, 1970) draws for its data on work in this class. An excellent satire on this field is B. Vroom, "Weekend Confrontation with the Soc Rels," *The New Yorker*, 43, December 2, 1967, 199–212.

[6] C. Argyris. Personal communication.

[7] One film, *Fathers and Sons* (centering around the problems of authority and dependence), is completed and available from Dr. Mills.

reading and the discussion were in part centered on exactly those problems which the group process demonstrated. Were the students influenced by the theory and the content of their reading and encouraged to act-out those parts that seemed congenial to them, or did they act this way spontaneously? The revolt against the leader may be a case in point. It had been described earlier in an article by Bennis and Shepard.[8] This article was assigned classroom reading in the groups, which Slater discusses. The occurrence of the revolt in Slater's group is then taken as evidence for revolt in his subsequent book. In the film that Mills produced, the same revolt is shown occurring very graphically, but at the climax of the revolt, one of the students is reading to the class the relevant passages from Slater's book. Does the group follow the theory because it knows the theory? Can the student get an understanding of general group process from groups of this kind, when he knows how groups are supposed to act? It must be admitted, however, that another group in Mills' film, instead of reading from Slater's book was listening to a recital of a song by Bob Dylan, which said about the same thing. It might be that the influence of the theory of sensitivity training is greater than that which can be directly traced to assigned readings in the class (Slater or Bennis and Shepard), and manifests itself through influence on popular songs and other parts of popular culture.

Through the normal dissemination process as well as mobility of university faculty, and the fact that students become faculty in time, the model of Social Relations 120 spread to other universities in the country and was imitated widely. Correspondent to this course there had been other attempts, especially in schools with more emphasis on human relations. For instance, McGregor had organized his introductory psychology course in a similar way. He had the class discuss human relations problems and try to interpret their own reactions, and find in them applications of group dynamics principles to management problems. Having groups work completely on their own and discussing problems in this context was, however, only done for research purposes, in order to collect data for a Ph.D. dissertation.[9] From all these sources, this kind of teaching method in human relations and social psychology has spread widely in many colleges and universities. It is hard to evaluate, just as effectiveness in teaching on a college level in general is never evaluated. Like much of

[8] W. Bennis and H. Shepard. "A Theory of Group Development," *Human Relations*, 9, 1956, 415–437.

[9] M. Deutsch. "The Effect of Cooperation and Competition upon Group Process," *Human Relations*, 2, 1949, 124–152 and 190–231.

college and other teaching, success depends more on the ability of the teacher than on the specific technique used. The group may become either a ridiculous game for students, a somewhat dangerous half-therapy, or a laboratory experience in conjunction with somewhat abstract teaching in social psychology. As in other teaching techniques, it depends on what else the students do in the course, and on whether this kind of experience can be tied into a more general learning experience.

The experience-learning kind of approach is becoming accepted in professional training as well as in academic training. It fits into the tendency in professional training to have some mechanism between classroom work and practical experience, a pre-practice, so to say. This approach fits easily into the kind of interpersonal relations training that nurses and doctors take as part of their general education. Different from academic training, these professional courses adapt easily to the experiential kind of training of human relations, and are a natural way for doctors and nurses to be trained at the bedside for their future professions. Like any part of a curriculum, most of these courses are compulsory for anybody going into the program, and thus the membership in the course is not freely selected. Here again, the problem arises of voluntary vs. compulsory participation. Some schools try to meet the problem by providing alternate ways of obtaining training in human relations by which a choice is given between classroom and experience-based human relations training. But it is questionable whether the minority who would choose the alternate classroom approach might not be subjected to some social pressure. "What's wrong with you that you don't dare it?" Another approach was taken at the University of Puerto Rico where a course of this type is compulsory. Dr. Juan Rosselló, the instructor, defended this approach by giving the example of the necessity for medical students to go through some traumatic experiences in their training, such as anatomy.[10] For many students the initial anatomy demonstrations are a great shock. If they want to become physicians they have to be able to stand those shocks, and this is just as true in the human relations field as in physical medicine. This is a possible point of view, having as its basis the conviction that commitment to enter a profession involves certain risks a person must be willing to take.

Be this as it may, the techniques of sensitivity training have become important parts of much of professional training, and many teachers who are dissatisfied with the difficulties of teaching sociol-

[10] Personal interview.

ogy or psychology in an abstract way to a group of student nurses have found it convenient and more fascinating to teach through some technique of intensive group experience. Here are people qualified in their own occupation employing sensitivity training as an interesting technique. We can see that, in many cases, it might be just a subsidiary part of the teaching and, therefore, does not exert too much pressure on the students. If it does exert pressure, however, there may be some question as to whether a well-intentioned teacher, who has read a few books, should let students undergo a possibly traumatic experience.

In another context, professionals have felt that in many circumstances it might be advisable to teach people in a firsthand way how to deal with others and how other people might react to them. During periods of civil rights demonstrations and confrontation, many civil rights activists have had sensitivity training in workshops. It was felt that training new recruits to know what might happen to them if they engage in a demonstration of civil disobedience could be valuable. Experience at this type of clinic has shown that it may be good training when the participants really need it and want to have a somewhat safe introduction to the kind of violence they might encounter. As things get serious, however, this generalized technique is rejected in favor of training related specifically to the problem at hand.

An example was an attempt to give sensitivity training to prospective civil rights workers for the 1964 "Mississippi Summer." The program was designed to make the volunteers better able to face hostile encounters and to deal more efficiently within the framework of nonviolent action, as well as to make them more conscious of their own feelings. The participants rejected the proffered training, however, and even the trainers became doubtful about its relevance. Specific stronger concerns overrode general niceties of human relations training.[11]

This kind of training for professional activists is something between occupational training and training for general social situations. In this context, sensitivity training has been used as a method of understanding interracial and interethnic feelings. This is, in a sense, a return to the origins of sensitivity training in intergroup relations workshops. The original social concerns of these workshops had

[11] M. Lakin. "Human Relations Training and Interracial Social Action: Problems of Self and Client Definition" (with a commentary by Robert F. Allen), *Journal of Applied Behavioral Science*, 2, 1966, 139–148.

almost been forgotten in the subsequent development of the personal growth wing. Even in the present interracial and interethnic workshops the training is not done to teach people what to do but to enable them to understand better their own feelings and reactions to people of a different race or belief.

One good example of work of this kind is the C-group (confrontation group), part of the training workshops conducted by the Boston University Human Relations Center, under the direction of Kenneth Benne. C-groups are like regular T-groups with the exception that, during the actual interaction, the leader and sometimes the members throw people back on their self-identification—ethnic, sex, age, or whatever. Feedback occurs in this form: "You are reacting to whatever the other person is saying because he is white and you are black, or he is a man and you are a woman," and so on. This, then, would make persons hyperconscious of their identity, and in this way train them to interact better with members of a different group. For people engaged in intergroup work, this may be a way of making conscious their residual feelings of antagonism and prejudice, which many people think they have completely overcome. On a more positive side, it may also make them accept their own identity. Positive feelings toward one's identity might include a sharp differentiation from somebody else's identity, but this might be necessary for engaging in genuine intergroup work.[12]

While C-groups are apparently unique to Benne's work at the Boston University workshops, similar interracial encounters are now conducted in many circumstances. Again we find the curious attempt to concretize general social and interpersonal relationships, the rejection of the symbol in favor of the direct feeling. Two examples show how this might work.

In one of the sessions at the Boston University seminar, nonverbal exercises were conducted. The group sat in a large circle, and two members were supposed to go into the center of the circle and meet each other in any way they wished. The two members in this exercise were a white man and a black man who had shown some antagonism toward each other during the previous course of the workshop. Before it was definitely determined whether the exercise was starting, the white man fell off the chair, and apparently collapsed. The black man came over, tried to lift him up to see whether anything was really wrong with him, and then started to guide him

[12] Cf. I. Rubin. "The Reduction of Prejudice through Increased Self-Acceptance." Boston University Human Relations Research Reports and Technical Notes No. 83, 1966.

toward the middle of the circle. At this point the white participant gave his partner a swift kick, freed himself, and went on his own to the center. This inauspicious start, of course, eventually resulted in a fight. As he commented later on the episode, the black participant explained: "You see, that's the trouble with you whites in general. You act as if you needed us and as if we could get together; and then when we come more than halfway across, all you do is kick us."

A second example was told to me by a minister who is running an encounter center and is now more involved in the encounters than in his religion. He told me about a session he had been in where he got into a wrestling exercise with a black participant who had finally gotten him down on the floor. In describing this incident he concluded: "Being down there and having to watch for his possible aggression, I could understand more what a black man must feel than any study of class relations had taught me before."

These are examples of complete denial of the possibility of verbal communication, the use of symbols, and general understanding beyond the purely physical and direct sensory level. The mythology that anything nonverbal is true and only nonverbal effort can really get to the heart of the matter, whereas words falsify, is shown very strongly in these educational groups. People really believe that the physical contact and physical acting-out of these somewhat general and complicated social relationships help both in understanding the problems and in dealing with them.

There are many groups of this kind conducted now; for instance, marathon groups between whites and blacks often reach the point of expressing strong hostilities and recognizing many hostile feelings people might have. They have been conducted in California, especially, in potentially explosive situations, and may be good ways of training people who have to deal with racial problems, such as policemen or other public officials. On the other hand, one might question how release of emotions in some situations might produce later harmony. The experiences of aggressive attack by the other might remain more strong in a person's mind than anything done in the later course of the exercise.

The question at this point is really whether these encounters involving the release of strong emotion may add fuel to the fire or may be a technique to control potentially festering conflicts. A case in point is an interesting experiment Martin Lakin conducted in Israel.[13] He took, within Israel, Jewish and Arab participants into

[13] M. Lakin. *Arab and Jew in Israel*. Washington, D.C.: NTL Publications, 1970.

sensitivity training groups. In the nature of the case, the ethnic identification was paramount in everybody's mind. The main topics of
discussion were the ethnic conflicts within the country. In a sense,
the whole exercise failed, and the two sections never became one
group but remained two parties debating. The exercise showed that
the ethnic identification of the group was stronger than any immediate situation within the group could overcome. Or, to put it in another way, none of the participants could ever take the role of the
other ethnic group. On the positive side, the members learned something about the feelings of the other people, and again, as usually
happens in sensitivity training groups, everybody thought at the end
that it was a good idea. The trainer himself followed mainly the strict
Bethel technique, and did not hold with the more extreme California
point of view. Partly for this reason, he never used any strong emo-
tion-arousing techniques, no physical activity, combat or otherwise.
But he also avoided those techniques because of the delicate situation
of the country; and he was not particularly eager to add more conflicts to the conflict already existing. Whether this conservative technique is in a sense self-defeating, as it does not allow the strong emotion which might overcome the conflict, or whether the stronger
techniques in a critical situation are frivolous games of people who
do not know whether they could control the situation if it got out of
hand, must be judged in each case, and no general criteria are
available.

An even more ambitious enterprise was attempted by Leonard
Doob and a team of trainees from Yale and UCLA at the Hotel
Fermeda in South Tyrol (Italy).[14] The participants were six intellectuals each from Somalia, Kenya, and Ethiopia to aid in settling
the border conflict of Somalia with Ethiopia and that of Somalia
with Kenya. The two-week program included eight days of T-group
meetings supplemented by social get-togethers and a weekend break.
Two T-groups were conducted concurrently consisting of three participants from each of the countries. The last two days were devoted
to a general assembly trying to integrate the work of the two T-
groups and leading to a unifying conclusion.

Although some agreement was reached in the T-groups, the general assembly at the end was characterized as a failure. T-group
members either spoke against the solution reached in their groups,
returning to their national identification, or failed to speak up for
their groups, causing resentment between the erstwhile group mem-

[14] L. W. Doob, *Resolving Conflict in Africa*. New Haven: Yale University Press, 1970.

bers. The formal post-meeting evaluations showed the familiar pattern of general medium satisfaction with the experience, and little future effect. The report includes chapters written by the African participants, one from each country, and by the several American trainees and organizers. An interesting contrast emerges. The T-group participants, the Africans, speak frankly of the failure of the program culminating in the fiasco of the final session. The trainers discuss with satisfaction the process of the groups, e.g. the fact that T-groups could be run at all, and excuse and play down the final outcome. The reader is left wondering under what, if any, conditions the trainers would consider the exercise to be a waste of time.

Convictions about the importance of sensual understanding as contrasted with verbal understanding have brought some people into the movement to try to revamp the whole educational system and put stronger emphasis on sensual education and less on symbolic and verbal instruction. Their educational proposals for the future would include having people "really" understand their senses, having them work on vision, touch, and so on; using education much more for feeling than for understanding. The Esalen group is working seriously in this direction; some Esalen-trained teachers in San Francisco and faculty members from San Francisco State College are introducing sensory exercises into grade school. Some of them are quite interesting, such as making children understand the importance of the hand. They might do an exercise consisting of going around for a day or so without using their right hand or keeping their right hand taped up. The whole emphasis here is on understanding the body, its potentiality, and how to enhance sensations. Apparently, Esalen is going to produce a series of textbooks for children in elementary schools on how to do this kind of work. At present only a report of the whole study is available.[15] It would be interesting to see the outcome of this experiment. Some advocates already see education going principally in this direction. This is partly a reflection of the idea that what is wrong with society is the excessive reliance on symbols and on indirect communications, the end being strong technology. They may be confusing the excesses of a hyper-technological culture with the general principle of anti-intellectualism. Non-organized reliance on feeling may result in uncontrollable collective action, while the technical knowledge that has been able to maintain today's economy also maintains the standard of living which makes it possible for many people to spend days and weeks in

[15] G. Brown. *Human Teaching for Human Learning*. New York: Viking, 1971.

encounter group centers. Using the schools more and more for sensual experiences might be an extreme remedy for excesses.

One of the strictures made against standard educational practice is its stifling of creativity in favor of rote learning or, at best, skill training. The radically different emphasis of sensual training is often looked at as a way to reach the creative potential. Especially psychologists who have been influential in the sensitivity training movement have equated the kind of development in a human potential center with development of creativity. Thus, Maslow would define the self-actualizer as creative practically by definition, and Moustakas, a clinical psychologist swept up in the movement, defines a therapeutic encounter as leading to a creative experience.[16] The terms encounter, self-actualizing, and creativity seem to be almost interchangeably used.

Because of this point of view, the influence of sensitivity training on education has been expected to lead into training in creativity. It has had some attraction to artists; the lack of criticism which is a standard of sensitivity training groups helps members in proposing very novel ideas in art, science, or technology. The technique of "brainstorming," which was very popular for a while in industry, was very similar to T-groups. Members would, for a specified period, propose ideas without internal control or external criticism. Then the ideas would be listed, combined, and organized for possible novel solutions. Some companies have combined this kind of approach with T-groups: one chemical company used NTL advisers to organize teams of research and development and marketing people, make them function better together in a personal way, and then "brainstorm" new products. It happened that a new, best-selling pill resulted from this session, and therefore the approach still has high prestige there.[17] It is unlikely that this is what Maslow meant by "self-actualizing."

Within the educational field itself probably the most extensive work of this kind was the Ford-Esalen study conducted in several schools in California.[18] Descriptions of the classes show that some of the sensual techniques used in adult groups were used successfully. This is not surprising, as many of these exercises give the impression

[16] A. Maslow. "The Creative Attitude," in R. Mooney and T. Razik (eds.), *Explorations in Creativity*. New York: Harper, 1967, 47–54. C. Moustakas. *Creativity and Conformity*. Princeton, N.J.: Van Nostrand, 1967.

[17] Personal interview. The respondent requested that neither the company nor the product be identified.

[18] Brown. *Op. Cit.*

of children's games. The effect on the pupils is shown in more descriptive passages, showing some of the classroom work and evaluation by the teachers. The impression one gets from these passages is of intense commitment of the staff of the study to their work with consequent close supervision and encouragement of the teachers which was transmitted to the attitude of the students. Whether any specific techniques led to creativity more than the team spirit of the study group itself is questionable.

In his report on the study, George Brown includes a chapter, "Proceed with Caution." In it he warns that half-trained leaders or purely expressive techniques may do more harm than good. In fact, these warnings show one of the difficulties of training for creativity in general. Creativity has been shown to consist of several stages, one being the creation of a novel product and another its acceptance by social consent. The interaction in sensitivity training disregards old standards frequently to lead to new ways of thinking and acting and induces people to act in a new pattern.[19] This novelty may be exciting to immediate groups, but—like so much in this field—may be inconsequential soon afterward. In the criticism of current education, any new technique may be effective in breaking the mold, but the application of the technique for genuine creativity remains to be proved.

The clearest avenue of approach has been art, and many art forms, especially the theater, have evolved useful ways of getting at the emotions of the audience. Theater groups have been using group techniques both for the training of the company and for a new kind of involvement with the audience. Some of these approaches, especially in training actors (such as the Stanislavski technique), predated work in sensitivity training and influenced the people who started it. Moreno, too, started by training actors. One can see again a general cultural phenomenon which has pervaded the culture and was also accepted in sensitivity training. The dramatic emphasis, moreover, is implicit in much of the work in sensitivity training, and many of the published transcripts of encounter groups are edited to achieve a dramatic form. In addition, professional dramatists use these techniques to some advantage, and theaters as diverse as Grotowski's Poor Theater in Poland and the Performance Group in New York use encounter methods.[20] Here, sensitivity training may

[19] M. Stein. "Creativity and Culture," in R. Mooney and T. Razik (eds.), *Explorations in Creativity*. New York: Harper, 1967, 109–119.

[20] Cf. T. Grotowski. *Toward a Poor Theater*. New York: Simon and Schuster, 1969.

have found its new home. In general encounter groups, one always suspects that people play at sincerity. It is doubtful whether one can be sincere merely by trying to be so, or whether sincerity is something that comes along as a by-product of ulterior aims. In the theater groups, we have a carefully rehearsed performance, and the good groups are strictly trained to look spontaneous. Some feedback principles are operative, though; the play may have different developments depending on the reactions of the audience. This kind of drama may best exemplify the balance between control and spontaneity which occurs in real sensitivity training. In the same way as the reality behind apparent spontaneity is a carefully rehearsed piece of theater, the trainer in sensitivity training instructs his group in a performance. Training techniques in sensitivity training are, as in modern theater, attempts to use spontaneous techniques to lead to a predetermined conclusion. Slater's interpretation of his Harvard class in mythological terms is an idealized way of explaining the teaching process in the form of mythological drama. As the mythology becomes stronger, this same educational technique can be put into a touching theatrical performance.

Chapter 13

The Elusive Search

"It's too bad you're not a 'self-actualizing' person, Charlie Brown. Self-actualizing persons are free from fears and inhibitions. They accept themselves and they accept others. . . . They have self-esteem and confidence."

"Can I become a self-actualizing person?"

"No way! Five cents, please."[1]

Let us recapitulate how far we have come. We have considered sensitivity training as a social movement that, in contrast to older social movements, has taken its authority in the name of science. In earlier sections we have described it by discussing its place as a social movement in the society, the needs in society that it makes explicit and tries to meet, and the mythology in society it expresses. This way of looking at sensitivity training is the way one would look at social movements of different types. Sensitivity training can also be looked at as a scientific procedure, however. In the last few chapters we have described several specific applications in which it has been used and in which it has tried to be effective. In this chapter, we can summarize what kinds of effects it has been shown to have, whether it can be judged by the scientific procedure, and which different categories of description should be used.

If we look at sensitivity training just as a social phenomenon,

---

[1] C. Schulz. "Peanuts," fall, 1969. Tm. Reg. U.S. Pat. Off. © 1969 by United Features Syndicate, Inc.

a symptom of social stress which erupts in society from time to time, then we could treat it simply as a social fact without dealing with evaluation procedures. In its application to the various fields we have discussed, however, proponents of sensitivity training act as professionals relying on scientific procedures. They profess a profound belief that the procedures have beneficial results for the participants or for the organizations in which they are active. This faith can be found in every field of application studied, in psychotherapy, in personnel management, and in training methods, and proponents testify to the strong experience of finding a new way, of opening new vistas, or whatever terms they want to use. The way in which the effect is described varies from situation to situation. In the more individual impact of the regular encounter group, in recreational experiences, and even in psychotherapy, the subjective experience is paramount. The individual reaction can be described in such vague terms as a new way of looking at things, personal regeneration, openness, or general terms that have been used since ancient times for similar experiences. On the other hand, in management procedures of business and government and in other training techniques, an objectively noticeable effect is received. Following the training, one has the right to expect the better adjustment of trainees to the new conditions of the job, easier adaptation to change conditions (as in the Peace Corps), or better methods to keep an organization running smoothly. In these cases, evaluation procedures have shown some kinds of effect, but the effects are very specialized and usually not as broad as the whole procedure would have warranted. In our interviews with clients of sensitivity training in industry, we have found general expressions of approval of the technique itself, usually accompanied by some implied apologies that it just did not fit this particular organization.

In effect, if one considers the length of time it takes to undergo sensitivity training, the amount of interaction during this time, the extent of efforts on the part of many people, the strong emotions they express, the deep experiences they sometimes report, it is surprising how little long-range effect this procedure has. One might assume that any treatment of this length or intensity, especially that undergone by self-selected, susceptible persons, would have some lasting effect. The tortuous way in which most program evaluations have to go about proving any lasting effects shows by itself how little these deep experiences affect a person's future actions.

The contrast between what observer, participant, and trainer feel should have happened and what really happened in the long run is remarkable and surprising. Similar discrepancies have been observed in other experiments attempting change in behavior, however. Some of the programs studied used methods similar to sensitivity training, and their lesson may be instructive. Studies have been done comparing the effect of group meetings with mass communications, for instance, in the introduction of birth control methods.[2] The group meetings used a variety of techniques, some close to sensitivity training: discussions, commitment, small-group action and interaction, and visual aids. Observers in these groups always felt that the groups would be extremely effective. The participants went away from the groups convinced that they would start using contraceptive measures.

Almost as a control, some mass media were used in other areas, usually the distribution of pamphlets stressing the points made in the group meetings. It always turned out that actual beginning and continued use of contraceptive measures were more strongly induced by the distribution of a few pamphlets than by the strong experience of the group meeting. Following up these surprising results, it was seen that the strong experience of the group meeting was partially self-defeating. People took the whole experience as a performance and had difficulty seeing its relevance to their real lives. There was an implicit assumption that what is taught with great impact in a meeting, and what is really meaningful in a home situation, are very different. A pamphlet, on the other hand, stays in the home, can be reread, and is low key enough to seem sensible in later use. In this case, and in some similar ones, it can be seen in retrospect that the immediate impression and strong experience were not necessarily the best way of inducing any change, beneficial or not.

To assess the over-all effort of evaluation of sensitivity training and the conclusions to be reached, we did a survey of the evaluation attempts that have been made. A search of studies from 1945 to 1970 yielded 149 items. They were collected from comprehensive critiques of research by Stock, Campbell and Dunnette, and House,[3] and

---

[2] R. Hill, J. Stycos, and K. Back. *The Family and Population Control.* Chapel Hill: University of North Carolina Press, 1959.

[3] R. House. "T-Group Education and Leadership Effectiveness: A Review of the Empiric Literature and a Critical Evaluation," *Personnel Psychology*, 20, No. 1, 1967, 1–32. J. Campbell and M. Dunnette. "Effectiveness of T-Group Experiences in Managerial Training and Development," *Psychological Bulletin*, 70, No. 2, 1968, 73–104. D. Stock. "A Survey of Research on T-Groups," in L. Bradford, J. Gibb and K. Benne (eds.), *T-Group Theory and Laboratory Method.* New York: Wiley, 1964.

supplemented by the *Journal of Applied Behavioral Science* and *Psychological Abstracts*, with additions from recent individual studies.[4]

The data on these studies are necessarily fragmentary. Some reports are available only in manuscript, some are unpublished dissertations. The original report could be examined in only two-thirds of the cases (99). The rest were summarized either in a review article or in a dissertation abstract. In addition, even if the article was available, the nature of the data collected and of the results were not always given in sufficient detail to extract needed information. Thus, complete data on methods and outcomes are not available for all studies.

In each case, the data are generally based on few training groups. More than half of the available studies included four or fewer groups, and more than one-third used only one or two groups. Only about one-third included any control group. These fractions are based, however, on only 93 of the studies, because data on the number of groups used in each study were frequently omitted. While three-quarters of the studies reported measures before and after the sessions, only one-quarter used any follow-up study. Besides the obvious difficulty of follow-up work, this discrepancy shows the predominant concentration of interest on the events occurring in the sensitivity training groups, as compared to enduring change.

The kinds of data collected show the same trend. The most popular are self-reports, questionnaires, and tests; then follows ratings by others, such as trainers or co-members, and then objective data on behavior in the group. The two kinds of measures that could show actual change, ratings by outsiders and measures of performance outside the group, are the least frequent in the studies—the latter being used in only 16 of the studies.

There has been a change in emphasis during the time period covered. The quantity of studies increases gradually from 6 in the 1945–50 period to 32 in 1961–65. In the five years following, the number of studies more than doubled, to 74. The later years saw a progressive use of control groups, number of groups in a study, and use of follow-up data. The greatest shift has occurred in the measures employed. Before 1960, 23 of 39 studies relied on rating measures during the group sessions, while after 1960, only 37 of 106 studies used them. By contrast, follow-up measures have been used almost entirely in the last decade, although they still constitute only about one-quarter of the total number in this period. They were

[4] The studies are listed in Appendix II.

hardly used at all before. There is little interest, however, in comparing process observation with objective outcome measures; only 14 studies have used this combination, almost all of them quite recent ones.

The techniques used limit the possibility of finding measurable changes. We can look, however, at the pattern of results that emerges from the studies. Depending on whether or not there was a control group, the investigator will determine changes within the group before and after sensitivity training or changes in sensitivity training groups compared to a control group. Immediately after the training, 18 studies showed definite improvement, while 14 studies gave no positive results. Where there were control groups, the evidence is similar: 19 studies showed positive results and 14 showed negative or mixed results. Of the remainder, 59 studies had no after-training measures, concentrating only on process, and 24 had no before-training measures to assess the change. When follow-up is considered, of course, the number of relevant studies became smaller; of those without control groups, 12 studies showed sustained or incipient improvement during the follow-up, and 7 showed either reverses or continued nonimprovement. The equivalent numbers among studies with control groups is 5 with positive results and 6 without.

As mentioned earlier, only 14 studies used process observation and follow-up, a combination of methods that would make it possible to relate any effects found to events during the training sessions. These studies, too, divide about evenly between successful and non-successful studies in terms of finding lasting changes.

Research and evaluation studies tend to show that something happens as a consequence of sensitivity training, but that the effect is not reproducible and that intended benefits are as likely as not to result. The general tendency of publication procedures as well as the natural inclination of the researcher would be to stress positive results and to neglect no-difference findings. The mixed evidence, therefore, probably reflects an even bleaker reality. Thus it is not surprising that with so little positive evidence collected, there has been hardly any effort to see how any particular effect occurred. Lack of research of this kind has prevented sensitivity training from having influence on the mainstream of social psychology and group dynamics, but it has not impeded its growth in popularity.

There seems to be a built-in resistance against accepting negative evidence. After a deep experience of this kind, one wants to believe that some change occurred. Change agencies for ages past have had little effect. The Sunday Christian who goes to church once a week and acts against the precepts of the church the rest of the time is almost proverbial. Consequently, one of the defenses of sensitivity training is that the competing techniques, such as psychotherapy, have also not been shown to be very effective when evaluated, or that there is too little evaluation research to affect ongoing experimental procedures. Evidence would suggest that there is a need to believe in the efficacy of strong experience for the general good and for behavioral changes that are beneficial. Perhaps people are afraid of admitting the need for the experiences themselves, which may be ridiculed or else feared as addiction. The best parallel for the belief in the efficacy of sensitivity training groups may well be the ineradicable belief in the effectiveness of alcohol for snake bites. It gives a good feeling, and hence people want to believe in its effectiveness.

The various leaders in sensitivity training react to this curious situation in different ways. Probably the frankest explanation and justification for it comes from Richard Farson who has been active in the encounter movement in industry and for a while was director of the Western Behavioral Sciences Institute.

> This whole notion of sensitivity training, the whole concept of training, period, which has been with this thing from the start, has unfortunately been hooked up with change. I think that's been a big bugaboo. It does not change people. The kind of work that you're exploring now, sensitivity training, does not bring about changes in behavior. The overwhelming research finding in this area—and there have now been twenty or so years of research on this problem (and I'm not talking about just sensitivity training, but I'm talking about *all* of the experiential modes of dealing with people; that would include, for example, deep psychoanalysis and other things like that)—there is one overwhelming finding, and that is that you can show monumental changes *subjectively,* that is, in terms of what people report about themselves. It's not uncommon to have a person say that experience, even if it was a weekend at Esalen or whatever it was, was so important to me. It changed my life in ways that you can't imagine. I will never be the same. I turned a corner. It was the best thing that ever happened. That is not an uncommon statement. Fact is, you get positive statements of that sort from roughly 80 to 90 percent of all the people who go through these experiences.
>
> If this whole field had developed not out of education and therapy but out of, say, the theater, out of drama, which it might have, could have, then we would be valuing the experience for what it does while it's going on, not what it does after it's over, and we would treat it as a marvelous, exciting human experience, an aes-

thetic experience, which is what it is. It's a beautiful moving experience that qualifies with any of them. And then we would ease off on the whole idea that it's somehow supposed to fix you, change you, or improve you, or everything like that. I mean it doesn't do that any more than the other things, symphony concerts, or sexual intercourse, or looking at a sunset or reading a book, whatever it is. No matter what the aesthetic experience is, they only work while they are going on, and I feel it's unfortunate that we haven't seen that that is not something *negative* about the group, it's something very positive about it. The things we value most in our world are those experiences. The things we value least are the things that are designed to change you, like training, for example. Who cares about training? Advertising. Who cares about advertising? Those are the things that we *don't* care about in our society. Higher education we *do* care about. That's not supposed to change anybody. No *specific* changes are supposed to result from higher education. Romance is not supposed to change you. It's too important to change people.[5]

This frank statement accepts the situation and tries to justify it. Unusually enough, some extreme groups in the sensitivity training field, the proponents of the human potential movement, are also pushing to have the hardest possible data collected within a scientific framework; for example, there have been recent attempts at Esalen to establish a research program that uses physiological measures, electroencephalography, and muscle potential to establish scientific truths about the impact of encounter training.[6] It may be a sign of the times that those same people who are frankly anti-intellectual in their appeal to the general public, and whose success with sensitivity training groups was independent of any proved effects, are also trying so desperately to adopt the language of the prestigious physical and biological sciences.

Between these two extremes of accepting experience as experience and of trying to find backing in the prestigious sciences, other practitioners have found different compromises. The early high hopes of finding techniques within social science for a rational method of conducting change have mainly vanished or at least been toned down. Hardly any of the sensitivity training centers have a research component built-in, as had been the case at the beginning of the movement. In some group sessions, mainly of the variety of the personal growth centers, evaluative attitudes are taken to be an ag-

[5] R. Farson. Personal interview.

[6] J. Silverman. "When Schizophrenia Helps," *Psychology Today*, 4, September, 1970, 63–65. He is planning a book entitled *The Value of Psychotic Experience*.

gression against the principle of the center itself. Even social psychologists who would not go that far make a great distinction between their experiences with encounter at the centers and the rational approach which they might use later or in different parts of their work. Within a great part of the movement today research and measurement are treated as fiddlefaddle.

On the other hand, the researchers persist. Many studies are being done to show the effect of sensitivity training sessions on questionnaire responses or on behavior. Many of those studies show some effect, at least as far as behavior within the group is concerned, or answers to personality questionnaires. Measures of this kind show only that people have learned how to behave in the situation and know what the ideal behavior and questionnaire responses are. One of the striking phenomena apparent in the research literature over the years is the appearance of new researchers who do one or two studies and then stop. This seems to be an indication of the overwhelming belief that there should be something there. Everybody tries, over and over, to look for the same effects, getting partial confirmation at best and becoming satiated with the rigors of the evaluation procedure. The former researcher becomes either a convinced sensitivity trainer, forgetting the satisfactions of research and the notions of proof of effectiveness, or he goes into a different field of research and gives up sensitivity training entirely.

Besides these evaluation studies, persistent attempts are made to tie in sensitivity training with other fields of social science. As we have seen before, originally social psychology and sensitivity training were linked through the field of group dynamics. Today, group dynamics can be considered as having divided itself into two different fields, one the laboratory experimental social psychology, and the other the development that became sensitivity training. Today, there is very little connection between the two, although some people are able to bridge both fields.

Perhaps from a research point of view the question of the effect of sensitivity training is too general and asked in the wrong way. The research of Lieberman, Yalom, and Miles may point the way to the solution;[7] it is probably the best available investigation in this field. Students were randomly placed in groups using different training techniques with two groups for each technique. The over-all effect of

[7] M. Lieberman, I. Yalom, and M. Miles. "The Group Experience Project: A Comparison of Ten Encounter Technologies," in L. Blank, G. Gottsegen and M. Gottsegen (eds.), *Encounter: Confrontations in Self and Interpersonal Awareness.* New York: Macmillan, 1971.

sensitivity training compared with control groups was not significant. Nevertheless, certain leaders were able to effect quite striking results which could be validated in the later testimony of back-home associates. What was found was that the leader and his personality were more significant than the particular brand of sensitivity training used.

Extrapolating from these results, we may see that there are certain actions by certain people which are able to produce changes in members of the group. This is true not only of sensitivity training per se, but is true in the general framework of interaction with different kinds of people, some of whom are good healers and some of whom are not. This hails back again to Jerome Frank's theory of persuasion and healing.[8] In fact, the changes are produced by the healer, independently of the ideological framework in which he claims to be working. The ideological framework is important to justify to the client what influence he is willing to accept, however. To say that certain gestures and certain actions of a skilled person might produce beneficial effects, independent of the system that the practitioner may profess, is not saying that either the healer or the patient is deceiving himself. In the society in which we live, given our culture and our cultural needs, a technique, and even more, an ideology such as sensitivity training is necessary to attract people, to keep them as participants, to make them accept leaders' influence. "Evaluation" and "research" may be the useful terms for participants to express and understand their experiences.

[8] J. Frank. *Persuasion and Healing*. Baltimore, Md.: Johns Hopkins, 1961.

Part V

IRONIC DILEMMA

Chapter 14

Beyond Science

"The sleep of reason brings forth monsters."[1]

In this section we will summarize the views of sensitivity training that derive from the tension between its internal and its external aspects. Its internal aspect is a technique and belief system with a particular purpose, some theoretical background, and a proved method. Externally, it developed because it corresponded with some needs of society, a symptom of a deficiency in society, as it were. We can, therefore, look at sensitivity training as an indication of what society needs, what people need and want, and what the present situation is unable to give them.

Within the movement, basic conflicts have arisen between its different functions. The more popular sensitivity training has become, the more necessary it has been to endure or try to deny these disputes. The dilemmas have led to some basic ironies which are the hallmarks of the movement in its present stage. Probably the greatest irony is the relation of sensitivity training to science. Sensitivity training was born in a scientific setting; it was originally developed as an application of the newly found insight of social scientists into human and interpersonal problems. It is still advertised as an application of behavioral science to social problems, and it looks to science for validation of its claims. On the other hand, its basic kernel is the generation of a strong emotional experience, the kind of experience sought in previous times through the discipline of mysticism, and

[1] F. S. Goya. Title inscribed on the etching of one of his "Caprichos."

constitutes exactly that aspect of life which has tried to free men from the bonds of rationality.

In the long run, this inner contradiction has become more and more noticeable. Sensitivity training has ranged farther and farther away from traditional scientific work. It is treated at best as the outer fringe of group dynamics in discussions of social psychology, and research efforts and theoretical input by people in the movement have decreased almost continually since its inception. By contrast, some adherents of the movement still claim allegiance to social science. Many of them are professionals in the field. Requirements for some sensitivity practitioners include academic training, for example, becoming fellows of NTL, and trainers continue their efforts to legitimize the enterprise through the traditional channels. The relevant professions are becoming more involved in establishing social control. The basic irony lies in the discrepancy between ends and means. Sensitivity training basically aims at the regeneration of man through a deep, almost spiritual, experience, the kind of effort that has traditionally been part of the field of religion. It uses, however, the methods, the language, and some of the ritual of scientific work. One could almost say that, here, science is used to overcome the scientific view of man.

Sensitivity training can be related to the problems of social science and may be seen as a reaction to some of its developments. The central feature of sensitivity training, the strong experience in group interaction, is a very real event, and the conditions that lead to it are central to the concerns of social psychology. During a great part of their history, however, social psychologists have been looking at emotional events, describing them, and talking about their importance, and then gradually giving up the topic in favor of exact language describing other topics. Thus, group processes have been studied for a long time and discussed by many scholars with interesting ideas. Nevertheless, further work following their pioneering efforts has led them to exact but impersonal laboratory experiments or extremely abstract mathematical models. The Lewinian school, from which at least the Bethel experience started, has gone this course. Although Lewin was extremely concerned with human interaction and social problems and the study of real groups, the basic principles he developed have succumbed more and more to detailed analysis. Lewin's successors in group dynamics have gone from natural groups, then from groups of any kind, to work with individuals. The large laboratories supposed to contain whole groups for observation were gradually subdivided into cubicles where one person could be measured in interaction with a tape recorder or a message that presumably came from another person.

It may be argued, and most practitioners in the field of group dynamics would grant it willingly, that this gradual shift in emphasis has led to increased methodological and theoretical precision, the development of several logical, intricate, but consistent miniature theories, and an amount of cumulative research rare in social science. By the same token, however, many topics that could not be treated in this way, that might depend on the actual functioning of groups or somewhat subtle emotional interchanges, have been lost and neglected. Many practitioners in the field, eager young students, and laymen concerned with problems of everyday living have felt a great loss when they compared what they thought was being done in group dynamics with what was actually being done. Recurrently, in the history of the field, less exact but more encompassing new approaches have arisen, even within academic social psychology, to treat such topics as ethnomethodology and associated techniques. However, sensitivity training has also been ready to receive scientists disappointed in rapid progress by traditional methods. Sensitivity training has been sanctioned by its ancestry in group dynamics as a legitimate field for treating group interaction. It has kept up its reputation by advertising itself as able to treat both practically and experimentally the concerns of many in dealing with their personal problems, with the functioning of groups, and especially with the emotional aspects of man and society. It has been ready to receive them in its centers and workshops and to give them the support and experience they needed.

For many people who have come to the sensitivity training centers in search of a rational understanding of group processes, the experience has been a revelation. Many stay for the experience itself, for the enjoyment of working in the field, and forget the original concern with hard science that brought them there. It has become more and more true with sensitivity training that one is either in it or out of it, and that attraction to it has been in the nature of a conversion experience. Within the field of social science, a person who has followed this school and has become a member of the in-group will neglect any doubts or investigations that may undermine the experience. The social support given to sensitivity training, the proliferation of the centers, the attention given to them in the press and other mass media, the attempts of all kinds of organizations to hire consultants and to institute something like sensitivity training in their fields, has made it easy for people to become full members of the movement and to reject any inside analysis. The field given up by experimental group dynamics has been pre-empted with a vengeance.

This development may explain the paradox of much of sensitivity training, namely, that it is an anti-intellectual movement in the name of science. Its strengths, as well as its weaknesses, derive from this fact. At its best it is an attempt to integrate two aspects of man's existence that are usually kept separate—the analytical, intellectual function and global feelings, emotional attempts to understand man's place in the world. A neat balance between the two may lead to fruitful cross-fertilization. At its worst, however, it may tamper with the procedure of science, introduce questionable emotional practices, and disguise easy excitement as experimental research or proved professional practice. Between these extremes, the system frequently becomes exasperating. Believing the language of the movement, one might look for research, proof, and the acceptability of disproof. In fact, the followers of the movement are quite immune to rational argument or persuasion. The experience they are seeking exists, and the believers are happy in their closed system which shows them that they alone have true insights and emotional beliefs. Given the cultural context in which they are working, however, the high prestige of science, and the necessity of professional control, sensitivity training in general does not want to sell itself as purely a new awakening. Thus it wants not only to become a cult, a new religion of the age of Aquarius, but also to stay on good terms with the scientific establishment. From this dual effort arise certain tensions and new attempts which may show best the place of sensitivity training within social science.

Seen in this light, the history of sensitivity training is a struggle to get beyond science. The motivations of many of those who founded the movement and who nurtured its early steps were purely scientific. Sensitivity training was designed to help in understanding group processes and to use the new field of group dynamics as a teaching aid in helping people work better within groups. However, the participants as well as some of the staff members were caught up in an intense emotional experience, the strength of which really provided the nucleus of the workshops. The whole field of group dynamics and of social psychology was quickly recognized as having two aspects, the scientific, experimental, theoretical aspect, and the human relations, group workshop aspect. Although some people were able to work in both areas, everyone knew quite clearly which field was which, and what the two different fields meant. Thus, when group dynamics was recognized as a field in social psychology, the Bethel type of approach was usually not mentioned. Some people who talked about workshops and wrote about them used some of the empirical findings of social psychology as part of their ideas, but the rest argued mainly on the testimonial of the people who had attended and the strong experience provoked. At first the laboratories were used as sources for research. The most successful studies had little connection with the idea of the workshop itself, but used it simply as a place with easy access to subjects where experiments could be conducted in a semi-realistic situation.

Much of the subsequent history of sensitivity training can be viewed as a struggle on the part of the people from a strong pragmatic, science-oriented background to hold off the more experiential kind of convert. Of course, they had to realize that the real popularity of the movement came from the experiential features, and even the scientists themselves did not work according to the canons of science. The techniques developed more and more into advanced laboratories using nonverbal communication systems which evoked strong feelings, and left the practical application to later life undiscussed. The attraction of the laboratory as a special experience became stronger and stronger, and the new branches of sensitivity training stressed those more and more, until sensitivity training became allied with anti-rational movements.

For many of the people who are searching, it is important that the scientific language persist. While some of the extreme groups value the experience for its own sake, most of the participants are attracted by the fact that they can get the experience and still keep a semblance of scientific language. Thus the movement has been trying to combine the cult of pure experience with the language of hard scientific fact.

This ambiguity or ambivalence can turn up in many places, and we have seen it especially in the acceptance of nonlogical thinking, the tendency toward experiential learning, and in the attitude toward research. When we map the fields in society closely connected with the intensive group experience (the cells $A'-H'$ of the chart in Chapter 8), we find that they also comprise a list of those fields in which science has failed or constitutes a threat. On the one hand, science has undermined the rational basis of mysticism and ritual. Here the sensitivity training movement can give another foundation for the mystical experience and ritualistic expression man seems to need. In the other expressive fields, such as art, science and the scientific approach have had little to contribute. The remaining fields were those in which human change was an important feature, and here science has been both a failure and a threat. In fact, the effect of scientific method in purposefully changing human beings has been relatively small in most areas. Education and training in professional fields or organizations have been unsuccessful in many ways, and more immediate remedial efforts, such as psychotherapy, have also left much to be desired. People faced with these problems have adopted new methods on the emotional or "gut" level, and reject professional training and all the accoutrements of science. We need only remember a movement such as Synanon (see Chapter 10).

Thus we can summarize the whole application of sensitivity training as either giving underpinnings to expressive activities that had lost their old foundations in mythology or religious belief, or as finding some way to produce change. In both areas, of course, it is impossible to overlook the relevance of the developments of the last few hundred years and simply to deny the existence of science. Although some of the facets of the movement make interesting attempts to rescue the old truths, such as magic, astrology, or witchcraft, this is not the general approach. The usual method is to accept the experience of scientific explanation, which has been the experience of a race or society, but to go beyond it and combine it with older types of exercises and activities, or to invent new ones in old guises. In this way we can understand the different uses of gymnastics and physical exercises in encounter centers. The conscious use of the body for spiritual exercises has been the stock in trade of most mystical movements; on the other hand, the importance of the body has pervaded psychotherapy from Charcot and Freud, and especially in Reich and Lowen (cf. Chapter 6). Thus, encounter centers are close both to Chinese, Indian, and Persian kinds of rhythmic activities and to modern kinds of physiotherapy, physical exercises, and gymnastics.

The relation between mind and body, which has been fundamental for the development of modern science, may also be the best example of what can be called the post-scientific attitude within the encounter movement. The contrast between mind and body, and the separation of the two, is probably one of the characteristics of Western culture. In part the distinction is implied in Christianity; Descartes used this fact and made the distinction absolute in order to gain freedom for physical science from theological restrictions. One of the effects of this separation has been the development of physical and biological sciences, separate from psychology, psychoanalysis, and the social sciences, keeping the mental and physical aspects as separate and closed systems. It was only after both kinds of science developed that attempts were made to show a relationship between the two and to integrate the two systems. In the late nineteenth and early twentieth centuries, the theories of emotion by James, Lange, and Cannon, Pavlov's conditioning theories, and Freud's theory of symptom formation showed the relationship between the two. The same period saw a frank acknowledgement of the importance of the body and of bodily needs. The original split between mind and body was made with the assumption that the mind was superior and the body was something weak, bad, which one should be ashamed of. Further development in psychosomatic medicine has stressed the profound interaction between mind and body, the importance of bodily well-being for mental adjustment, and the influence of psychic disturbances on physical expression.

The sensitivity training movement has been influenced by several strands of this development. It accepts the importance of the body, and expends much effort in physical exercises. These exercises are there to develop bodily skills, to get a greater variety of new sensations, and also to use physical conditions to attain certain mental states. On the other hand, partly through the influence of Oriental philosophy and religion, encounter centers also use mental control and techniques such as meditation and, perhaps, trancelike states. The movement seems to have had two influences in its consideration of mind-body relationships: the medical, psychosomatic influence which gives an almost physiological definition for mental changes and uses all kinds of techniques to produce those, and the Oriental one with all its attempts to direct training to achieve new and supposedly superior mental states.

Perhaps the common thread underlying and uniting these different points of view is the rejection of the intellectual aspect of life or, in somatic language, the influence of the cortex. All the attempts to produce a changed state of mind, such as physical exercises, are directed toward the appreciation of the body before the central nervous system developed, relaxing the brain by relying on the importance of other centers of man's physical activity. One of the books put out by Esalen is even called *Sensory Awareness below Your Mind*,[2] and this could be an applicable slogan for much of the activity of this kind within sensitivity training. It is a concerted effort to turn away from the emphasis on intellect, on tool-making abilities of the

[2] B. Gunther. *Sensory Awareness below Your Mind.* New York: Collier, 1968.

human animal, on classification, in short, on mediation of any experience through reflection, and to push the participants toward a direct experience that is not thought about and not analyzed.

Thus the current problem of the relation of sensitivity training to society and to science has developed. On the one hand, sensitivity training is advertised as the movement that rids man of his over-reliance on his overdeveloped brain, especially the cortex, which reverses history, especially the Western history of dominance over nature, and which returns man to his lost garden of innocence. On the other side, sensitivity training is sold to diverse clients as a problem-solving technique, and as a new way of working on the traditional problems of behavioral science. The more the movement expands and becomes part of the popular culture, the more both aspects arouse public attention and concern.

The different factions within sensitivity training have looked for ways to maintain, or regain, scientific respectability. In the activities at NTL and Bethel and their associated laboratories, a continuous attempt has been made to keep in contact with academic science. Faculty delegates are recruited from university or similar professional settings. The failure of concrete evaluation attempts has been especially crucial here. A reaction has been to proclaim that people trained in these laboratories will become special people, members of an invisible, or perhaps visible, fraternity who have experienced something that may or may not be appropriate in their own work or profession. Connected with this are the attempts to introduce sensitivity training as part of the curriculum in some schools or in professional training. This may be an example of the familiar phenomenon of converts proselytizing to maintain the social reality of their own experience. We have seen (in Chapter 12) the different forms this may take, such as a general reform in instruction which fits a lack that the present malaise of academic life has created.

Attempts to teach some of the concepts of human interaction, especially in courses similar to sensitivity training, combine the sometimes dry textbook psychology with immediate experience. This balance is difficult to maintain, and frequently such teaching leads to excitement for excitement's sake and attracts people who are looking either for therapy or a strong emotional experience. The age of most of the students and the general setting would guarantee in any case the occurrence of some rapid change, and the students who experience this change are greatly impressed by the procedure. It is noticeable, however, that many of the main protagonists of this classroom approach have left sensitivity training and say they are no longer part of the movement, that what they are doing is *not* sensitivity training.

A good example of this trend is Richard Mann, who has taught experientially directed courses in group interaction at Harvard and Michigan.

> I don't have interest in training people how to give feedback or get feedback, or make a good group or be democratic, or be open and honest, or any other damn thing. I mean, that is not my goal. My goal is to go in there and let a group develop. You know, groups aren't all that different, and when I think I understand something, I will say, "Hey, I think I see something happening." Or when I feel something, I will say, "Hey, that is really getting me mad," but it is not, it seems to me, with some underlying purpose of training everybody in the new etiquette of how you say, in this kind of somber tone, "Yes, I have a little feedback to give you, and blah, blah, blah." I don't like it. I think it is Boy Scout moralism, and I think that's the sensitivity training tradition.[3]

Attitudes of this kind exemplify one aspect of the conflict between the emotional experience that is sensitivity training and the demands of hard science. Unwilling to give up the regular procedures in social science, protagonists reject their membership in the clique of sensitivity training and admit only that they use group methods, some more or less orthodox and some of their own devising. In the same way, some of the personnel management people at NTL have left the fold and use group methods in a different context. Among these people, the conflict and ambiguity of the whole field of human relations has led them through different schools of thought, and they may have learned something by having had the experience of having considered sensitivity training.

Perhaps it is the more extreme groups that are looking harder for new ways to adopt scientific respectability. The balance between faith and reason has been precarious wherever one has looked. It is instructive to see how this balance has been worked out in various instances. Recent developments at Esalen are an interesting case in point.

The adoption of the encounter movement by the mass media has in part overwhelmed the encounter centers as well as influenced their development. After all, at a time when restaurants advertise themselves as group encounters with food, going to an encounter session is hardly a novelty and even somewhat conventional. Pure

---

[3] Personal interview.

encounter groups have diminished, and the participants at Esalen meetings, as well as at the meetings Esalen holds in San Francisco, are demanding new kinds of programs. The response has been in several directions. One has occurred at Esalen itself, by creating a residential community and acceding in this way to the demand for a complete cultural isolation and riding with the so-called counter-culture. This regime includes work time for the paying customer, organic food, and similar cultural patterns. The second is the more pronounced drive toward occultism, mysticism, and the adoption of cult exercises from the extreme branches of religion around the world. The basic premise of Esalen has always been, at least in the eyes of the founders, an adaptation of Eastern modes of thought into Western science. Encounter groups used this implicitly within the framework of group dynamics and social science. The newer developments have been more explicit about this heritage but lean also on the work of experimental psychology, psychophysiology, and biological sciences. These developments include the new interest in all kinds of physical exercise, massage, osteopathy, and chiropractic, which have all found a home at Esalen.

Thus, interest in group experience per se has decreased at Esalen, and encounter groups are played down in favor of working with individuals. In this work there is a search for exact, scientific instrumentation, the kind of data that can be measured by electronic machines. Science here means neglect of the emotional experience once thought essential for the understanding of groups. However, these experiences still persist with their aura of mystical anti-intellectualism. Thus the attempt is made to obtain the regular data of experimental psychology with the procedures of growth centers and to measure changes within an individual after various forms of treatment. But at the same time, interpretation of these data is made almost intuitively, and the procedure is only used to validate the beliefs of the faithful.

A demonstration of the scientific value of sensitivity training was put on at Esalen for a group of visiting behavioral and biological scientists. A popular Esalen technique was demonstrated, a kind of chiropractic developed by Ida Rolfe ("structural integration," cf. Chapter 5) but evaluated only by photographs, without any measuring devices or any standardized conditions. The idea that tape measures or other simple devices could be used was rejected emphatically and almost emotionally. One reason given was lack of funds (apparently the cost of tape measures in comparison with that of Polaroid cameras); another was that measurement was impossible because change depended not on simple linear measures but on the ratio of several such measures. Even under these anti-scientific conditions, however, coordinated attempts are being made to attract reputable scientists whose cautious statements can then be easily generalized into wholesale endorsements. Here again, the development has been similar to the one in teaching human relations discussed above. Some interesting research areas, such as the physiological and psychological effects of meditation, have been taken out of the setting of the growth centers and into the laboratory by people who are not necessarily part of the movement. Psychologists and physiologists not necessarily connected or identified with the movement may find some of the ideas enriching.[4] Here also, an individual must choose at some point whether he wants to be a scientist or stay within the encounter movement. Some people are able to do both part-time, at least for a while.

One of the reasons for this complicated relationship between sensitivity training and organized scientific enterprise is a matter of economics. A great amount of funds is channeled these days from different sources for scientific endeavor. These funds are not obtainable in any other way. Records show that few funds have been used for support of sensitivity training and encounter centers.[5] The main contributions came rather early in the development of the movement. Thus, the Carnegie Corporation supported the National Training Laboratory in its early years; during the same years, NTL was able to obtain government funds, especially through the Office of Naval Research. Since this time little support from government or private foundations has been given. Records of the National Institutes of Health and the National Institute of Mental Health show hardly any support for sensitivity training or research in it as such. Only very recently has NIMH shown interest in the sensitivity training movement, encounter groups, and the new cultural phenomena that were analogous to the rise of the drug culture in the 1960's.

Private foundations have been equally cautious. The Carnegie Foundation followed up its initial grant to NTL by an internal small study evaluating the movement which resulted in a privately circulated research report; the researcher has since joined the encounter movement. Other support has come for specific programs of the Western Behavioral Sciences Institute from the Mary Reynolds Bab-

[4] Cf. C. Naranjo and R. Ornstein. *On the Psychology of Meditation*. New York: Viking, 1971.

[5] Data on funding were obtained from government listings and correspondence with relevant foundations.

cock Foundation for a study of a school system, and from government sources for research on family structure. In addition, some foundations interested in community work have supported sensitivity training as a specific technique in community organization. In general, however, the share of sensitivity training in the general financial support of science has been extremely small in comparison to that of other endeavors.

Thus the main support of sensitivity training has come from clients. The National Training Laboratory, through different contracts with industry and government such as the Peace Corps and State Department, has made NTL more a service than a scientific organization. This connection has also served as a conservative check on NTL's activities as they must avoid shocking the potential customer by becoming engaged in some far-out kind of work. The reaction to some financial difficulties in which NTL has recently found itself has been to separate different training functions and to spin off different organizations that can serve specific customers, such as communities or industry. In conformity with its tradition, Esalen has met the challenge of raising money by putting more effort into performances. Benefits in New York and Los Angeles are being mounted; in 1970, the first benefit Esalen held in New York City netted $100,000 for development funds. However, in 1971, the attendance dropped in a catastrophic fashion. In addition, publications, records, tapes, and movies bring income to the organizations and to some of the leaders. The financial picture, therefore, enforces the impression of the whole function of the sensitivity training movement. It is not being supported as a scientific endeavor but is filling a cultural need for people dissatisfied with the efforts of social scientists on their behalf.

Chapter 15

Playing with Fire

"You can't make an omelette without breaking eggs."[1]

A main tenet of sensitivity training has been the need to care for others, the use of group experiences to learn again the meaning of community, to take man out of the isolation into which technology has cast him. This humanistic concern has clashed with the fact that the essence of sensitivity training has been the manipulation of little-understood but intense emotional forces.

The experiences of sensitivity training are not new; they have been found in many circumstances in many societies. Essentially, the argument runs that in our science- and technology-dominated society, we have forgotten those experiences important to individual development and social solidarity. We may accept as evident that intensive group experiences have been part of the human society and the human experience far and wide. In whatever guise we have seen them, they have been tied into a wider system, whether religious, social, or in other ways specialized, and have thus been under a strict social control. It is likely that, until this present time, it has not been realized that these techniques could be executed just for the worth of the experience, instead of as part of an intricate system of beliefs. We have seen that the decline of these global systems, especially of religious inspiration, has made the sensitivity training movement possible and has even given it its function in modern times.

[1] M. Robespierre. Epigram quoted in B. Stevenson, *The Home Book of Quotations*. New York: Dodd, Mead, 1967, 532.

The group leader in sensitivity training has thus assumed the function of the healer, priest, or shaman in earlier societies. With these functions he also assumed certain responsibilities. Societies have in the past exerted strong controls over the individual who exercised this kind of influence. This was done through selection, training, and continuous supervision against abuse of this special power. The experiences aroused by the modern technique are as intense as the religious and healing experiences, and leave their mark on the participants. They can be aroused at will. What are the necessities for social control, and how can it be exercised? There are two important circumstances in the consideration of the possible effects of these experiences. The first is the peculiar nature of the group relationship within sensitivity training, and the second is the scientific rhetoric connected with the movement.

The sensitivity training or encounter group is dominated by the philosophy of the here and now. This is not only true of the content of the sessions; discussions and actions are made to relate to the present situation, and escape from it is frowned upon. It is also true of the relationships within the groups themselves and their meaning. Thus, characteristically, these groups are comprised of strangers who have come together for a session of a weekend or a few weeks, or a course taken for a few hours a week, who have never seen each other before, have not selected each other for coming together, and presumably will not see each other again. Even for groups of people in which some know each other, or who are selected from the same organization, the same principle holds in a certain way. Although in this case there is a past and a future in the relationship, this past and future is separate from the relationship itself and the condition of the group. The members will not view each other in these same circumstances again. We have discussed the difficulties this assumption may bring about (see Chapter 10).

The striking feature of all of sensitivity training is how people come to care for each other in these groups and how they seem to become important to each other for the short time the group lasts. This show of genuine affection (as well as aggression) is the mainstay of the experience; however, all this ends with the group. The same is true for the leader who has been able to manage the group and guide it through the difficulty of its work. Intensity without permanence is a characteristic of encounter groups. In the worst cases, we can say that the participants are a group of people using each other for their own purposes. The group is really a commercial relationship that counterfeits real interpersonal feelings. In the best

214

cases, it becomes a strong experience that will leave behind memories to be cherished. In any case, however, the implicit definition of care precludes future responsibilities.

As we mentioned earlier, limited intense relationships have been seen as an advantage of encounter groups by such advocates as Carl Rogers. He says that in the highly mobile, high-density society of the future, the ability to make short-range strong, effective relationships and to relinquish them easily, that is, to invest in the meaning of brief encounters, will be one of the preconditions of psychic survival, and that a society of this kind will have its special beauties and charms. The arguments that an immediate experience can be interesting and beautiful may be tenable. Nevertheless, one of the claims of promoters of this intense experience, which is part of a whole body of rationalization, has been that the experience leads to a beneficial change in the individual. Traditionally, the practitioner, the companion through the process of change, has assumed a special responsibility toward the person to guide him into this new status and to help him if there are any unforeseen consequences. In encounter groups, however, the responsibility ends with the final session. The here-and-now atmosphere does not carry any further.

Even the professional group leaders have a *laissez faire* attitude toward possible breakdowns and other detrimental effects. Jane Howard, in *Please Touch*, has noted the casual acceptance of many events, such as death or psychotic commitment, which are considered traumatic in most circumstances.[2] In a magazine account of the encounter group training of the Company of Young Canadians in which six members developed serious troubles and two were hospitalized, the psychiatrist in charge was quoted as saying, "There is always a danger in bringing people from a structured society into an unstructured society where there are no rules, no authority."[3] In the therapy method closest to encounter groups, Gestalt therapy, the same unconcern prevails. Perls states in his book, "Sir, if you want to go crazy, commit suicide, improve, get turned on, or get an experience that would change your life, that is up to you. You came here out of your own free will."[4]

This professional unconcern brings us to the second important aspect of the encounter group, namely, the use of scientific rhetoric

[2] J. Howard. *Please Touch*. McGraw-Hill, 1970.

[3] "Stress and Strength at Crystal Cliffs" (Toronto), *Globe Magazine*, Aug. 6, 1966, 3–12.

[4] F. Perls. *Gestalt Therapy Verbatim*. Lafayette, Calif.: Real People Press, 1969, 75.

to justify the action. Associations resembling encounter groups or consisting of intense group experiences have usually been part of the religious sector of society, and the ritual, myth, and surrounding social events give social support to the change that might be occurring. At present, scientists, particularly social scientists, have succeeded the priest as guides to personal change and, it might be said, to spiritual search. Scientific authority enforces its own rules and sanctions, and these guarantee society protection against abuse of special power and knowledge. People who are organizing encounter groups claim their competence mainly through their insight into the procedures that constitute the scientific method which they apply as the essence of their profession. The ethics of their practice come from scientific and professional codes.

Professional responsibility is a relation of trust between client and practitioner. The client must be able to believe that the practitioner is well qualified, that there is a body of knowledge the practitioner can draw on, that a definite service can be performed, that possible dangers are kept at a minimum, and that these dangers stand in sensible relation to the possible benefits. These are the requirements for any scientifically based profession. The professional encounter group organizer assumes this responsibility within the framework of behavioral science. Psychology, social psychology, sociology, and psychiatry provide the basis on which he can rest his procedure and activities. Encounter groups do more, however, or they at least aim to do more, than most rational professional relationships in modern life. The practitioners' use of intense emotional experiences, and exercises of a ritualistic nature, and their talk of treating alienation, existential despair, and the dislocation of contemporary living puts them also into the role of spiritual adviser. To the general problem of a professional's competence is added his responsibility as a "guru" to his following. He combines some of the charisma of the religious healer with the language of the scientist, profiting by his emotional impact as well as the prestige of science. Thus, he assumes both the responsibility of the competent professional and the moral compassion of shared emotion.

This double role of the sensitivity group leader results in an ambiguous position regarding criteria by which to judge his performance. Discussions by protagonists of sensitivity training typically start with a denunciation of the current intellectual, fragmented, technological, manipulating society, and a promise of a new way of life based on feeling, bodily enjoyment, and unity with

216

nature. This exalted level is mainly inspirational and exudes a somewhat religious atmosphere. Questions about evidence or misstatement of fact are clearly inappropriate here. After this tone is set, the group leader can then take the professional route, quoting some results of training, testimonials of satisfied customers, and description of the training procedures. If his defense of sensitivity training as a procedure is challenged on the basis of the danger of the procedures in comparison with low evidence of success, the leader can return to the high road and deprecate these picayune concerns in the context of the aim of spiritual regeneration. If one dares to puncture this mood, however, there is always the comeback of comparing sensitivity training with other procedures of personal change, such as psychoanalysis; attacking the competition by pointing to the lack of hard research proving its effectiveness. Between claiming to be beyond evaluation and quibbling over the relative merit of their own and others' research results, the question of the responsibility of the sensitivity training leader remains unanswered.

To a lesser degree, a similar responsibility devolves upon the other members of the group. During the conduct of encounter groups, people delve deeply into each other's lives, tell what they like and don't like about each other, and in general undermine each other's defenses. After this, the person is supposed to go out and apply what he has discovered under the supposition that something he has learned in the group is true and correct.

The question of what sensitivity training promises and what its real nature is has become important in determining the propriety of publicity for different events. In 1969 the *Village Voice* started to refuse advertising for groups which implied therapy; this was done on the basis that advertising therapy is against professional standards and, in general, unethical. Because of its audience this newspaper is an important publicity outlet for sensitivity training in the New York area.

A lengthy controversy has resulted, with the paradoxical result that the sponsors of encounters, sensitivity training, or similar workshops argue that they do not conduct therapy or provide psychological sessions in the sense of aiming at changing character of the psychological state of participants in a fundamental way, while the publisher claims they do. The publisher could point to such advertisements as workshops on myopia, on overcoming creative blocks and on the use of such terms as "sociotherapy." On the other hand, a committee of encounter group leaders supplied the description that, "the purpose of our groups is to provide a *social environment* for people who prefer not to relate to others in the distracting and sometimes artificial environments of bars, parties, dances, etc." (that is, a singles' bar for people who do not like bars), and disseminated this statement in an open letter to the publisher, staff, and stockholders of the *Village Voice*. The Committee for Scientific and Professional Ethics and Conduct of the American Psychological Association has supported the publisher on the general point, but has been unable to clarify each instance, especially borderline cases, as therapy or not. Here we have a practical result of effect of the multiplicity of claims for sensitivity training; it is unlikely to be resolved early and is at present leading to angry confrontation and resort to the courts.[5]

Against the scientific model of the professional, then, there is the whole content and stance of the movement. The stance of the movement stresses feeling, the strong experience *as experience,* and also the gratifications that come out of this experience. We have seen how, despite the scientific language, the ideology promotes in many ways a return to nonscientific thinking, and that there has been little systematic evaluation. Many people in the movement have become more and more impatient with the lack of evaluation techniques and the lack of standardized attempts to establish definite results. Thus, according to their own claims, we may be reluctant to accord many practitioners scientific competence. They do not claim any particular knowledge of the outcome of their procedures, but only spiritual insight. We are again returning to a central point within the movement, namely, that the extreme kind of process orientation, or the orientation to the direct experience, leaves the practitioners finally without any claim for long-range benefits, or anything more than the value of the experience itself. The other, more interpersonal, kind of responsibility is also rejected by the trainer, as we have seen quite explicitly in quotes from some of them, and is never really accepted by the other members of the group who share a great amount of concern for each other during the group experience.

We are left here with a situation in which people are induced to undergo a strong experience which historically has been controlled and has frequently been part of the sacred aspect of society. This has

[5] The author thanks Dr. Edwin Fancher, publisher of the *Village Voice,* and Ed Mentkin, Coordinator, Ad Hoc Committee for a Public Dialogue on Encounter Groups, for the opportunity of inspecting part of the relevant correspondence.

been taken over now as pure technique, subject only to the general social controls of society, science, and the professions. Thus, it has become a general social problem, and as a social problem, we have to weigh its possible benefits and dangers. As has been shown in the earlier discussion of evaluative research in the field, there is not very much evidence about the dangers, and we have to rely in part on anecdotal experience in both.

The principal benefits derived from encounter groups can be defined only negatively. The group is an experience different from ordinary life in which people may shed their old restraints and try new patterns of behavior and experience. This may be viewed as fulfilling a religious need for people who have rejected formal religion. We must leave the question of benefits in this uncertain state; benefits are possible, but the ways they are derived and the goals achieved are unknown. Positive testimony on the immediate effects of encounters is similar to that in other procedures where the over-all result is quite problematic, such as drug usage. Of course, there is nothing intrinsically wrong with feeling good, but we must examine the possible and reported dangers.

Data on dangers and adverse effects of encounter groups and sensitivity training in general have been collected even less systematically than those on beneficial results. Evidence exists of the occasional incidence of serious emotional breakdowns which may require hospitalization. How high this incidence is, is hard to ascertain. One of the lower estimates given is 1 in 1,500; a study at Yale showed that the incidence of psychiatric disorders was lower among the students who participated in sensitivity training than in a general sample of students. Other estimates, however, are much higher. Odiorne has stated that there is likely to be one person with a serious problem in practically every encounter group, and Juan Rosselló, who was for several years the psychiatrist for the National Training Laboratory, estimates about five serious problems during each summer.[6] The official data given by NTL lists 25 serious psychiatric incidents out of 11,000 participants in 22 years of summer programs and 8 incidents out of 3,000 participants in 13 years of industrial laboratory programs.[7]

A recent, intensive evaluation study by Lieberman, Yalom, and Miles dealt with identification and estimation of psychiatric casual-

[6] Personal interviews.
[7] NTL release.

ties.[8] They found, using a variety of techniques and two groups led by different trainers representing each technique, an over-all psychiatric casualty rate of 9.6 percent, compared to none in a control group. Casualties were defined carefully as evidence of definite harm occurring as a consequence of the sessions. Although the rate looks high, this result itself is less important than the fact that the group leaders were least able to identify the casualties as compared to the trainees themselves, peers, or associates. This finding casts doubt on many of the low estimates given, which are mainly derived from the leaders or the organizations conducting the programs.

These data, fragmentary as they are, are cited mainly to show that there is a recognized danger in encounter groups. We find many anecdotal reports of the complete breakdown of persons who previously had been functioning quite effectively. Quotes from one panel discussion illustrate three cases.

> As a matter of fact, I am personally familiar with a program manager, which in the . . . industry is a very responsible job, an aggressive guy, who was sent by one of the . . . companies to one of these programs. He was stripped of all of his strength and left with nothing. He is now in the Veterans Administration Hospital and is a total wreck. His wife cannot even see him. This is an actual case in point.

> *Business Week* sent a reporter to Bethel last summer, who was an executive of a . . . company in New Jersey, who began to show very aberrant kind of behavior in the group and particularly in the dormitory. And the person who was with him, an executive of . . ., documented this for me. He was acting very erratically, and the staff wouldn't listen and they didn't discover it. They went to his T-group trainer and tried to tell him this man was in trouble. Finally, about four o'clock one morning, he tried to commit suicide. He took it to the staff next morning; they called the State Police and the State Police said they would put him in a strait jacket, and take him ninety miles to a mental institution. (A vice president of a major company!) So these two executives left the lab, took the man back to New Jersey and committed him to a sanitarium.

> An executive of a very large . . . company, the manager of their [testing laboratory], a very rigid man, a man with previous psychiatric history, was sent to a lab. He has a complete breakdown be-

[8] M. Lieberman, I. Yalom, and M. Miles. "The Group Experience Project: A Comparison of Ten Encounter Technologies," in L. Blank, G. Gottsegen and M. Gottsegen (eds.), *Encounter: Confrontations in Self and Interpersonal Awareness.* New York: Macmillan, 1971.

cause he was in with engineers. And what did he discover from these engineers is that anyone who runs a [testing laboratory] is a bastard, and you always have been, and you are fifty-eight years old, and now we are going to let you know about it. He committed suicide.[9]

These are extreme cases; they are quoted to show that group encounters can have serious effects, even as other interventions on a person's mind and body do. Statistics show that they are relatively rare, but almost every person who has been involved in encounter groups knows of at least one case of serious breakdown. This is, therefore, certainly a point to bear in mind when evaluating encounters.

Psychotic breakdowns are the most visible casualties of encounter groups, but they are not likely to be the only ones. Minor damages may occur, ranging from unpleasant experiences to various degrees of impairment of functioning. The anguish of a person excluded from the group can be quite traumatic; just as traumatic can be the situation of a group member who does not conform to the group norms of openness, spontaneity, and involvement. This group-induced stress might be justifiable in a technique where definite gain can be expected, or where the training follows a procedure whose workings the practitioner understands. As Rodney Luther said, "We are concerned that 25 to 40 percent of persons sent to sensitivity gain nothing and very possibly lose some highly valuable behavioral assets. Even in actual war, win-loss ratios of this order of magnitude are impossible to justify."[10]

A more subtle, but pervading, detriment is the invasion of privacy. Everybody has built up, over the years, an internal structure in which certain concerns are regarded as more or less accessible to others. The right to privacy is a legal as well as a human right. The norms of encounter groups frequently treat this right as obnoxious, and the social pressure within these groups is to persuade the person to surrender it. The damage this frontal attack on the person's defenses can do is not known, but is certainly worth consideration. Here, as elsewhere, we meet with a lack of concern on the part of encounter group leaders for what happens to a person after he leaves the group, how he reconstructs his defenses.

In our earlier discussion, we found that claims of benefits from encounter groups were most reasonable if they were put under the

[9] Sensitivity Training Panel of the 1967 meeting of the Personnel Association of Southern California, transcript.
[10] *Ibid.*

heading of recreation, or regarded as limited adjuncts to definite training programs. That is, the value of encounters is highest either as a restrained technique or as pure enjoyment. Against this limited success we must set the reported dangers; the balance is not encouraging. It might be most useful, then, to look at encounter groups as frankly experimental. Benefits cannot be established in more than a tentative way, but the leaders and organizers of the groups believe they have discovered a new dimension of human experience which has potential value for today's mass society. They also believe that their new techniques are worth experimenting with, even if there is little underlying theory in the rigorous sense of the word.

If we accept this, then we must consider encounter groups in the same light as any other experimentation with human subjects. The ethics of experimentation has been a controversial subject, but gradually some standards have emerged. The three main principles that guide experimentation with human subjects are voluntary participation, informed consent, and compensating value.[11]

The first principle states that nobody should be forced to be an experimental subject. Correspondingly, we must ask whether everyone who participates in an encounter group does so voluntarily. In many cases, participants sign up individually for encounter groups from a variety of motives, so no problem arises. In other cases, however, an encounter group program is accepted by an entire business or school as a training procedure. This is done, for example, in some medical schools. Here we cannot speak of voluntary participation. Even if there is no formal requirement or direct order by the boss to participate, it is clear to many people that participation is preferred and can lead to great advantages for the participant within the organization. Even without any pressure from authority figures, simple group pressure might influence a person to attend an encounter group if most of his peers have done so. In none of these situations can we speak of voluntary participation.

This problem is aggravated by the fact that many adverse effects of encounter groups are recognized as the result of defective screening. Some people will be threatened very much by the procedures used in encounter groups; some may even go into these groups as a desperate last gamble before commitment to an institution or suicide. Encounter groups are usually not equipped to deal with the

[11] "Ethical Aspects of Experimentation with Human Subjects." *Daedalus*, Spring, 1969, 219–594. Issued as Vol. 98, No. 2 of the *Proceedings of the American Academy of Arts and Sciences.* H. Jones (ed.). *Law and the Social Role of Science.* New York: Rockefeller University Press, 1967.

special problems of persons of this kind. They do not explore and guide people systematically through deep-seated problems. Even with the current limited knowledge, it may be possible to screen out people who obviously could be harmed. But this simple precaution, which is so seldom observed, is made more difficult to enforce if pressure of any kind brings whole groups involuntarily to an encounter. In volunteers it may be relatively easy to check on at least some morbid motivations. People who come under pressure are likely to include those for whom participation would be dangerous and who normally would have stayed away. Aside from simple moral reasons for condemning enforced participation, pressure to participate increases the dangers inherent in the technique.

The principle of informed consent brings up another knotty problem. Since the workings of encounter groups are so little understood even by their practitioners, it is extremely difficult to describe to a layman what is involved. The problem of trying to explain the actual workings and possible dangers of a procedure to laymen is faced by many experimenters, and real understanding is often not achieved. Nevertheless, the principal safeguard is the professional competence of the experimenter. In effect, the prospective subject trusts the experimenter implicitly and has faith that no real harm will come to him. This trust is based on the belief that the experimenter has the training to know what is harmful and the ethical standards not to want to harm the subject.

Encounter groups frequently have professional leaders who are trained and responsible. Even they cannot know much about the factors operating in encounter groups, however, because so little is known. No formalized, agreed-upon provisions have been made regarding how to introduce the participants to the encounter experience, how to guide them through the difficulties they face in the group, or how to provide suitable closure at the end. In addition, there are few requirements or professional standards for leading encounter groups. Looking at the different encounter group centers one finds that their directors have a variety of backgrounds and no common fund of knowledge and experience, nor do they share a common set of professional ethics. The fact is, unfortunately, that the prospective participant generally has little knowledge about the professional background of his trainer. He must check on the professional competence of the trainer for himself, either through a feeling of reassurance based on personal contact or by trying to get information about the trainer's previous encounter groups. There is an urgent need for encounter centers to provide prospective participants—

actually prospective subjects—with relevant information of this kind.

According to the principle of compensating value, the subject must receive either personal benefit from the experiment or social benefit through the creation of knowledge that might help him or others in similar circumstances. As we have seen, except in special cases, it is impossible to promise personal benefits to the participants. If encounters are looked on as experimentation or research in a wider sense, it is just at this point that the orientation of the group leader becomes important. In exchange for the invasion of privacy, temporary anguish, and risk of danger that the participants are experiencing, the group leader cannot promise anything like a personal reward, such as a physician does when he uses an experimental, high-risk treatment. If the group leader is a serious researcher, he must, therefore, commit himself to a valid study design which can give possible future benefit, and help in understanding the strong emotional forces he releases in his groups.

The problem of responsibility has faced sensitivity training for a long time. On the one hand, the leaders can point to examples of novel developments in human culture suppressed by advocates of the established order; they assert a freedom to experiment with new ways of feeling, encounter, and human organization. And clearly, no critic wants to be part of a modern inquisition. On the other side, society has a stake in protecting the public from untested and potentially dangerous techniques which the layman may be unable to judge. One has only to compare the care and supervision demanded for the introduction of a new drug. The need for the activity of the Food and Drug Administration is not questioned. If sensitivity training can have effects of comparable strength, are not equivalent measures for protection of the public necessary? Recent events have pointed up the general irony of the position of sensitivity training.

Heightened visibility of the movement has provoked attention from government agencies. Several state legislatures have devoted some time to sensitivity training, especially in California, and Congress has seen some comments made on this topic.[12] Most of these comments are leveled at the ideological orientation of sensitivity training, and they should be treated in this context. Some of the interest has centered on the question of protection of the public, however. The California investigation involved lengthy committee hearings giving voice to advocates as well as to opponents of sensitivity training and discussing some of the dangers of the treatment as well as the use of captive audiences. With telling effect, witnesses described the introduction of sensitivity training into high schools without the possibility of consent of either students or parents. Nevertheless, no legislation has resulted from these hearings. Inquiries of this sort show an increasing readiness for some regulatory legislation which could easily be triggered by the wake of some well-publicized incident.

It is not surprising, therefore, that professional organizations, too, have become concerned with the impact of sensitivity training. The American Psychiatric Association has established a task force whose report mirrored the concern of the profession and urged more research on actual achievements and shortcomings of sensitivity training as a group psychiatric technique. Psychiatry as a profession is especially vulnerable in this respect; opposition to psychiatry stems from the same sources as that to sensitivity training, and stringent regulation of the one could also hamper the work of the other. One of the borderline topics is sex education which has been advocated as an important mental health program but has been opposed by more conservative groups. The combination of sex education with techniques of sensitivity training, especially nonverbal techniques, can bring down the wrath of some pressure groups on entire mental health programs.[13]

The American Psychological Association has established a standing committee to study the ethical implications of sensitivity training. The general attitude many psychologists have was brought out in a study by Verplanck who wrote department heads in several universities for their positions in regard to the use of sensitivity training. Only one respondent in 138 checked that he had no problems with its use but few (19) could report concrete incidents; however, of the rest, more than one-quarter had "heard of difficulties." The whole set of responses added up to a general uneasiness, but without enough concrete evidence to take definite steps.[14]

The organizations involved in sensitivity training have also taken steps to police their own activities. NTL has been in the forefront of this effort; it has publicized a set of standards to guard

[13] "Stress and Strength at Crystal Cliffs."

[14] W. Verplanck. "How Do You Track Down Rumors?" *American Psychologist*, 25, 1970, 106–107. I am grateful to Dr. Verplanck for letting me use a copy of his original tabulations.

against untoward incidents and to make the group leaders responsible. The main portion of this effort has been concentrated on the qualifications of the trainers themselves; these are specified as advanced academic training in behavioral science, productive work in one's field, completion of a specialized training program on group participation and leading, and examination and review by an NTL board. This rigorous screening program insures some control over the trainers. Even within NTL it is attacked as being too narrow professionally, however, and of practically excluding those people who would be in close contact with minority groups and who would be open to radical changes.[15]

By contrast, the personal growth centers, and especially Esalen, have countered the challenge by elaborating the concept of responsibility. This builds on the ideas of Fritz Perls discussed earlier; it has been worked out by William Schutz. A statement by him at a New York workshop gives the general idea:

> I'd like to state first that, whatever happens, you are responsible for yourself. That is, if during the course of these things you want to become physically injured, then you can do that if you want to; if you want to bow to group pressure, you can do that. If you want to not bow to group pressure, you can also do that. But I want to underline clearly at the outset that you are responsible for whatever happens to you here.[16]

Given this basic philosophy, the task of the trainer is only to do what he thinks is best; his responsibility ends there, and the responsibility of the group member who came to the session on his own takes over. This interpretation of responsibility goes so far that one hears of opposition to having resident psychiatrists or counselors available. Only if the participant is thrown back on himself, if he sees nobody who can take the load off his back, can he assume his rightful responsibility to sink or swim.

This radical revival of the ancient maxim, "Let the buyer beware," may perhaps initiate a novel way of interpreting the professional relationship, but it does not fit today's practice. Even under current legal conditions, without additional controls, sensitivity training may be in trouble on the Coast. Even Esalen had to dissociate itself from some practitioners who claimed "Esalen training"

[15] *Standards for the Use of the Laboratory Methods in NTL Institute Programs.* Washington, D.C.: NTL, 1969.

[16] "Encounter v. Psychotherapy." Transcript of workshop held in New York City, February, 1970.

and got involved in malpractice suits. Thereby Esalen implied that its mark of approval meant something and referred to a specific training; this may be a first step along the road to certification similar to what the more conservative NTL has done. But even in NTL, damage suits have become a mounting problem. Several suits, until now for physical rather than psychological damage, have been settled out of court, but training organizations have convened and tried to make arrangements to counter this threat.

The irony of the situation is apparent. The basic rhetoric of sensitivity training and encounter groups rails against the alienation of modern man: alienation from other people, from nature, and from genuine emotion. In working out procedures to make man more involved with others, problems of the potential effect of these techniques arise. These are the problems the purveyors of many means of improving life have faced in a technological society. The political and ideological leanings of the leaders and many partisans of sensitivity training have then led them to inveigh against the manufacturers of DDT, Thalidomide, and the SST, against selfish technocrats who unleashed these artifacts without taking responsibility for possible consequences to man and nature. It is only when the advocates' own techniques become widespread with effects that cannot be predicted that they retreat to the morality of the marketplace, catering to public demand, sometimes created by their own publicity, and looking with dismay at consumer protection.

Chapter 16

Escape or Movement

". . . Tell us, as Horace would of old,
If man should fight or follow his set fate;
If I have erred in the aim or in the path;
If toward wisdom there is yet another road,
And if perhaps the art of joy is life's whole art." [1]

Sensitivity training was born out of a search for a new technique, a new way of conducting human relations training in and through groups. The fundamental principle was process, what happened in the group; it was felt that a democratic, involving, meaningful experience could not lead to objectionable ends. This principle represented the then dominant philosophy of pragmatism and instrumentalism, the retreat from ultimate aims, be they religious or ideological.

This process orientation considers only the time period covered by the sensitivity training program. It implies that if sensitivity training is conducted according to valid rules, then one does not have to worry about any ultimate ends of the program itself. Attention to the means of providing change is better than invoking a utopian ideal and using any means to achieve it. This principle causes its followers to adhere to a middle-range time perspective rather than a long or short time perspective. If the time perspective is length-

[1] A. de Lamartine. "Farewell to Poetry: Philosophy," in *Méditations Poetiques*. Paris: Furne, Jouvet, 1875, 262. Author's translation.

229

ened, then the resulting goals and world-encompassing belief systems can be included in the justification of the process. If it is shortened, then single acts, feelings, and pure sensation tend to be valued for themselves alone. The intermediate position, while the most conducive to rational planning, is hard to maintain. Previous chapters have discussed the increasing emphasis on the short-range goals, on the cult of pure experience and sensualism. Nevertheless, a countertrend can also be discerned, toward the development of an all-encompassing ideology of the movement, toward placing sensitivity training into the framework of a new philosophy that will regenerate man, bring about a new kind of society, and find a new center of being which will transcend the traditional faith.

With its explosion in the 1960's, sensitivity training has attracted prophets, philosophers, and Utopians who see in sensitivity training at least some chance for the fulfillment of their future goals. It is also true that the experiences provided by sensitivity training fit well with some of the trends of the decade: the turning away from the technological society, from goal orientation, and from exploitation of nature toward emphasis on individual expression, life based on small groups, cooperation, and lack of social structure. It can be seen that these new aims represent an almost conscious departure from traditional middle-class values or the values of a technological society. That is, productivity in the material sense, long-range time perspective, trust in institutionalized structures, and privacy of the individual are precisely those features within society that are rejected by the sensitivity training movement. In contrast, the ideal group is more expressive than instrumental, has faith in the here and now, is dependent on the needs of the individual, and does not believe any safeguards are necessary either to protect the group procedure from disruption and terror by its members or to protect the individual from being crushed by the group. In this way, sensitivity training has become part of a new radical outlook, and in some respects has been used to symbolize it.[2]

This conjunction brings up the question of the aims of sensitivity training within traditional politics. It is hard to place sensitivity training in this framework, as it has been attacked from both the left and the right. The somewhat anti-materialistic stance of sensitivity training does not conform with orthodox Marxism. Clearly, sensitivity training does not believe purely in economic determinants

[2] A. Hampden-Turner. *Radical Man*. Cambridge: Schenckman, 1970.

or even in the importance of economic determination for any behavior. It is a product of a period of relative affluence. It has attracted members of the wealthy middle class who did not find complete happiness with affluence, and were looking for more meaning in life than the satisfaction of primary needs could give. Thus, the kinds of problems sensitivity training faces are not the problems of leftist politics.

In addition, the whole aim of sensitivity training is, if not the denial, then the overcoming of conflict. Within labor relations, therefore, the suspicion is always present that sensitivity training is really just a technique used by management to give workers anything else but money. The fact that sensitivity training has been used to obviate union organizing has aroused the suspicion within unions that the whole movement is more a tool of management than of labor. The general theory of labor organizers is a theory of conflict, negotiation, and accommodation. The exact point of accommodation will be based on the relative power position that might have to be established through confrontations such as strikes; and labor organizers are cynical, or at least skeptical, about any attempts to arrive at solutions through some emotional or complicated discussion method.

Even within sensitivity training similar conflicts occur, and sensitivity training organizations have trouble solving them. The current conflicts about minority groups, blacks, and women rear their heads within sensitivity training centers and are not acted upon in accordance with sensitivity training techniques but by the general techniques of conflict, confrontation, and power relationships. This makes the movement very suspect by the new left, and not only from the purely Marxist point of view.

In spite of all these reservations on the part of the left, the strongest attack on the movement has come from the right. The reason seems to be not because of any particular objectionable features of sensitivity training, but because of its association with, and use as, a medium for the whole complex of changing social standards. Sensitivity training can be seen as part of the progressive movement in education, especially since it was originally sponsored by the National Education Association. Its sensual approaches can be seen as part of the loosening of moral standards; and its attempt to change both persons and society as threatening personal integrity as well as the current social system.

In fact, sensitivity training has been exposed frequently to intense attacks from the right, including extensive documentation in the *Congressional Record* and hearings of the California legislature.[3] In these documents it is attacked mainly for two reasons. First, its form implies a loosening of traditional standards; the more conspicuous kinds of sensitivity training, such as nude therapy groups and nude encounters, receive a disproportionate share of attention. Second, the procedure is accused of being analogous to brainwashing, and the idea of influencing people that strongly is attacked as insidious. Attacks of this kind usually lump sensitivity training together with other procedures, such as group psychotherapy. Therefore, they are taken seriously not only by people in sensitivity training, but also by psychiatrists who would generally be quite skeptical about it themselves.

We might wonder why this violent attack on sensitivity training comes so much more strongly from the right than from the left. After all, as an ideologically neutral method, it should be as useful in convincing people to hold extreme right-wing stances as to hold middle-of-the-road or left-wing stances. In great part, the violence of the attack is aimed at the type of people who promote sensitivity training, rather than at anything particular that they are doing. In addition, the organizations promoting sensitivity training, such as the National Education Association and others, have also been the targets of right-wing groups in general, who feel that anything they are supporting is therefore suspect. Finally, not the technique itself but the atmosphere in which it is executed is suspect. Especially the more publicized paraphernalia such as sensual interaction, the forms of Oriental mysticism, and the deliberate flouting of social taboos would offend those right-wing groups not particularly on any political but rather on a cultural basis.

Perhaps the attacks by both sides of the political spectrum on sensitivity training spring from the same cultural sources. Sensitivity training is neither a method to solve the dire social problems and disadvantages of the poor, as the orthodox left would want it to be, nor is it a method for teaching conformity to traditional values, as the right would want. It is a symptom of the new middle class, of the affluent society, and of the explosion of, and the search for, joy and new kinds of excitement. Thus its escape from the traditional problems of economic need and the dictates of necessity can be the source for the attacks by both sides.

[3] California State Legislature, *Sensitivity Training*, Dec. 5, 1968, San Diego. *Congressional Record*, House of Representatives, June 10, 1969, 4660–4679 and Jan. 19, 1970, 1424–1429.

The ideology of sensitivity training, therefore, stands outside the conventional arrangement of political ideologies. This is a carry-over of its origin, which was a combination of techniques for producing change, encouraging participatory leadership, promoting sensual awareness, and expanding the ranges of human (especially non-intellectual) potentiality. It is apparent that the first two aims are at loggerheads with the last two. The first set is derived from a rational concern with the pragmatic problems of society. The second set promotes a regeneration of man and, in the extreme, a change of the whole direction of the development of human society. These two aspects we have noted as the two aims of the sensitivity training movement have frequently been irreconcilable. The fact that the movement continues to maintain both wings makes it difficult to fit its basic philosophy to traditional political categories.

How can we describe the ideology of a movement born out of a reaction against ultimate aims, the long-range aim of a movement whose slogan is "here and now"? We can begin with the concept which has been the sacred term of the movement from the beginning: "change." Change was the stated purpose of the early NTL labs, change has been the commodity sold to clients by diverse organizations, and it is what the psych-resorts sell today. The feeling of change can be an immediate experience, but it implies a future effect, however unspecified. The inclusive term for all professionals working in sensitivity training is "change agent," referring again to the process but presumably implying some purpose as well.

An ideology based on change for change's sake can encompass the different schools of sensitivity training, but it is set off from other ideologies. Those, too, accept change; after all, nobody assumes a present state of perfection. But other ideologies, religious as well as secular, assume a direction, an ideal state first, and then chart the changes that must occur for this state to be achieved. By contrast, sensitivity training seeks change as a good in itself, in this way producing an ideology for the sensation of the moment.

This ideology of change implies a constant search for novelty for its own sake. Previous chapters have shown how the fascination with new techniques by encounter group centers leads to neglect of the client's problem and his immediate needs. However, the readiness of sensitivity training to be on the side of change against tradition in any context and its willingness to enlist the powerful group methods for this purpose is seen as a threat by proponents of the established order as well as by those who have some specific change in mind. In its lack of ideology, sensitivity training is not too different from the radical mood of the 1960's.

Many attacks on sensitivity training from laymen stress its similarity to brainwashing techniques, the process of leading innocent people away from old traditions to new values. Ironically, criticism from the scientific community comes from the fact that no real change has been shown, and that probably what is looked at as the destruction of values is mainly the result of the self-selection of participants. The more extreme behavior and expression of surprising new values is less the result of sensitivity training than the use of encounter centers as places to express long-felt ideas and desires by people who elect to attend. Thus, many of the strongest attacks on sensitivity training look very strange to people who have examined the evidence for the effectiveness of sensitivity training (see Chapter 13).

The philosophy of the movement has developed from an abnormal situation, a situation in which, on the one hand, economic needs were not as salient as they had been, and on the other hand, the traditional religious and cultural values no longer affected a great part of the population. Sensitivity training has become a symbol of the search for new types of positive values, for a new "center" within man, and for similar social expressions. The movement starts from the regeneration of the individual, the way most religions start. In this context, its main claim is the fact that a reconstructed individual, an individual who can express his own feelings, has a chance through sensitivity training to create his own society. According to this view, there is no distinction between social needs and needs of the individual.

This attitude expresses the view of the affluent society, especially the affluent middle class within it, which needs no materialistic help from society but feels only the restrictions that come from it. A final irony is that this ideology represents a return to problem solving. It expresses the same optimism that has carried the rise of technology so far and leads to hope that the intense group experience will solve society's remaining problems. As the rise of technology has satisfied physical needs, while restricting the social needs and helping to mechanize man, so the new social technologists are trying to change man by giving proper attention to change in the expression of man's needs, intense experiences, or other claimed effects of sensitivity training. They say that we can solve all our social problems by abolishing them altogether. This optimistic view amounts to a denial that there is a tragedy within man which arises from the fact that, at some point, social needs and human needs are contradictory, the good of the individual and of the group cannot always be identical, and then one of them has to give.

DILEMMAS OF THE FUTURE

At the end of the 1960's, organizationally as well as ideologically, sensitivity training reached the end of an era. The ideas of sensitivity training are no longer new. A movement committed to change and novelty cannot subsist even on its own innovations. The glamour has faded. Clients have seen intensive group techniques introduced and abandoned; social scientists are waiting for hard research results; even the popular media are abandoning the wide-eyed picture of the breakthrough in human relations and the equally exaggerated picture of the sinister group leader manipulating the group for his nefarious ends. Nevertheless, the groups still attract many participants who need, if only for a short time, a feeling of purpose and meaning in the universe which they have not found in their secular middle-class life.

Projecting the present trends in sensitivity training into the future, the movement is likely to be less a separate movement within or at the borderline of the scientific enterprise. Some of its features are likely to be absorbed by traditional enterprises. The more extreme aspects, on the other hand, are going to become more purely religious or recreational exercises, separated from the present areas of application. Conflicting demands might lead to a split, to separate movements for separate purposes.

Let us see how this would be accomplished in different fields. As far as scientific research is concerned, social psychologists are showing more interest in the nature of affection, love, and trust, as well as hate and aggression. Some aspects of encounter groups as well as some of their terminology may well be taken over for this purpose. In the same way, psychophysiologists are beginning to study meditation and its effects in the laboratory and are returning to experimental psychology's heritage of introspection, to describe meditation and similar exercises in their own terms (see Chapter 14). At the same time, however, sensitivity groups are coming more and more to approximate religious retreats, Sufi and Yoga centers, halfway houses, and singles' weekends at mountain and beach resorts.

Similarly, group therapists have begun to incorporate exercises first used in sensitivity training into orthodox therapy groups. Management has adopted some intensive techniques without purchasing the whole sensitivity training approach. This selective acceptance of a few new techniques has been the fate of many panaceas and may constitute their essential function. Originators of new systems prepare a whole new package, supposedly theoretically and technically integrated. After some experience, it is found that the main values lie in some of the system's new techniques which are then incorporated under other current systems. Instead of a breakthrough in effecting massive change we have acquired a few useful tools. We might remember that even differential calculus was introduced as an important aspect of a philosophy of the perfection of God.

On the other hand, we might expect some offshoots of therapeutically oriented sensitivity training procedures to exist for a long time. These techniques will become more esoteric and be surrounded by a tighter and tighter clique of true believers. And we may be sure that they will always find some willing customers.

Finally, what of the future of the movement in the history of ideas? Prediction here is most hazardous; proponents of the movement frequently rely on analogy with previous times. A favorite analogy is the breakdown of classical civilization, the loss of values which had served the Mediterranean people for more than a millennium. They can see sensitivity training as the cutting edge of a movement which brings forth new beliefs, new values, new ways of life that would be as radically different as Christianity was from Classicism. The religious flavor of the movement points in this direction.

Perhaps. But it is always a little presumptuous to see oneself at the moment of supreme crisis at the start of a new era. Other historical analogies may be less grandiose. One which comes to mind is the "Splendid Century" in France. The aristocracy had amassed great affluence but lost its function and purpose and thereby gained a great amount of leisure. Aristocrats spent their time in sensual play and in close examination and discussion of the minutiae of interpersonal relations, which they endowed with enormous meaning. They also were looking for less harmless diversions, such as occultism and intense emotional release. In the meantime the real work of the state was carried on by the establishment of the time.

In the same vein, Peter Berger has predicted that the meaning of the "counterculture" is the surrendering of power positions by the youths of the upper classes to the lower-middle and lower classes. He also maintains that for the ones who do not want to drop out completely, there will always be jobs available as T-group leaders.[4]

Neither of the two analogies fits exactly. We have neither the social nor economic conditions of the Roman Empire or of the French monarchy. Our wealth as well as our leisure are based on the rapid rise of technology and science, and much of our spiritual motive may spring from the need to come to grips with the implications of science. Sensitivity training represents a movement in this context. We can be sure that it will not be the last of its kind. But whether it represents a transition to a new era or merely the sensibility of the newly affluent and leisured, only the future historian can tell.

[4] P. Berger and B. Berger. "The Blueing of America," *New Republic, 164,* No. 14, Apr. 3, 1971, 20–23.

Appendix I

Bibliography

Alchen, D. *What the Hell Are They Trying to Prove, Martha?* New York: John Day, 1970.

Alvarez, A. *Under Pressure.* Baltimore, Md.: Penguin, 1965.

Argyris, C. *Interpersonal Competence and Organizational Effectiveness.* Homewood, Ill.: Dorsey, 1962.

Austin, B. *Sad Nun at Synanon.* New York: Grossman, 1970.

Bales, R. *Personality and Interpersonal Behavior.* New York: Holt, 1970.

Barker, R., T. Dembo, and K. Lewin. "Frustration and Regression: An Experiment with Young Children," *University of Iowa Studies in Child Welfare.* Vol. 18. New York, 1941.

Beckhard, R. *Organizational Development: Strategies and Models.* Reading, Pa.: Addison-Wesley, 1967.

Bellah, R. "Civil Religion in America," *Daedalus,* 26, Winter, 1967, 1–21.

Benne, K. *Education for Tragedy.* Lexington: University of Kentucky Press, 1967.

——. "History of the T Group in the Laboratory Setting," in L. Bradford, J. Gibb, and K. Benne, *T-Group Theory and Laboratory Method.* New York: Wiley, 1964.

Bennis, W. *Organizational Development: Its Nature, Origins and Prospects.* Reading, Pa.: Addison-Wesley, 1967.

——, K. Benne, and R. Chin (eds.). *The Planning of Change.* 2nd ed. New York: Holt, 1970.

——, and H. Shepard. "A Theory of Group Development," *Human Relations,* 9, 1956, 415–437.

——, and P. Slater. *The Temporary Society.* New York: Harper, 1968.

Berger, P., and B. Berger. "The Blueing of America," *New Republic, 164,* No. 14, April 3, 1971, 20–23.

Berne, E. *Games People Play.* New York: Grove Press, 1964.

——. *Transactional Analysis in Psychotherapy.* New York: Grove Press, 1961.

Bion, W. *Experiences in Groups.* New York: Basic Books, 1961.

Blake, R., and J. Mouton. *Corporate Excellence through Grid Organizational Development.* Houston: Gulf Publishing, 1968.

Blank, L., G. Gottsegen, and M. Gottsegen (eds.). *Encounter: Confrontations in Self and Interpersonal Awareness.* New York: Macmillan, 1971.

Blankford, M. *The Big Yankee: The Life of Carlson of the Raiders.* Boston: Little, Brown, 1947.

Blumer, H. "Collective Behavior," in A. M. Lee (ed.), *Principles of Sociology.* New York: Barnes and Noble, 1951, 165–222.

Bogue, D. *The Population of the United States*. Glencoe, Ill.: Free Press, 1959.

Bradford, L., and J. French (eds.). "The Dynamics of the Discussion Group," *Journal of Social Issues*, 4, No. 2, Spring, 1948, entire issue.
———, J. Gibb, and K. Benne. *T-Group Theory and Laboratory Method*. New York: Wiley, 1964.

Brown, G. *Human Teaching for Human Learning*. New York: Viking, 1971.

Burke, K. *A Grammar of Motives*. New York: Prentice-Hall, 1952.

Burton, J. (ed.). *Encounter*. San Francisco: Jossey-Bass, 1969.

California State Legislature. *Sensitivity Training*. San Diego, Dec. 5, 1968.

Campbell, J., and M. Dunnette. "Effectiveness of T-Group Experiences in Managerial Training and Development," *Psychological Bulletin*, 70, No. 2, 1968, 73–104.

Camus, A. *The Stranger*. New York: Knopf, 1946.

Chapple, E. *Culture and Biological Man*. New York: Holt, 1970.

Chase, S. *Roads to Agreement*. New York: Harper, 1951, 83–99.

Coch, L., and J. French. "Overcoming Resistance to Change," *Human Relations*, 1, 1948, 512–532.

Davis, S. "An Organic Problem-Solving Method of Organizational Change," *Journal of Applied Behavioral Science*, 3, 1967, 3–21.

De Grazia, S. *Of Time, Work and Leisure*. New York: Twentieth Century Fund, 1962.

Deutsch, M. "The Effect of Cooperation and Competition upon Group Process," *Human Relations*, 2, 1949, 124–152 and 190–231.

Dicks, H. V. *50 Years of the Tavistock Clinic*. London: Routledge and Kegan Paul, 1970.

Doob, L. W. *Resolving Conflict in Africa*. New Haven: Yale University Press, 1970.

Durkheim, E. *The Elementary Forms of Religious Life*. London: Allen and Unwin, 1915.

Eldredge, H., and D. Thomas. *Demographic Analysis and Interrelations*. Vol. III of *Population Re-Distribution and Economic Growth in the United States*. Philadelphia: American Philosophical Society, 1965.

Ellis, A. "A Weekend of Rational Encounter," in J. Burton (ed.), *Encounter*. San Francisco: Jossey-Bass, 1969, 112–127.

"Encounter versus Psychotherapy." Transcript of workshop held in New York City, February, 1970.

"Ethical Aspects of Experimentation with Human Subjects," *Daedalus*, Spring, 1969, 219–594. Issued as Vol. 98, No. 2 of the *Proceedings of the American Academy of Arts and Sciences*.

Fagen, J., and I. Shepherd. *Gestalt Therapy Now*. Palo Alto, Calif.: Science Behavior Books, 1970.

Farber, S., and R. Wilson. *Control of the Mind*. New York: McGraw-Hill, 1961.

Fellin, P., and E. Litwak. "Neighborhood Cohesion under Conditions of Mobility," *American Sociological Review*, 28, 1963, 364–376.

I. Bibliography

Fensham, P., and D. Hooper. *The Dynamics of a Changing Technology.* London: Tavistock, 1964.

Frank, J. D. *Persuasion and Healing.* Baltimore, Md.: Johns Hopkins, 1961.

Freud, S. *Civilization and Its Discontents.* Garden City, N.Y.: Doubleday, 1930.

———. *Totem and Taboo.* London: Kegan Paul, Trench, Trubner, n.d.

Fülöp-Miller, R. *The Jesuits.* New York: Capricorn Books, 1963.

Galbraith, J. *The Affluent Society.* Boston: Houghton Mifflin, 1958.

Glock, C., and R. Stark. *Religion and Society in Tension.* Chicago: Rand McNally, 1965.

Goldstein, K. *The Organism.* New York: American Book, 1939.

Goodman, P. *The New Reformation.* New York: Random House, 1970.

Gray, T. "On a Distant Prospect of Eton College."

Green, H. *I Never Promised You a Rose Garden.* New York: Holt, 1964.

Grotowski, T. *Toward a Poor Theater.* New York: Simon and Schuster, 1969.

"Groups," *American Journal of Psychiatry, 126,* 1968, 223–277.

Gunther, B. *Sensory Awareness below Your Mind.* New York: Collier, 1968.

———. *What to Do until the Messiah Comes.* New York: Collier, 1971.

Gustaitis, R. *Turning On.* New York: Macmillan, 1969.

Hampden-Turner, A. *Radical Man.* Cambridge, Mass.: Schenckman, 1970.

Heinlein, R. *Stranger in a Strange Land.* New York: Putnam, 1963.

Henry, W. E. "Social Mobility as Social Learning: Some Elements of Change in Motive and Social Context," in M. B. Kantor, *Mobility and Mental Health.* Springfield, Ill.: Thomas, 1965.

Herzberg, F. *Work and the Nature of Man.* New York: World, 1966.

Hesse, H. *Siddhartha.* Berlin: S. Fischer, 1935.

Hill, R., J. Stycos, and K. Back. *The Family and Population Control.* Chapel Hill: University of North Carolina Press, 1959.

House, R. "T-Group Education and Leadership Effectiveness: A Review of the Empiric Literature and a Critical Evaluation," *Personnel Psychology, 20,* No. 1, 1967, 1–32.

Howard, J. *Please Touch.* New York: McGraw-Hill, 1970.

Huxley, A. *Brave New World.* Garden City, N.J.: Doubleday, 1932.

———. "Human Potentialities," in S. Farber and R. Wilson, *Control of the Mind.* New York: McGraw-Hill, 1961.

Jacques, E. *The Changing Culture of a Factory.* London: Tavistock, 1951.

Jones, H. (ed.). *Law and the Social Role of Science.* New York: Rockefeller University Press, 1967.

Kahn, M. "The Return of the Repressed." Conference on Intensive Group Techniques organized by the Foundations' Fund for Research in Psychiatry, Puerto Rico, June, 1969. Mimeographed.

Kaiser, R. "Letting Go," *Playboy, 16,* 1969, 80–82+.

Kantor, M. B. *Mobility and Mental Health.* Springfield, Ill.: Thomas, 1965.

Katz, D. "The Functional Approach to the Study of Attitudes," *Public Opinion Quarterly*, 24, 1960, 163–204.

Keene, S. "Sing the Body Electric" and "My New Carnality," *Psychology Today*, 4, October, 1970, 56–62.

Kesey, K. *One Flew over the Cuckoo's Nest.* New York: Viking, 1962.

Klapp, O. *The Collective Search for Identity.* New York: Holt, 1969.

Klein, M. *Contributions to Psychoanalysis, 1921–1945.* London: Hogarth, 1948.

———. *Developments in Psychoanalysis.* London: Hogarth, 1932.

———. *Our Adult World.* London: Heineman, 1962.

Koch, S. "The Image of Man in Encounter Group Theory." Unpublished manuscript (*Journal of Humanistic Psychology*, in press).

Ladinsky, J. "Occupational Determinants of Geographic Mobility among Professional Workers," *American Sociological Review*, 32, April, 1967, 258–264.

Laing, R. *The Divided Self: A Study of Madness.* Chicago: Quadrangle, 1960.

Lakin, M. *Arab and Jew in Israel.* Washington, D.C.: NTL Publications, 1970.

———. "Human Relations Training and Interracial Social Action: Problems of Self and Client Definition" (with a commentary by Robert F. Allen), *Journal of Applied Behavioral Science*, 2, 1966, 139–148.

Lamartine, A. de. *Méditations Poetiques.* Paris: Furne, Jouvet, 1875, 262.

"Landmarks," *Journal of Applied Behavioral Science*, 3, No. 2, 1967.

Landsberger, H. *Hawthorne Revisited.* Ithaca, N.Y.: New York School of Industrial and Labor Relations, 1965.

Lapassade, G. *Groupes, Organizations, et Institutions.* Paris: Gauthier-Villars, 1970.

Lathen, E. *Pick-Up Sticks.* New York: Simon and Schuster, 1970.

Lee, A. (ed.). *Principles of Sociology.* New York: Barnes and Noble, 1951.

Levi-Strauss, C. *The Savage Mind.* Chicago: University of Chicago Press, 1966.

Lewin, K. *Dynamic Theory of Personality.* New York: McGraw-Hill, 1935.

———. *Field Theory in Social Science.* New York: Harper, 1951.

———. "Forces behind Food Habits and Methods of Change," *Bulletin of National Research Council*, 108, 1943, 35–65.

———. "Frontiers in Group Dynamics I: Concept, Method and Theory in Social Science; Social Equilibrium," *Human Relations*, 1, 1947, 5–40.

———. "Frontiers in Group Dynamics II: Channels of Group Life and Social Planning and Action Research," *Human Relations*, 1, 1947, 143–153.

———. *Principles of Topological Psychology.* New York: McGraw-Hill, 1936.

———. *Resolving Social Conflicts.* New York: Harper, 1948.

I. Bibliography

Lieberman, M., I. Yalom, and M. Miles. "The Group Experience Project: A Comparison of Ten Encounter Technologies," in L. Blank, G. Gottsegen, and M. Gottsegen (eds.), *Encounter: Confrontations in Self and Interpersonal Awareness*. New York: Macmillan, 1971.

Likert, R. *New Patterns of Management*. New York: McGraw-Hill, 1961.

Lippitt, R. *Training in Community Relations*. New York: Harper, 1949.

Loomis, C. "Sociometrics and the Study of New Rural Communities," *Sociometry*, 2, 1939, 56–76.

Lowen, A. *The Betrayal of the Body*. New York: Macmillan, 1967.

———. *Love and Orgasm*. New York: Macmillan, 1965.

Luce, G. Unpublished manuscript.

McGregor, D. *The Human Side of Enterprise*. New York: McGraw-Hill, 1960.

McKelvay, St. C. "A Reporter with the B–29's," *The New Yorker, 21,* June, 1945, 33–36.

Mann, J. *Encounter*. New York: Grossman, 1970.

Mann, R. *Interpersonal Styles and Group Development*. New York: Wiley, 1967.

Marrow, A. *The Practical Theorist*. New York: Basic Books, 1969.

Maslow, A. "The Creative Attitude," in R. Mooney and T. Razik (eds.), *Explorations in Creativity*. New York: Harper, 1967, 47–54.

———. *Eupsychian Management*. Homewood, Ill.: Dorsey, 1965.

———. *Motivation and Personality*. New York: Harper, 1954.

———. *Toward a Psychology of Being*. Princeton, N.J.: Van Nostrand, 1962.

Merton, R. "Science and the Social Order," in *Social Theory and Social Structure*. Glencoe, Ill.: Free Press, 1957.

Miller, H. *Income of the American People*. New York: Wiley, 1965.

Mills, C. *White Collar*. New York: Oxford University Press, 1951.

Mills, T. *Group Transformation*. Englewood Cliffs, N.J.: Prentice-Hall, 1964.

Mooney, R., and T. Razik (eds.). *Explorations in Creativity*. New York: Harper, 1967.

Moreno, J. "The Concept of the Here and Now, Hic et Nunc: Small Groups and their Relation to Action Research," *Group Psychotherapy, 22,* Nos. 3–4, 1969, 139–141.

———. *Einladung zu einer Begegnung* (Invitation to an Encounter). Vienna, 1916.

———. *Psychodrama*. Vols. I and II. Beacon, N.Y.: Beacon House, 1946 and 1959.

———. *Who Shall Survive?* 2nd ed. Beacon, N.Y.: Beacon House, 1953.

Moustakas, C. *Creativity and Conformity*. Princeton, N.J.: Van Nostrand, 1967.

Naranjo, C., and R. Ornstein. *On the Psychology of Meditation*. New York: Viking, 1971.

Nash, O. "The Seven Spiritual Ages of Mrs. Marmaduke Moon," in *The Face Is Familiar*. Boston: Little, Brown, 1940.

New York Times, Feb. 18, 1971.

News of the World, Aug. 21, 1970.

Orwell, G. *Nineteen Eighty-Four.* New York: Harcourt, Brace, 1949.

Panshin, A. *Heinlein in Dimension.* Chicago: Advent, 1968.
Perls, F. *Ego Hunger and Aggression.* New York: Random House, 1964.
———. *Gestalt Therapy Verbatim.* Lafayette, Calif.: Real People Press, 1969.
———. *In and Out of the Garbage Pail.* Lafayette, Calif.: Real People Press, 1971.
Personnel Association for Southern California. Sensitivity Training Panel, 1967 Meeting. Transcript.
Poppy, J. "It's OK to Cry in the Office," *Look,* July 9, 1968, 64–76.
Potter, D. *People of Plenty.* Chicago: University of Chicago Press, 1954.

Reich, C. *The Greening of America.* New York: Random House, 1970.
Reich, W. *Character Analysis.* New York: Farrar, Straus, 1949.
"Report of the Clinical Area: Special Commission on T-Groups," University of Michigan, n.d. (1968–1969). Mimeographed.
Rice, A. *The Enterprise and Its Environment.* London: Tavistock, 1963.
Rieff, P. *The Triumph of the Therapeutic.* New York: Harper, 1966.
Roethlisberger, F., and W. Dickson. *Management and the Worker.* Cambridge, Mass.: Harvard University Press, 1939.
Rogers, C. *Client-Centered Therapy in Current Practice, Implications and Theory.* Boston: Houghton Mifflin, 1951.
———. "Interpersonal Relationships U.S.A. 2000," *Journal of Applied Behavioral Science,* 4, 1968, 208–269.
———. *On Becoming a Person.* Boston: Houghton Mifflin, 1961.
———, and B. Stevens. *Person to Person: Problems of Being Human.* Lafayette, Calif.: Real People Press, 1967.
Rubin, I. "The Reduction of Prejudice through Increased Self-Acceptance." Boston University Human Relations Research Reports and Technical Notes No. 83, 1966.
Russell, B. *In Praise of Idleness.* New York: Norton, 1935.

San Diego Magazine, June, 1969.
Schott, W. "Review of *Please Touch* and *Encounter.*" *New York Times Book Review,* June 28, 1970.
Schutz, W. *Here Comes Everybody.* New York: Harper, 1971.
———. *Joy.* New York: Grove Press, 1968.
Schutzenberger, A. "Observation et Psychotherapie de Groupe et en Formation." Mimeographed.
———. *Precis de Psychodrame.* Paris: Press Universitaire, 1966.
Segal, M. *Introduction to the Work of Melanie Klein.* New York: Basic Books, 1964.
Shepard, M., and M. Lee. *Marathon 16.* New York: Putnam, 1970.
Silverman, J. "When Schizophrenia Helps," *Psychology Today,* 4, September, 1970, 63–65.
Slater, P. *Microcosm.* New York: Wiley, 1966.
———. *The Pursuit of Loneliness.* Boston: Beacon Press, 1970.

I. Bibliography

Smelser, N. *Theory of Collective Behavior*. New York: Free Press, 1963.

Sohl, J. *The Lemon Eaters*. New York: Simon and Schuster, 1967.

Standards for the Use of the Laboratory Methods in NTL Institute Programs. Washington, D.C.: NTL Publications, 1969.

Steele, F. "Can T-Group Training Change the Power Structure?" *Personnel Administration*, 33, 1970, 118–153.

Stein, M. "Creativity and Culture," in R. Mooney and T. Razik (eds.), *Explorations in Creativity*. New York: Harper, 1967, 109–119.

Stock, D. "A Survey of Research on T-Groups," in L. Bradford, J. Gibb, and K. Benne (eds.), *T-Group Theory and Laboratory Method*. New York: Wiley, 1964.

Storer, N. *The Social System of Science*. New York: Holt, 1966.

"Stress and Strength at Crystal Cliffs" (Toronto), *Globe Magazine*, Aug. 6, 1966, 3–12.

Toffler, A. *The Culture Consumers*. New York: St. Martin's Press, 1964.

———. *Future Shock*. New York: Random House, 1970.

Trist, E., G. Higgin, H. Murray, and A. Pollock. *Organizational Choice*. London: Tavistock, 1963.

U.S. *Congressional Record*. 91st Cong., 1st Sess., 1969, Vol. 115, Part 12, 15, 322–15, 335.

———. 91st Cong., 2nd Sess., 1970, Vol. 116, No. 1, H24–H28.

U.S. Department of Commerce, Bureau of the Census. *Population Characteristics*. Series P–20, No. 188.

Verplanck, W. "How Do You Track Down Rumors?" *American Psychologist*, 25, 1970, 106–107.

Vroom, B. "Weekend Confrontation with the Soc. Rels," *The New Yorker*, 43, Dec. 2, 1967, 199 212.

Watts, A. "Divine Madness" (tape recording). San Rafael, Calif.: Big Sur Recordings, 1969.

———. *Psychotherapy East and West*. New York: Pantheon, 1961.

———. *The Wisdom of Insecurity*. New York: Pantheon, 1951.

Weaver, R. "Ultimate Terms in Contemporary Rhetoric." *Perspectives USA, 11*, 1955, 122–141.

Wilson, B. *Religion in a Secular Society*. Baltimore, Md.: Penguin, 1966.

Wolfe, T. *The Electric Kool-Aid Acid Test*. New York: Farrar, Straus, 1968.

Yablonsky, L. *Synanon, the Tunnel Back*. New York: Macmillan, 1965.

Yalom, I. *The Theory and Practice of Group Psychotherapy*. New York: Basic Books, 1970.

———, J. Fidler, J. Frank, J. Mann, M. Parloff, and L. Sata. *American Psychiatric Association Task Force Report on Recent Developments in the Use of Small Groups*. Washington, D.C.: American Psychiatric Association, 1969.

Reports of Research Evaluating Sensitivity Training, 1945 to 1970

Alderfer, C. P. "Relatedness Need Satisfaction and Learning Desires in Laboratory Education," *Journal of Applied Behavioral Science, 6,* 1970, 365–368.

Anderson, B. R. "A Study of Educational Change Based on a Strategy of Teacher Self-Assessment: Trial of a Strategy of Change in a Bolivian Setting," *Dissertation Abstracts, 28,* No. 12-A, 1968, 4839–4840.

Argyris, C. *Interpersonal Competence and Organizational Effectiveness.* Homewood, Ill.: Dorsey, 1962.

——. "Explorations in Interpersonal Competence—I," *Journal of Applied Behavioral Science, 1,* 1965, 58–83.

——. "Explorations in Interpersonal Competence—II," *Journal of Applied Behavioral Science, 1,* 1965, 255–269.

——. *Organization and Innovation.* Homewood, Ill.: Dorsey, 1965.

——. "The Incompleteness of Social-Psychological Theory: Examples from Small Group, Cognitive Consistency, and Attribution Research," *American Psychologist, 24,* 1969, 893–908.

Back, K. W. "Interpersonal Relations in a Discussion Group," *The Journal of Social Issues, 4,* No. 2, 1948, 61–65.

Barron, M. E., and G. K. Krulee. "Case Study of a Basic Skill Training Group," *Journal of Social Issues, 4,* No. 2, 1948, 10–30.

Bass, B. M. "Mood Changes during a Management Training Laboratory," *Journal of Applied Psychology, 46,* 1962, 361–364.

——. "Reactions to *Twelve Angry Men* as a Measure of Sensitivity Training," *Journal of Applied Psychology, 46,* 1962, 120–124.

——. "The Anarchist Movement and the T-group: Some Possible Lessons for Organizational Development," *Journal of Applied Behavioral Science, 3,* 1967, 211–227.

Baumgartel, H., and J. W. Goldstein. "Need and Value Shifts in College Training Groups," *Journal of Applied Behavioral Science, 3,* 1967, 87–101.

Beer, M., and S. W. Kleisath. "The Effect of the Managerial Grid Lab on Organizational and Leadership Dimensions," in S. S. Zalkind, Chairman, *Research on the Impact of Using Different Laboratory Methods for Interpersonal and Organizational Change.* Symposium at APA, Washington, D.C., 1967.

Bennis, W. G. "The Relationship Between Some Personality Dimensions and Group Development." Unpublished material, Boston University Human Relations Center, 1956.

——, R. Burke, H. Cutter, H. Harrington, and J. Hoffman. "A Note on Some Problems of Measurement and Prediction in a Training Group," *Group Psychotherapy*, 10, 1957, 328–341.

——, and D. Peabody. "The Conceptualization of Two Personality Orientations and Sociometric Choice," *Journal of Social Psychology*, 57, 1962, 203–215.

Ben-Zeev, S. "Sociometric Choice and Patterns of Member Participation," in D. Stock and H. Thelen (eds.), *Emotional Dynamics and Group Culture*. New York: New York University Press, 1958, 84–92.

Blake, R. R., and J. S. Mouton. "Personality Factors Associated with Individual Conduct in a Training Group Situation." Human Relations Training Laboratory Research Monograph No. 1, Printing Division, University of Texas Press, 1956.

——. "Some Effects of Managerial Grid Seminar Training on Union and Management Attitudes Toward Supervision," *Journal of Applied Behavioral Science*, 2, 1966, 387–400.

——, L. B. Barnes, and L. E. Greiner. "Breakthrough in Organization Development," *Harvard Business Review*, 42, No. 6, 1964, 133–155.

——, and B. Fruchter. "A Factor Analysis of Training Group Behavior," *Journal of Social Psychology*, 58, 1962, 121–130.

Blansfield, M. G. "Depth Analysis of Organizational Life," *California Management Review*, 5, No. 2, 1962, 29–42.

Blumberg, A., and R. T. Golembiewski. "Laboratory Goal Attainment and the Problem Analysis Questionnaire," *Journal of Applied Behavioral Science*, 5, 1969, 597–600.

Bolman, L. "The Effects of Variations in Educator Behavior on the Learning Process in Laboratory Human Relations Education," *Dissertation Abstracts*, 29, No. 4-B, 1968, 1492.

——. "Laboratory versus Lecture in Training Executives," *Journal of Applied Behavioral Science*, 6, 1970, 323–335.

Boyd, J. B., and J. D. Elliss. *Findings of Research into Senior Management Seminars*. Toronto: The Hydro-Electric Power Commission of Ontario, 1962.

Brook, R. C. "Self-Concept Changes as a Function of Participation in Sensitivity Training as Measured by the Tennessee Self Concept Scale," *Dissertation Abstracts*, 29, No. 6-A, 1968, 1700.

Browne, S. A., and M. Crowe. "Personality Structure as a Determinant of Sociometric Choice." Dittoed material, Research Center for Group Dynamics, University of Michigan, 1953.

Buchanan, P. C. "Organization Development Following Major Retrenchment." 1964. Mimeographed.

——, and P. H. Brunstetter. "A Research Approach to Management Development, Part II," *Journal of the American Society of Training Directors*, 13, 1959, 18–27.

Bunker, D. R. "Individual Applications of Laboratory Training," *Journal of Applied Behavioral Science*, 1, 1965, 131–148.

——, and E. S. Knowles. "Comparison of Behavioral Changes Resulting from Human Relations Training Laboratories of Different Lengths," *Journal of Applied Behavioral Science*, 3, 1967, 505–523.

Burke, R. L., and W. G. Bennis. "Changes in Perception of Self and Others during Human Relations Training," *Human Relations, 14,* 1961, 165–182.

Carron, T. J. "Human Relations Training and Attitude Change: A Vector Analysis," *Personnel Psychology, 17,* 1964, 403–424.
Cherlin, D. L. "Anxiety and Consultant Differences in Self-Study Groups," *Dissertation Abstracts, 29,* No. 11-B, 1969, 4364.
Clark, J. V., and S. A. Culbert. "Mutually Therapeutic Perception and Self-Awareness in a T-Group," *Journal of Applied Behavioral Science, 1,* 1965, 180–194.
——, and H. K. Bobele. "Mutually Therapeutic Perception and Self-Awareness under Variable Conditions," *Journal of Applied Behavioral Science, 5,* 1969, 65–72.
Culbert, S. A. "Trainer Self-Disclosure and Member Growth in Two T-Groups," *Journal of Applied Behavioral Science, 4,* No. 1, 1968, 47–73.
Culver, C. M., F. Dunham, J. W. Edgerton, and M. Edgerton. "Community Service Workers and Recipients: A Combined Middle Class–Lower Class Workshop," *Journal of Applied Behavioral Science, 5,* 1969, 519–535.

Delaney, D. J. "A Study of the Effectiveness of Sensitivity Training on the Perception of Non-Verbal Communications in Counselor Education," *Dissertation Abstracts, 27,* No. 4-A, 1966, 948.
DeMichele, J. H. "The Measurement of Rated Training Changes Resulting from a Sensitivity Training Laboratory of an Overall Program in Organization Development," *Dissertation Abstracts, 27,* No. 11-A, 1967, 3578–3579.
Draeger, C. "Level of Trust in Intensive Small Groups," *Dissertation Abstracts, 29,* No. 10-A, 1969, 3457.
Dunnette, M. D. "People Feeling: Joy, More Joy, and the 'Slough of Despond,'" *Journal of Applied Behavioral Science, 5,* 1969, 25–44.
Dyer, R. D. "The Effects of Human Relations Training on the Interpersonal Behavior of College Students," *Dissertation Abstracts, 28,* No. 6-A, 1967, 2068–2069.
Dyer, W. G., R. F. Maddocks, J. W. Moffitt, and W. J. Underwood. "A Laboratory-Consultation Model for Organization Change," *Journal of Applied Behavioral Science, 6,* 1970, 211–227.

Eisenstadt, J. W. "An Investigation of Factors which Influence Response to Laboratory Training," *Journal of Applied Behavioral Science, 3,* 1967, 575–578.

Foundation for Research on Human Behavior. "An Action Research Program for Organization Improvement. Ann Arbor, Mich., 1960.
French, J. R. P., Jr., J. J. Sherwood, and D. L. Bradford. "Changes in Self-Identity in a Management Training Conference," *Journal of Applied Behavioral Science, 2,* 1966, 210–218.
Friedlander, F. "The Impact of Organizational Training Laboratories

upon the Effectiveness and Interaction of Ongoing Work Groups," *Personnel Psychology, 20,* 1967, 289–307.

Gage, N. L., and R. V. Exline. "Social Perception and Effectiveness in Discussion Groups," *Human Relations, 6,* 1953, 381–396.

Gassner, S. M., J. Gold, and A. M. Snadowsky. "Changes in the Phenomenal Field as a Result of Human Relations Training," *Journal of Psychology, 58,* 1964, 33–41.

Geitgey, D. A. "A Study of Some Effects of Sensitivity Training on the Performance of Students in Associate Degree Programs of Nursing Education," *Dissertation Abstracts, 27,* No. 6-B, 1966, 2000–2001.

Gibb, J. R. "Effects of Role Playing upon (a) Role Flexibility and upon (b) Ability to Conceptualize a New Role," *American Psychologist, 7,* 1952, 310 (Abs.).

——, and A. W. Gorman. "Effects of Induced Polarization in Small Groups upon Accuracy of Perception." Paper read at APA, September, 1954.

——, and G. N. Platts. "Role Flexibility in Group Interaction," *American Psychologist, 5,* 1950, 491 (Abs.).

——, E. E. Smith, and A. H. Roberts. "Effects of Positive and Negative Feedback upon Defensive Behavior in Small Problem-Solving Groups." Paper read at APA, 1955.

Glidewell, J. C. "Changes in Approaches to Work Problem Analysis during Management Training." Mimeographed manuscript. Washington, D.C.: Second American National Red Cross School for Management Development, 1956.

Gold, J. S. "An Evaluation of a Laboratory Human Relations Training Program for College Undergraduates," *Dissertation Abstracts, 28,* No. 8-A, 1968, 3262–3263.

Gradolph, I. "The Task Approach of Groups of Single-Type and Mixed-Type Valency Compositions," in D. Stock and H. Thelen (eds.), *Emotional Dynamics and Group Culture.* New York: New York University Press, 1958, 127–130.

Haiman, F. S. "Effects of Training in Group Processes on Open-Mindedness," *Journal of Communication, 13,* 1963, 236–245.

Hall, J., and M. S. Williams. "Group Dynamics Training and Improved Decision Making. *Journal of Applied Behavioral Science, 6,* 1970, 39–68.

Harrison, R. "Impact of the Laboratory on Perceptions of Others by the Experimental Group," in C. Argyris, *Interpersonal Competence and Organizational Effectiveness.* Homewood, Ill.: Dorsey, 1962, 261–271.

——. "Cognitive Change and Participation in a Sensitivity-Training Laboratory," *Journal of Consulting Psychology, 30,* 1966, 517–520.

——, and B. Lubin. "Personal Style, Group Composition, and Learning," *Journal of Applied Behavioral Science, 1,* 1965, 286–301, two studies.

Hartley, J. A. "A Semantic Differential Scale for Assessing Group Process Changes," *Journal of Clinical Psychology, 24,* 1968, 74.

Herod, J. "Characteristics of Leadership in an International Fraternity for Women and Influence on the Leaders' Attitudes of a Group-Centered Leader Training Experience. *Dissertation Abstracts, 29,* No. 10-A, 1969, 3461–3462.

Hill, W. F. "The Influence of Subgroups on Participation in Human Relations Training Groups." Unpublished Ph.D. diss., University of Chicago, 1955.

Himber, C. "Evaluating Sensitivity Training for Teen-Agers," *Journal of Applied Behavioral Science, 6,* 1970, 307–322.

Horowitz, M. W., J. Lyons, and H. V. Perlmutter. "Induction of Forces in Discussion Groups," *Human Relations, 4,* 1951, 57–76.

Horwitz, M., and D. Cartwright. "A Projective Method for the Diagnosis of Group Properties," *Human Relations, 6,* 1953, 397–410.

Johnson, D. L., P. Rothaus, and P. G. Hanson. "A Human Relations Training Program for Hospital Personnel," *Journal of Health and Human Behavior, 7,* 1966, 215–223.

Johnson, J. J. "Some Effects of Three Kinds of Groups in the Human Relations Area," *Dissertation Abstracts, 28,* No. 5-B, 1967, 2172.

Johnson, L. K. "The Effect of Trainer Interventions on Change in Personal Functioning through T-Group Training," *Dissertation Abstracts, 27,* No. 12-A, 1967, 4132.

Kassarjian, H. H. "Social Character and Sensitivity Training," *Journal of Applied Behavioral Science, 1,* 1965, 433–440.

Kepes, S. Y. "Experimental Evaluations of Sensitivity Training," *Dissertation Abstracts, 27,* No. 6-B, 1966, 2121–2122, two studies.

Kernan, J. P. "Laboratory Human Relations Training—Its Effect on the 'Personality' of Supervisory Engineers," *Dissertation Abstracts, 25,* No. 1, 1964, 665–666.

Klaw, S. "Inside a T-Group," *Think, 31,* November–December, 1965, 26–30.

Koile, E. A., and C. Draeger. "T-group Member Ratings of Leader and Self in a Human Relations Laboratory," *Journal of Psychology, 72,* 1969, 11–20.

Kolb, D. A., and R. E. Boyatzis. "On the Dynamics of the Helping Relationship," *Journal of Applied Behavioral Science, 6,* 1970, 267–289.

Kolb, D. A., S. K. Winter, and D. E. Berlew. "Self-Directed Change: Two Studies," *Journal of Applied Behavioral Science, 4,* 1968, 453–471.

Krear, M. L. "The Influence of Sensitivity Training on the Social Attitudes of Educational Leaders of Racially-Imbalanced Schools," *Dissertation Abstracts, 29,* No. 6-A, 1968, 1954–1955.

Lakin, M. "Participants' Interpretations of a Group Sensitivity Training Experience: A Case Study." Typescript, Duke University, 1960.

——, and R. C. Carson. "Participant Perception of Group Process in Group Sensitivity Training," *International Journal of Group Psychotherapy, 14,* 1964, 116–122.

Lee, W. S. "A Study of the Effectiveness of Sensitivity Training in an In-service Teacher-Training Program in Human Relations," *Dissertation Abstracts, 28,* No. 5-A, 1967, 1680.

Lieberman, M. A. "The Relationship of Group Climate to Individual Change." Unpublished Ph.D. diss., University of Chicago, 1958.

———. "Some Preliminary Findings: Group Experience Project." Presented in symposium entitled Human Relations Laboratory Training—A Critical Evaluation. 78th Annual American Psychological Association Convention, Miami Beach, Fla., September, 1970.

Lippitt, G. "Effects of Information about Group Desire for Change on Members of a Group," *Dissertation Abstracts*, 20, No. 10, 1960, 4200.

Lohmann, K., J. H. Zenger, and I. R. Weschler. "Some Perceptual Changes during Sensitivity Training," *Journal of Educational Research*, 53, 1959, 28–31.

Lott, A. J., J. H. Schopler, and J. R. Gibb. "The Effects of Feedback on Group Processes." Paper read at Rocky Mountain Psychological Association meetings, 1954.

———. "Effects of Feeling-Oriented and Task-Oriented Feedback upon Defensive Behavior in Small Problem-Solving Groups." Paper read at APA, 1955.

Lubin, B., and M. Zuckerman. "Level of Emotional Arousal in Laboratory Training," *Journal of Applied Behavioral Science*, 5, 1969, 483–490.

Lundgren, D. C. "Interaction Process and Identity Change in T-Groups," *Dissertation Abstracts*, 29, No. 3-A, 1968, 961–962.

Massarik, F., and G. Carlson. "The California Psychological Inventory as an Indicator of Personality Change in Sensitivity Training." M.A. thesis, UCLA, 1960. Mentioned in M. D. Dunnette, "Personnel Management," *Annual Review of Psychology*, P. R. Farnsworth (ed.), 13, 285–314. Palo Alto, Calif.: Annual Reviews, 1962.

Mathis, A. G. " 'Trainability' as a Function of Individual Valency Pattern," in D. Stock and H. Thelen (eds.), *Emotional Dynamics and Group Culture*. New York: New York University Press, 1958, 150–156.

Miles, M. B. "Factors Influencing Response to Feedback in Human Relations Training." New York: Horace Mann-Lincoln Institute of School Experimentation, Teachers College, Columbia University, 1958.

———. "Changes During and Following Laboratory Training: A Clinical-Experimental Study," *Journal of Applied Behavioral Science*, 1, 1965, 215–242.

———, S. K. Cohen, and F. L. Whitam. "Changes in Performance Test Scores after Human Relations Training." New York: Columbia University Teachers College, 1959. Mimeographed.

Morton, R. B., and B. M. Bass. "The Organizational Training Laboratory," *Journal of The American Society of Training Directors*, 18, 1964, 2–15.

Myers, G. E., M. T. Myers, A. Goldberg, and C. E. Welch. "Effect of Feedback on Interpersonal Sensitivity in Laboratory Training Groups," *Journal of Applied Behavioral Science*, 5, 1969, 175–185.

Nadler, E. B., and S. L. Fink. "Impact of Laboratory Training on Socio-

Political Ideology," *Journal of Applied Behavioral Science,* 6, 1970, 79–92.

Norfleet, B. "Interpersonal Relations and Group Productivity," *Journal of Social Issues,* 4, No. 2, 1948, 66–69.

NTL Institute for Applied Behavioral Sciences. *Explorations in Human Relations Training.* Washington, D.C.: NEA, 1953, two studies.

Orsburn, J. D. "Sensitivity Training versus Group Lectures with High School Problem Students," *Dissertation Abstracts,* 28, No. 2-A, 1967, 503–504.

Oshry, B. I., and R. Harrison. "Transfer from Here-and-Now to There-and-Then: Changes in Organizational Problem Diagnosis Stemming from T-Group Training," *Journal of Applied Behavioral Science,* 2, 1966, 185–198.

Pollack, H. B. "Change in Homogeneous and Heterogeneous Sensitivity Training Groups," *Dissertation Abstracts,* 28, No. 11-B, 1968, 4762–4763.

Powers, J. R. "Trainer Orientation and Group Composition in Laboratory Training," *Dissertation Abstracts,* 26, No. 7, 1966, 4065.

Rinn, J. L. "Dimensions of Group Interaction: The Cooperative Analysis of Idiosyncratic Descriptions of Training Groups," *Educational and Psychological Measurement,* 26, 1966, 343–362.

Roberts, A. H., J. H. Schopler, E. E. Smith, and J. R. Gibb. "Effects of Feeling-Oriented Classroom Teaching upon Reactions to Feedback." Paper read at APA, September, 1955.

Rosenberg, M. "A Preliminary Report on the Relation of Personality Factors to Sociometric Position in Bethel Groups 5 and 6." Research Center for Group Dynamics, University of Michigan, 1950. Dittoed material.

Rubin, I. "The Reduction of Prejudice through Laboratory Training," *Journal of Applied Behavioral Science,* 3, No. 1, 1967, 29–50.

Rueveni, U., M. Swift, and A. A. Bell. "Sensitivity Training: Its Impact on Mental Health Workers," *Journal of Applied Behavioral Science,* 5, 1969, 600–601.

Russell, W. J. "A Study of Changes in Measures of Inner-Direction, Open-Mindedness, and Intraception During Laboratory Training Designs of the Methodist Church," *Dissertation Abstracts,* 29, No. 11-A, 1969, 3887–3888.

Schmuck, R. A. "Helping Teachers Improve Classroom Group Processes," *Journal of Applied Behavioral Science,* 4, 1968, 401–435, two studies.

Schutz, W. C., and V. L. Allen. "The Effects of a T-Group Laboratory on Interpersonal Behavior," *Journal of Applied Behavioral Science,* 2, 1966, 265–286.

Sikes, W. W. "A Study of Some Effects of a Human Relations Training Laboratory," *Dissertation Abstracts,* 26, No. 2, 1965, 1200.

Smith, A. J., J. Jaffe, and D. G. Livingston. "Consonance of Interpersonal Perception and Individual Effectiveness," *Human Relations*, 8, 1955, 385–397.

Smith, P. B. "Attitude Changes Associated with Training in Human Relations," *British Journal of Social and Clinical Psychology*, 3, 1964, 104–112.

——. "A Study of T-Group Training." Final report to the Social Science Research Council, April 1, 1965–June 30, 1968 (School of Social Studies, University of Sussex), three studies.

——. "Social Influence Processes in Small Groups." Progress report to the Social Science Research Council, Jan. 1, 1969–Dec. 31, 1969 (School of Social Studies, University of Sussex).

——, and T. F. Honour. "The Impact of Phase I Managerial Grid Training," *Journal of Management Studies*, 6, 1969, 318–330.

——, and H. B. Pollack. "The Participant's Learning Style as a Correlate of T-Group Learning," *Proceedings of the 16th Congress of the International Association for Applied Psychology.* Amsterdam, 1968.

Steele, F. I. "Personality and the 'Laboratory Style,'" *Journal of Applied Behavioral Science*, 4, 1968, 25–45, two studies.

Stock, D. "The Relation between the Sociometric Structure of the Group and Certain Personality Characteristics." Ph.D. diss., University of Chicago, 1952.

——. "Factors Associated with Change in Self-Percept," in D. Stock and H. Thelen (eds.), *Emotional Dynamics and Group Culture.* New York: New York University Press, 1958, 157–170.

——, and S. Ben-Zeev. "Changes in Work and Emotionality During Group Growth," in D. Stock and H. Thelen (eds.), *Emotional Dynamics and Group Culture.* New York: New York University Press, 1958, 192–206.

——, and W. F. Hill. "Intersubgroup Dynamics as a Factor in Group Growth," in D. Stock and H. Thelen (eds.), *Emotional Dynamics and Group Culture.* New York: New York University Press, 1958, 207–221.

——, and J. Luft. "The T-E-T Design." Typescript, NTL, 1960.

Taylor, F. C. "Effects of Laboratory Training upon Persons and Their Work Groups," in S. S. Zalkind, Chairman, *Research on the Impact of Using Different Laboratory Methods for Interpersonal and Organizational Change.* Symposium at APA, Washington, D.C., 1967.

Thelen, H., and W. Dickerman. "Stereotypes and the Growth of Groups," *Educational Leadership*, 6, 1949, 309–316.

Tolela, M. "Effects of T-Group Training and Cognitive Learning on Small Group Effectiveness," *Dissertation Abstracts*, 28, No. 12-A, 1968, 5175.

Underwood, W. J. "Evaluation of Laboratory Method Training," *Journal of The American Society of Training Directors*, 19, 1965, 34–40.

Valiquet, M. I. "Individual Change in a Management Development Program," *Journal of Applied Behavioral Science*, 4, 1968, 313–325.

Wagner, A. B. "The Use of Process Analysis in Business Decision Games," *Journal of Applied Behavioral Science, 1*, 1965, 387–408.

Watson, J. "Some Social-Psychological Correlates of Personality: A Study of the Usefulness of Psychoanalytic Theory in Predicting Behavior." Unpublished Ph.D. diss., University of Michigan, 1952.

———, R. Lippitt, D. Kallen, and S. Zipf. "Evaluation of a Human Relations Laboratory Program." Research Center for Group Dynamics, University of Michigan, 1961. Typescript.

Weschler, I. R., and J. Reisel. "Inside a Sensitivity Training Group." Industrial Relations Monograph No. 4, Los Angeles: Institute of Industrial Relations, University of California, 1959.

Wiens, A. N., R. G. Matarazzo, G. Saslow, S. M. Thompson, and J. D. Matarazzo. "Speech Interaction Patterns of Ward Nursing Personnel Before, During, and After Brief Sensitivity Training," *Journal of Applied Behavioral Science, 3*, 1967, 418–419.

Willis, C. G. "A Study of the Effects of Programmed Human Relations Training on a Selected Group of High School Dropouts," *Dissertation Abstracts, 27*, No. 12-A, 1967, 4144.

Zand, D. E., F. I. Steele, and S. S. Zalkind. "The Impact of an Organizational Development Program on Perceptions of Interpersonal, Group, and Organizational Functioning," in S. S. Zalkind, Chairman, *Research on the Impact of Using Different Laboratory Methods for Interpersonal and Organizational Change.* Symposium at APA, Washington, D.C., 1967.

Zenger, J. H. "The Effect of a Team Human Relations Training Laboratory on the Productivity and Perceptions of a Selling Group," *Dissertation Abstracts, 28*, No. 11-A, 1968, 4322.

Index

Index